FORMAL SEMANTICS AND LOGIC

FORMAL SEMANTICS AND LOGIC

Bas C. van Fraassen

UNIVERSITY OF TORONTO

The Macmillan Company, New York

Collier-Macmillan Limited, London

The Macmillan Company
866 Third Avenue, New York, New York 10022

Collier-Macmillan Canada, Ltd., Toronto, Ontario

Library of Congress catalog card number: 76–115294

First Printing

To my parents

PREFACE

This book is based on my lectures in advanced and intermediate logic courses at Yale University 1966–1968, Indiana University 1968–1969, and the University of Toronto 1969–1970. These courses were intended specifically for philosophy students with one previous course in formal logic.

The general aim of this book is to provide a broad framework in which both classical and nonclassical logics may be studied and appraised. The semantic approach adopted here was first systematically developed by Alfred Tarski; its development over the past forty years can only be very partially documented in our bibliographical notes.

After a preliminary chapter presenting the fairly elementary techniques to be utilized, Chapters II and III provide the general concepts and methods of formal semantics of logic. These chapters are illustrated throughout by the propositional calculus, the most familiar logical system we have. Chapters IV and V are devoted to applications to quantificational logic and to various nonclassical logics, respectively. In Chapter IV we develop first the usual semantics for quantificational logic. We then add a brief introduction to model theory, and a discussion of several forms of the Löwenheim–Skolem theorem. More than half of this chapter is devoted to standard material. In Chapter V also we present a fair portion of standard material: for example, Lindenbaum's theorem concerning characteristic matrices, and the usual Kripke-style semantics for modal logic.

But in view of the increasing influence of formal semantics on contemporary philosophical discussion, the emphasis is everywhere on applications to nonclassical logics and nonclassical interpretations of classical logic. In the Introduction I sketch a view of the nature of logic that is meant to accommodate the existence and importance of non-classical logics. In Chapter II the syntactic and semantic concepts used are purposely presented in a manner so general that they apply to languages of arbitrary structure. The calculus of systems as developed there and the problems of axiomatizability that are considered pertain to deductive systems formulated in any kind of formal language. The concept of compactness is dissected into a family of concepts, equivalent in the classical case but not elsewhere. Proof-theoretic methods are entirely avoided in this chapter, and the methods of proving compactness studied do not involve reference to any logical system.

Chapter III is devoted to the semantic appraisal of logical systems. As in the case for Chapter II, the concepts and methods introduced are illustrated throughout with reference to the most familiar logical system, classical propositional logic. Three kinds of interpretations of this system are considered: the usual one, interpretations through matrices, and interpretations through supervaluations. In Chapter IV, concerned with applications to quantificational logic, we only consider one unusual interpretation of the familiar logic: what Ruth Barcan Marcus calls the substitution interpretation. In Chapter V, devoted to nonclassical logics, there are also sections dealing with subjects that have so far been discussed only in the journals: transformation semantics for modal logic, supervaluations, and presuppositions. This chapter ends with an analysis of the concept of truth, in which it is argued that Tarski's theory of truth does not carry over unchanged to nonclassical cases.

In conclusion I would like to acknowledge gratefully my many debts to teachers, colleagues, and students: especially my teachers Karel Lambert and Nuel D. Belnap, Jr., but also Alan Anderson, Nino Cocchiarella, J. Michael Dunn, Frederic Fitch, Hugues Leblanc, Robert Meyer (who read an earlier draft of this book and made many valuable suggestions), Nicholas Rescher, Richmond H. Thomason, and many others. Whatever shortcomings this work has, it has in spite of what I learned from them.

Bas C. van Fraassen

CONTENTS

FORMAL SEMANTICS AND LOGIC

AIM AND STRUCTURE OF LOGICAL THEORY

Logical studies comprise today both logic proper and metalogic. We distinguish these subjects by their aims: the aim of logic proper is to develop methods for the logical appraisal of reasoning,[1] and the aim of metalogic is to develop methods for the appraisal of logical methods. In pursuing the aims of logic, it has been fruitful to proceed systematically, that is, to construct formal axiomatic systems of various kinds. These logical systems provide the immediate subject matter for metalogical investigation.

Metalogic can in turn be roughly divided into two parts: proof theory and formal semantics.[2] In proof theory, the logical systems are treated as abstract mathematical systems, and the questions dealt with relate directly to the specific set of axioms and rules used to formulate the system.[3] In formal semantics, the logical systems are studied from the point of view of their possible interpretations—with special reference to their intended interpretation, if such there be. This has led to a profound analysis of the structure of language, which has proved to be of importance for many philosophical discussions. While it is not possible to proceed with the semantic analysis of a logical system without due attention to some proof-theoretical results, it is important to emphasize their relative independence. This is nowhere clearer than with respect to the *compactness* problem, a central problem studied in this book. For the usual procedure in logic texts is to use proof-theoretic results concerning a system to establish a certain semantic result (strong completeness of the system) and then to deduce compactness as a corollary. But the statement of the compactness theorem involves no reference whatever to the logical system; it concerns only the language under discussion. (The system in question happens to pertain to that language, but there is no essential connection between a given language and any axiomatic system, as we understand those terms.) In such cases it seems important to attempt purely semantic proofs, without recourse to proof theory.

A certain amount of philosophical sound and fury has been raised by the question:[4] Which logic is the right logic? This question would not have made sense before alternative logics had been devised, but with the advent of intuitionistic, many-valued, and quantum logics it became important. The question clearly has a presupposition—that there is a unique right logic—which stands itself in need of philosophical scrutiny. Here the semantic point of view may help to clarify the issue.

In formal semantics, we deal with a class of structures called (*formal*) *languages*; they are called languages because they are believed to provide rational reconstructions of (parts of) natural languages and, indeed, adequate reconstructions relative to certain purposes. A logical system is considered correct for a language if it provides a catalogue of the valid inferences in that language. So the question "Which is the right logic?" may perhaps be rephrased as: Assuming that natural language is adequately represented by a certain formal language L, what logic is correct for L from the semantic point of view?

One task we now have is to clarify such notions as "valid inference in a language" and "correct for a language." These are basic concerns of formal semantics. But if the question raised above has a right answer, it would seem that in formal semantics we ought to consider only languages of a certain type: those which adequately represent natural language.

But the assumption that natural language is adequately represented, as a whole and for all relevant purposes, by a single known formal language no longer seems a very plausible assumption. This assumption was clearly made by ideal language philosophers, from Bertrand Russell, via the early Wittgenstein, to the Logical Positivists. It was thought that natural language has a certain discoverable skeleton, obscured at present only by the grammatical vagaries and *idiotismes* that grew in the mouths of the vulgar. Indeed, it was apparently thought that this hidden ideal language had an adequate reconstruction in *Principia Mathematica*, with minor additions needed to take care of nonmathematical subjects. The poet T. S. Eliot reports the enthusiasm with which this idea was received by young philosophers:

> Those students of philosophy who had not come to philosophy from mathematics did their best (at least, in the university in which my studies were conducted) to try to become imitation mathematicians—

at least to the extent of acquainting themselves with the paraphernalia of symbolic logic. (I remember one enthusiastic contemporary who devised a Symbolic Ethics, for which he had to invent several symbols not found in the *Principia Mathematica*.)[5]

Enthusiasm may still be found, but the ideal language paradigm has suffered somewhat in the intervening decades.

To the ideal language view we may oppose the view of the later Wittgenstein, that natural language provides us with the resources for playing a variety of language games of divergent structure. Ordinary language is then the collection of such games that are actually played, and it becomes a reasonable aim to provide rational reconstructions for some of these games. So different formal languages may represent different language games, and different logical systems may specify the valid rules of inference within different language games.

The use of the term "game" should not be taken to imply that the correct rules of inference are arbitrary. From the semantic point of view, the correct logic is always derivative: It is found by examining semantic relations (defined in terms of truth, reference, and so on) among statements. Thus, if what the intuitionist means by his statements is understood, it can then be seen that intuitionistic logic is the correct logic for his language.

Since we have now denied that there is a unique right logic we must face the charge of a self-defeating relativism. For what logical system shall govern the appraisal of our own reasoning in semantic inquiry? Our answer to this is fairly straightforward: In Metalogic we use a part of natural language commonly known as "mathematical English," in which we describe and discuss only mathematical (that is, set-theoretic) objects. When this language is understood it can be seen that classical logic (the theory of truth functions, quantifiers, and identity as taught in elementary logic courses today) is the correct logic for that language. To understand this language may involve understanding our beliefs concerning what sets are like and what sets exist—and some of these beliefs are rather audacious.[6] It may turn out that some of these beliefs are untenable; that is, they may have implications that are inconsistent by our own logical standards. But as an abstract possibility, this danger always exists—we cannot demonstrate the absolute consistency of our own logic without circularity. Nor is it necessary to counsel anyone to live dangerously; we do.

To sum up then, we accept classical logic as correct within a certain (perhaps rather limited) domain; and the language used in this book is within that domain. But we use this language to study and describe other languages and other logical systems, as well as our own. For our aim is to provide a framework for the appraisal of logical systems in general, classical and nonclassical.

NOTES

1. For an exposition of this view of logic, see P. F. Strawson, *An Introduction to Logical Theory* (London: Methuen, 1952).
2. The division is not exact; many questions have been dealt with from both points of view, and some proof-theoretic methods and results are indispensable in semantics.
3. The term "proof theory" was introduced by Hilbert; for surveys of recent work, see G. Kreisel, "Mathematical Logic," in *Lectures on Modern Mathematics*, Vol. III, T. L. Saaty, ed. (New York: Wiley, 1965) pp. 85–195, and "A Survey of Proof Theory," *Journal of Symbolic Logic*, *33* (Sept. 1968), pp. 321–388.
4. See, for example, P. Banks (apparently a pseudonym), "On the Philosophical Interpretation of Logic: An Aristotelian Dialogue," in *Logico-Philosophical Studies*, A. Menne, ed. (Dordrecht, Holland: Reidel, 1962), pp. 1–14; E. Beth, "Banks ab omni naevo vindicatus," *Contributions to Logic and Methodology in Honor of J. M. Bochenski*, A. Tymieniecka, ed. (Amsterdam: North-Holland, 1965), pp. 98–106; N. Rescher, *Many-Valued Logic* (New York: McGraw-Hill, 1969), chap. 3.
5. T. S. Eliot, Introduction to J. Pieper, *Leisure: The Basis of Culture*, A. Dru, trans. (New York: New American Library, 1963), p. 12.
6. We are deliberately speaking of mathematical objects in the idiom of naive platonism; the reader is asked not to infer that this is our position in philosophy of mathematics. After all, *any* philosophy of mathematics must eventually make sense of the common language of mathematical mankind.

CHAPTER I

MATHEMATICAL PRELIMINARIES

1. Intuitive Logic and Set Theory

The language to be used in this book is a part of natural language, and in this section we wish to make a few preliminary remarks on the conventions to be followed.

First, we shall use the common logical connectives in their truth-functional sense: "if . . . then" is the connective of material implication, and so on. Second, we shall use variables; if we say, for example, "For all sentences A of formal language $L, . . . A . . . ,$" then the letter A is used as a bound variable and the letter L as a free (substitutive) variable. The logic taught in elementary logic courses is the correct logic for the appraisal of our arguments involving these locutions.

The objects referred to (sentences, sets of sentences, formal languages, logical systems) always are or can be construed as mathematical objects. All mathematical objects are sets, and our main tool will be elementary set theory. Our use of this theory will be almost entirely intuitive, and many of our arguments concerning sets will be valid by the principles of logic alone. The reader need not have studied set theory per se to follow our arguments; if he knows quantificational logic, the remainder of this chapter should provide him with all the mathematical tools he will need.[1]

We shall read a sentence of the form $A \in B$ as "A is a member of B"; when this is true, B is a *set*. (We write $A \notin B$ for the negation of $A \in B$.) There is, in addition, a set that has no members, Λ, the *null set*. Synonymously with "set" we shall also use "class" and "family," and synonymously with "is a member of" we use "is in" or "belongs to," just to relieve the monotony of our already poverty-stricken jargon. When Fx is a sentence, possibly containing the variable x, then $\{x : Fx\}$ is a singular term, the name of the set of values of x such that Fx holds. That is, we accept the principle

(Abs.)   For all y, $y \in \{x : Fx\}$ iff Fy,

where "iff" abbreviates "if and only if." Let us hasten to add that "for all y" is to be taken as redundantly equivalent to "for all existent y," and that $\{x:Fx\}$ need not exist (in that case it is now sometimes called a *virtual class*, although "nonexistent class" would do just as well). For example, the Russell class

$$R = \{x: x \notin x\}$$

does not exist; for if it did, the principle (Abs.) would yield the contradiction

$$R \in R \quad \text{iff } R \notin R.$$

What sets do exist then? This question is answered, although not completely, by the axioms of set theory. For the time being the reader need only keep in mind that these axioms mean to guarantee the existence of any set seriously discussed in mathematics.

Using the *class-abstract* notation we have just introduced, and the notions of ordinary logic, we may characterize some of the common set-theoretic notions as follows:

null set: $\Lambda = \{x: x \neq x\}$.

inclusion: $X \subseteq Y$ iff every member of X is a member of Y.

complement: $\overline{X} = \{x: x \notin X\}$.

intersection: $X \cap Y = \{x: x \in X \text{ and } x \in Y\}$.

union: $X \cup Y = \{x: x \in X \text{ or } x \in Y\}$.

difference: $X - Y = \{x: x \in X \text{ and } x \notin Y\}$.

(If $X \subseteq Y$ we call X a *subset* of Y and Y a *superset* of X.) We read $x = y$ as "x is identical with y" and $x \neq x$ means *not* $(x = x)$. Many arguments about sets can be appraised simply by translating out these symbols and using ordinary logic, the principle (Abs.) and the *extensionality* principle

(Ext.) $X = Y$ iff $X \subseteq Y$ and $Y \subseteq X$, that is, iff X and Y have all members in common (where the variables X and Y range over sets). Venn diagrams are also a well-known aid for such appraisal.

Intersection and union have infinite counterparts. For example, if F is a family of sets, we may talk about the intersection of all the members of F:

$$\bigcap F = \{x : x \in X \text{ for every } X \in F\},$$

and about the union of all its members:

$$\bigcup F = \{x : x \in X \text{ for some } X \in F\}.$$

This notation may be abbreviated in various ways. If F is a finite family with as members exactly $A_1, \ldots, A_n$, we write

$$F = \{A_1, \ldots, A_n\},$$

$$\bigcap F = \bigcap_{i=i}^{n} A_i,$$

and so on. There are further obvious abbreviations; for example, if F is $\{X : X = \overline{Y} \text{ for some } Y \in G\}$, we also write F as $\{\overline{Y} : Y \in G\}$ and $\bigcap F$ as $\bigcap_{Y \in G} \overline{Y}$; similarly for other cases, The principles that govern infinite union and intersection are in general just the obvious analogues of their finitary counterparts; in any case, we can translate into more primitive notation when we wish to check this.

2. Mathematical Structures

We shall now introduce certain technical terms, such as "sequence," "relation," "function," and "operation," and explain the conventions that we adopt concerning their usage. Using these notions, we will be able to explain the general concept of a mathematical structure.

We denote by $\{x_1, \ldots, x_n\}$ the set whose members are $x_1, \ldots, x_n$.

The order in which these members are listed is of course irrelevant. But besides this set, there is also the sequence $\langle x_1, \ldots, x_n \rangle$; sometimes this is called the *ordered* set whose members are $x_1, \ldots, x_n$, to signify that here the order or listing is relevant. If the sequence has n members listed (not necessarily all distinct, of course), we also call it an *n-tuple*. A 2-tuple is also called a *couple* or ordered *pair*; a 3-tuple a *triple*, and so on.

A *binary relation* is a relation that holds between two objects, and we write "Rxy" or "xRy" for "x bears R to y." Similarly, an *n-ary relation* may be ascribed in a sentence of the form $Rx_1 \cdots x_n$; as in "x is the person sitting between y and z" or "points x and y separate point z from w." With an n-ary relation R we can associate the set of n-tuples that forms the extension of R,

$$\{\langle x_1, \ldots, x_n \rangle : Rx_1 \cdots x_n\},$$

and in set theory it is customary to identify the relation R with that set:

$$R = \{\langle x_1, \ldots, x_n \rangle : Rx_1 \cdots x_n\}.$$

Hence an *n*-ary relation is a set of *n*-tuples.

The set of all *n*-tuples taken from a given set X is denoted as X^n (the *n*th *Cartesian power* of X). The set of *n*-tuples of which the *i*th member is taken from X_i is denoted as $X_1 \times X_2 \cdots X_n$ (the *Cartesian product* of $X_1, \ldots, X_n$). So

$$R \subseteq X^2$$

means that R is a binary relation on X, and

$$R \subseteq X \times Y$$

means that R is a binary relation borne by members of X to members of Y. Happily the intuitive notion of relation is a good guide to its use in proofs; very seldom do we have to remember that R is to be identified with the set of ordered pairs $\langle x, y \rangle$ such that x bears R to y. The notions of sequence and Cartesian product also have infinitary analogues (denoted as $\langle x_1, x_2, \ldots \rangle$ and $X_1 \times X_2 \times \cdots$), of course.

A *function* is a relation; an *n*-ary function f being an $(n + 1)$-ary relation R satisfying the condition

If $Rx_1 \cdots x_n x_{n+1}$ and $Rx_1 \cdots x_n y$,   then $x_{n+1} = y$,

in which case we write

$$f(x_1, \ldots, x_n) = x_{n+1}.$$

Unary functions are most important; we say that f maps X *into* Y iff $f \subseteq X \times Y$ and $f(x)$ exists for every $x \in X$. Also, f maps X *onto* Y iff, in addition, Y has no proper subset Z such that $f \subseteq X \times Z$ ("every member of Y is the f-image of some member of X"). Finally, f is a *one-to-one mapping of X into Y* iff f maps X into Y and

If $f(x) = f(y)$,   then $x = y$,   for all $x, y \in X$.

When f maps X^n into X, we call it an *operation* on X. We sometimes use "transformation" or "mapping" instead of "function" and "operator" instead of "operation"; usage is not uniform here.[2]

We must now address ourselves to the rather elusive notion of a *mathematical structure* or *mathematical system*. Let us begin with a simple example. A group is a system that comprises a set of elements, a binary operation of "group multiplication," and a unary operation, the "inverse". Using $\wedge$ and $^{-1}$ to denote these two operations, respectively, the peculiar properties of a group are given by the axioms

1. $(x \wedge y) \wedge z = x \wedge (y \wedge z)$.
2. There is an element e such that
   (a) $x \wedge e = x$;
   (b) $x \wedge x^{-1} = e$.

What we have just given is an informal definition, because it uses the notions of "system" and "comprises," which we have not defined.

A formal definition of the notion of "group" is the following:

A *group* is a triple $\langle E, \wedge, ^{-1} \rangle$, where E is a nonempty set (the *elements*), $\wedge$ is a binary operation on E, and $^{-1}$ is a unary operation on E, and such that axioms 1 and 2 hold for all members x, y, and z of E.

This pattern of definition is today in common use. It leads to the following general notion of mathematical structure:

A *mathematical structure* (or *system*) is a sequence $\langle E_1, E_2, \ldots;$ $R_1, R_2, \ldots; f_1, f_2, \ldots; o_1, o_2, \ldots \rangle$, where $E_1, E_2, \ldots$ are sets; R_1, $R_2, \ldots$ are zero or more relations included in $E_1 \times E_2 \times \cdots; f_1$, $f_2, \ldots$ are zero or more functions included in $E_1 \times E_2 \times \cdots;$ and $o_1, o_2, \ldots$ are zero or more objects included in $E_1 \cup E_2 \cup \cdots$.

It is easy to see that by these definitions, a group is indeed a mathematical structure or system.

But this pattern of definition also has some drawbacks. For example, if $\langle E, \wedge, ^{-1} \rangle$ is a group, why isn't $\langle \wedge, E, ^{-1} \rangle$? Second, let us note that a *semigroup* is often defined as a system comprising a set of elements and a binary operation $\wedge$ such that axiom 1 holds. By the informal definitions, every group is also a semigroup. But by the formal pattern of definition, a semigroup is an ordered couple, and a group is a triple, so *no* group is a semigroup.

In other words, the formal pattern of definition provides us only with "typical representatives" of the intuitively constructed systems. Too much attention to these niceties would be pedantic, however. In our intuitive commentary we shall avail ourselves of the broader, intuitive notion, and in our formal theory of the formal pattern of definition.

There is one more topic that we must briefly consider here: the *cardinality*, or number of members, of a set. When a system comprises exactly one set, plus relations and operations on that set, we also talk of the cardinality of the system, meaning the cardinality of that set. What is that cardinality? Well, we shall make this notion partly intuitive and partly formal. The formal part is given by the principle

X has the same cardinality as Y iff there is a one-to-one mapping of X onto Y.

Because of this we can talk of X as having the cardinality of the set $\{1, \ldots, n\}$—which is just to say that X has n members, or that X's cardinality is n. We can also talk of X as having the cardinality of the (set of all) natural numbers. In the first case we say that X is *finite*, in the second case that it is *denumerable* or *countable* or *countably infinite*. Cantor showed that the set of real numbers is not finite or denumerable; hence it is said to be *nondenumerable* or *uncountable*.

The cardinality of a set X is denoted as $|X|$; thus $|X| = 3$ if and only if there is a one-to-one mapping of X onto $\{1, 2, 3\}$. The cardinality of the natural numbers is denoted as $\aleph_0$ (*aleph null*), so $|X| = \aleph_0$ if and only if X can be mapped one-to-one onto the natural numbers. A set X is uncountable exactly when $|X| > \aleph_0$, that is, if the set of natural numbers can be mapped one-to-one onto a proper subset of X but not onto X itself. Some principles of this generalized arithmetic are:

(a) If $X \subseteq Y$, then $|X| \leq |Y|$.

(b) The union of denumerably many countable sets is countable.

(c) If $|X| = \aleph_0$ then $|X^n| = \aleph_0$, but then the set of countable sequences of members of X is not countable.

(d) $|\{X : X \subseteq Y\}| > |Y|$.

Principle (d) is a famous result of Cantor's. The proofs of (a)–(d) we relegate to the exercises.

3. Partial Order and Trees

There is one set-theoretic axiom that we must mention, because of its strength and because of the amount of philosophical discussion it has generated. This is the Axiom of Choice. We shall not have too much occasion to use it, and when we do use it, one of its equivalents (such as Zorn's Lemma and the Well-ordering Principle) may be more convenient.

Axiom of Choice. *Given any nonempty family of mutually disjoint nonempty sets A_i there is a set B that contains exactly one member of each set A_i.*

To state some of its equivalents, we must define the notion of partial order.

DEFINITION.   A relation $\leq$ is a *partial ordering* of a set X iff
(a) $\leq$ is reflexive ($x \leq x$ for $x \in X$);
(b) $\leq$ is transitive (if $x \leq y$ and $y \leq z$, then $x \leq z$);
(c) $\leq$ is antisymmetric (if $x \leq y$ and $y \leq x$, then $x = y$).

The most important example of a partial ordering is $\subseteq$, which partially orders any family of sets. We call $\langle X, \leq \rangle$ a *partially ordered system* when $\leq$ is a partial ordering of X. A *chain* in a partially ordered system $\langle X, \leq \rangle$ is a nonempty subset Y of X such that if $x, y \in Y$, then $x \leq y$ or $y \leq x$. In addition, we define two special kinds of elements in a partially ordered system $\langle X, \leq \rangle$: An *upper bound* of a chain Y in this system is a member x of X such that $y \leq x$ for all y in Y, and second, a *maximal element* of the system is a member x of X such that if $x \leq y$, then $x = y$, for all y in X.

Now finally, we can state Zorn's lemma.

Zorn's Lemma. *If every chain in a partially ordered system $\langle X, \leq \rangle$ has an upper bound in X, then $\langle X, \leq \rangle$ has a maximal element.*

A well-ordering is a particular kind of partial ordering. By the following definitions, any chain is linearly ordered.

DEFINITION.   A relation $\leq$ is a *linear ordering* of a set X iff $\leq$ is a partial ordering of X and for any x, y in X, $x \leq y$ or $y \leq x$.

DEFINITION.   A relation $\leq$ is a *well-ordering* of a set X iff $\leq$ is a linear ordering of X and any nonempty subset Y of X contains a *least element*, that is, an element y such that $y \leq x$ for every x in Y, and y is in Y.

For example, when we give $\leq$ its usual meaning, the set of natural numbers is well-ordered but the set of real numbers is not well-ordered. Yet we accept the following equivalent of the axiom of choice:

Well-ordering Principle.   *For any nonempty set X there exists a well-ordering of X.*

We are now going to prove a theorem on the subject of *trees*, in which we will use the axiom of choice. Trees are a kind of partially ordered system: intuitively, the kind that can be represented by a treelike diagram (except that the tree might be infinite); see Figure 1. The

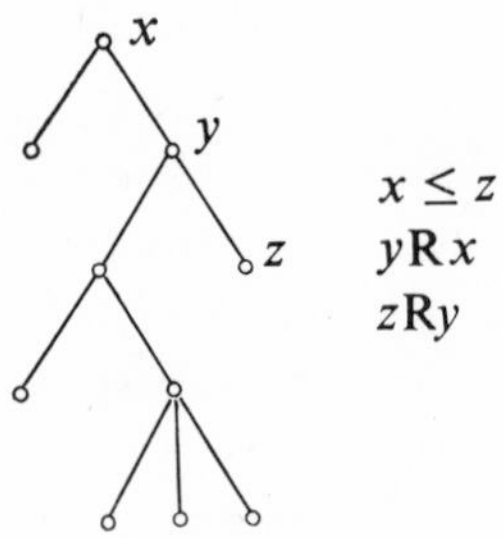

$$x \leq z$$
$$y\mathrm{R}x$$
$$z\mathrm{R}y$$

FIGURE 1

relation $\leq$ holds between two elements of the tree (called *nodes* and represented by dots) if you can get from the one to the other by following a path down the tree (branch). That we think of the trees as growing down rather than up is of course only an idiosyncracy. Genealogical trees are usually drawn this way.

In a tree there is an immediate descendant relation $\mathrm{R}: x\mathrm{R}y$ if $y \leq x$ and there is no z distinct from x and y such that $y \leq z$ and $z \leq x$. Now trees are most easily defined by using the relation R. (After the definition has been given the reader can define $\leq$ in terms of R.)

DEFINITION.   A *tree* is a class T of elements (nodes) on which is defined a binary relation R; one node is singled out as the origin O, and each node has associated with it one natural number (its *rank*) satisfying

(a) the rank of O alone is 1;
(b) the nodes of rank k are those which bear R to exactly one node of rank $k - 1$, where $k > 1$.

Condition (b) rules out circular paths, and also means that each node besides O bears R to something or other. We denote such a tree as $\langle T, R, O \rangle$. We say that a tree $\langle T, R, O \rangle$ has the *finite branching property* iff for every natural number k, there are at most finitely many nodes of rank k.

> DEFINITION. A sequence $\langle n_1, \ldots, n_k, \ldots \rangle$ is a *branch* of $\langle T, R, O \rangle$ iff
> (a) $n_1 = 0$;
> (b) $n_i R n_{i-1}$ for $i = 2, 3, \ldots$;
> (c) if there is an x such that $x R n_i$, then the sequence has an $(i + 1)$th element.

If the branch is finite it has a last element, called an *end point*. If all the branches of a tree are finite, and the tree has the finite branching property, then the tree as a whole is finite (has finitely many nodes). This is not obvious, because one might have branches of any finite length—the question is whether if you have arbitrarily long finite branches, it follows that you also have at least one infinite branch present. That this is so is stated by Koenig's lemma.[3]

Koenig's Lemma. *If a tree with the finite branching property has infinitely many nodes, then it has an infinite branch.*

Proof: Let $B = \langle T, R, O \rangle$ be such a tree. For any node x, we define $T(x)$ to be the class of nodes that lie on some branch passing through x. Now let $T^* = \{x : T(x) \text{ is infinite}\}$. Clearly O belongs to T^*, and if $y \in T^*$, and $y R x$, then $x \in T^*$. So $B^* = \langle T^*, R, O \rangle$ is again a tree: a subtree of B.

Suppose that $x \in T^*$. Could it be an end point of B? The answer is *no*, for then $T(x)$ would just contain the finite branch $\langle n_1, \ldots, n_k \rangle$ with $n_1 = 0$, $n_k = x$ (k being the rank of x)—so then x would not belong to T^*. Could x nevertheless be an end point of B^*? Then x, of rank k, would have infinitely many elements below it, but none of its descendants of rank $k + 1$ would be such. That would mean that x has infinitely many descendants of rank $k + 1$. But that contradicts out assumption that B has the finite branching property.

So B^* has no end points; each of *its* branches is infinite. And each of its branches is (part of) a branch of B. Now, B^* has at least one branch $\langle n_1, n_2, n_3, \ldots \rangle$, for O is in B^*; so let $n_1 = 0$, and O is not an end point; so we can choose n_2 in B^*, which is not an end point; so we can choose n_3 in B^*, which is not an end point; and so on. (Notice that we are making infinitely many choices, one from each rank in B^*; that the branch in question exists follows from the axiom of choice.) So B has at least one infinite branch.

4. Mathematical Induction

Natural numbers are a very important kind of mathematical object. The class of natural numbers may be defined on the basis of the notions *zero* and *successor*, as follows:

DEFINITION. (a) Zero is a natural number.
(b) If x is a natural number, so is the successor of x.
(c) Nothing is a natural number except in virtue of clauses (a) and (b).

This is a very special type of definition (*recursive definition*) not being of the more familiar form "x is a ... iff ...." Yet it defines, in some sense, the property of being a natural number, and hence the class of natural numbers. A further puzzling feature is the use of "in virtue of," which is not a notion it would be easy to define in general. Using the resources of set theory, we can replace the above recursive definition by one in a more familiar form:

DEFINITION. The *class of natural numbers* is the smallest class N such that
(a) $0 \in N$;
(b) if $x \in N$, then the successor of x is in N.

Here "smallest class N such that ... N ..." means "class included in every class X such that ... X ...." The use of this notion of smallest class takes over the function of clause (c).

Many other classes are recursively defined; for example, the class F of formulas of the language of the propositional calculus:

DEFINITION. (a) $p, q, r, p', q', r', p'', \ldots$ are in F.
(b) If $A \in F$, so is $\neg A$.
(c) If $A, B \in F$, so are $(A \ \& \ B), (A \lor B), (A \supset B)$.

Note that here are four ways of generating new elements (not just one way, by the successor function). This definition can now be concluded by adding a "nothing else" clause, or by saying that F is the smallest class satisfying these conditions.

In all the above definitions, clause (a) is a *basis clause*; the elements it introduces are the *basis elements* of the defined class. In each case, clause (b) introduces a *mode of generation* of further elements. For any recursively defined class, the following kind of argument is valid.

1. Each basis element has property P.
2. Each mode of generation preserves property P.
3. Therefore every element of the class has property P.

This proof technique is called mathematical induction. It has two variants: the one just described is *natural induction*; in addition there is *strong induction*, which we shall describe presently. First, let us give the schema for natural induction for the cases of natural numbers and formulas:

1. 0 has property P.

2. If k has P, then the successor of k has P.

3. Therefore, every natural number has P.

1. Each atomic formula (p, $q, \ldots$) has property P.

2. If A has P, so does $\neg A$. If A, B have P so do $(A \ \& \ B), (A \lor B), (A \supset B)$.

3. Therefore, each formula has P.

Usually the hard part of the proof lies in establishing 2 (the *inductive step*).

In the case of *strong induction*, we also think of each generated element coming after the elements from which it is generated, but for each element we consider the whole class of elements after which it comes (instead of merely its immediate predecessor). In the case of natural numbers, the ordering relation is just $<$ of course:

1. 0 has the property P.
2. If every natural number $i < k$ has P, then k has P.
3. Therefore, every natural number has P.

In the case of formulas, we count the number of symbols of which they are built up, calling this number their *length*; then they are ordered by the relation "is of length less than":

1. Each atomic formula has property P.
2. If all formulas of length less than A have P, so does A.
3. Therefore, each formula has P.

When 2 is being proved, "All formulas of length less than A have P" is called the *hypothesis of induction*. It is then generally necessary to consider each possible case (A is $\neg B$ for some formula B; A is (B & C) for some formulas B, C; and so on) separately. Clause 1 is usually proved as part of clause 2.

5. Algorithms

In the recursive definition of the class of natural numbers we think of that class as generated by a simple transformation procedure: we start with zero, and each element at which we arrive is transformed into its successor. This is a very simple case, and much more complicated transformation procedures may be used. When the procedure is still purely mechanical, and is applied only to expressions in some language, it is called an *algorithm*.

A venerable example of an algorithm is the *Euclidean algorithm*. This is a procedure that can be used to find the greatest common divisor of two natural numbers. More precisely, this algorithm is applicable to expressions of the form

$$(m, n),$$

where m, n are nonnegative integers. It has the following procedural rules:

R1. Arrange (m, n) so that the smaller number is on the right of the comma.

R2. If $n \neq 0$, divide m by n and write (n, r), where r is the remainder.

R3. If $n = 0$, change (m, n) into (m).

Starting with (m, n) and transforming the expression successively by these rules we finally arrive at an expression (k). The number k is then the greatest common divisor of m and n.

Example:

$$(4, 15)$$
$$(15, 4) \text{ by R1}$$
$$(4, 3) \text{ by R2, because } 15 = (3 \times 4) + 3$$
$$(3, 1) \text{ by R2, because } 4 = (1 \times 3) + 1$$
$$(1, 0) \text{ by R2, because } 3 = (3 \times 1) + 0$$
$$(1) \text{ by R3}$$

We now turn to a more general account.[4]

An algorithm is a specification of an effective process that transforms an expression E_1 successively into expressions $E_2, E_3, \ldots, E_k, \ldots$. This series may be finite or infinite. If it is finite, it may be because at some point the algorithm is "blocked" (not applicable), or because one of the rules is to stop at a certain point. The rules are called *commands*, and we write the ith command C_i in the form

$$C_i: A_i \rightarrow B_i$$

Sometimes B_i is not another expression, but a dot:

$$C_k : A_k \to \cdot$$

That is a *stop* command, which terminates the process. It says: Erase A_k; then stop.

The command C_i is applicable to an expression E if E contains a part of the form A_i. To apply C_i to E is to replace the leftmost occurrence of A_i in E by an occurrence of B_i. Thus if E is $(\times\ A_i\ \times\ A_i)$, the application of C_i to E consists in replacing E by $(\times\ B_i\ \times\ A_i)$. When carrying out an algorithm, the computing agent is to proceed as follows:

Step 1. Search for the first applicable command, and apply it (if found).

Step 2. If a command applied was a stop command, the resultant was the final expression, and the process terminates.

Step 3. If a command applied was not a stop command, begin again with step 1.

Step 4. If no applicable command can be found, write "blocked" and stop.

The Euclidean algorithm was stated very informally; we can roughly put it in the pattern described above by stating it as follows:

C1. $(m, n) \to (p, q)$, where $p = \begin{cases} m \text{ if } m > n \\ n \text{ if } n > m \end{cases}$ and $q = \begin{cases} m \text{ if } p = n \\ n \text{ if } p = m. \end{cases}$

C2. $, 0 \to \cdot$

C3. $(m, n) \to (n, r)$, where r is the remainder of division of m by n.

Note that C3 is never applied to an expression of form $(m, 0)$, because if $(m, 0)$ occurs, C2 is the first applicable command. Then C2 erases the comma and the zero, yielding the expression (m), and the process stops.

An algorithm sometimes uses auxiliary letters, foreign to the initial expressions to which it is meant to apply. An example is the *duplication algorithm*, which transforms an initial expression E into EE.

Duplication Algorithm. *Auxiliary symbols α, β. The symbols x, y, z stand for letters of the alphabet of the initial expression.*

C1. $\alpha x \rightarrow x\beta x\alpha$
C2. $\beta xy \rightarrow y\beta x$
C3. $\beta \rightarrow$
C4. $\alpha \rightarrow \cdot$
C5. $\rightarrow \alpha$

Here C5 is the starting command. It says: Write α to the left of whole expression. C3 and C4 are used to get rid of the α and the β's when they have done their job. C1 duplicates each letter, and C2 carries the duplicate to the right location. As an example we apply the algorithm to the expression *abb*. Note that x and y stand for *a* and also for *b*, so C1, for example, is really short for

C1a. $\alpha a \rightarrow a\beta a\alpha$
C1b. $\alpha b \rightarrow b\beta b\alpha$

and so on for the other commands.

Example of the duplication procedure:

abb	
αabb	C5
aβaαbb	C1 (C1a)
aβabβbαb	C1 (C1b)
aβabβbbβbα	C1 (C1b)
abβaβbbβbα	C2
abβabβbβbα	C2
abbβaβbβbα	C2
abbaβbβbα	C3
abbabβbα	C3
abbabbα	C3
abbabb	C4

When an algorithm is described with this degree of precision, it is easy to see that the procedure is purely mechanical. When we need to use algorithms later, we shall not aim for this degree of precision. We shall be content to describe the algorithm approximately as precisely as we described the Euclidean algorithm.

NOTES

1. We shall ignore the use/mention distinction except where that could cause confusion; we will, however, say more about this distinction at the beginning of Chapter II.
2. Thus "transformation" is sometimes used synonymously with "function" or "mapping," for example, by C. G. Cullen, *Matrices and Linear Transformations* (Reading, Mass.: Addison-Wesley, 1967), p. 78; but other authors use "transformation" as synonymous with "one-to-one onto operation."
3. Cf. E. W. Beth, *The Foundations of Mathematics* (Amsterdam: North-Holland, 1965), sec. 69, pp. 194–196.
4. Cf. H. B. Curry, *Foundations of Mathematical Logic* (New York: McGraw-Hill, 1963), sec. 2E, pp. 70–80.

CHAPTER II

STRUCTURE
OF
FORMAL
LANGUAGES

1. Logical Grammar

Throughout its history, the study of logic begins with a certain general grammatical analysis of language. The division of Ockham's *Summa*:

I. Terms
II. Propositions
III. Arguments

represents the pattern of almost every medieval and modern logic text.[1] The first division contains a logical analysis of terms (kinds of terms, logical relations among terms), the second of propositions (kinds of propositions, logical relations among propositions); only after such analysis is it fruitful to turn to the logical appraisal of argumentation. In the modern period, this was usually presented by means of a parallel, psychological analysis of acts of the mind; thus in Kant's logic text[2] we find

Part One. General Doctrine of Elements
I. Of Conceptions
II. Of Judgments
III. Of Syllogisms

But it was immediately added that concepts are expressed by terms, judgments by declarative sentences, and so on.

A more contemporary analysis,[3] developed by Ajdukiewicz and Curry, but parallel to many grammatical analyses of language found in the history of logic, divides expressions into three *categories*:

1. nouns   (*n*)
2. sentences   (*s*)
3. functors.

A noun is an expression that can be the grammatical subject of a sentence; a functor is any expression that is neither a noun nor a sentence. However, the use of a functor in combination with other functors and/or some nouns and/or sentences will yield a noun or sentence. There are clearly many kinds of functors; here are some important ones:

Type	Input (one or more)	Output	Example
Connector	*s*	*s*	...and...
Predicator	*n*	*s*	...is white
Operator	*n*	*n*	...+...
Subnector	*s*	*n*	that...

These are all called *first-order* functors, because their "input" does not include functors.

When we describe an artificial language, we do so in a natural language (say, English). The latter is called the *language in use*.[4] It is also, in that context, the *metalanguage* with respect to the artificial language being described. But we may formalize the description of a given artificial language. Then we have an artificial language L_1, and another artificial language L_2, which functions as a metalanguage with respect to L_1. In the meanwhile, the language in use functions as a metalanguage with respect to L_2, or perhaps with respect to both L_1 and L_2.

When describing an artificial language, it is seldom useful to *display* its symbols. Much more useful is the course of adding certain symbols and technical terms to the language in use, to *refer* to the symbols of the language described. This helps to avoid confusions of use and mention. But it also introduces new temptations: if *u* is introduced to refer to a symbol of *L*, we have often the temptation to use *u* as if it were the symbol that it designates, and sometimes the temptation to use *u* to refer to itself. As with many temptations, however, the most pleasant course is not to resist them too much, and giving in to them seldom does as much harm as one might fear.

2. Syntactic Systems

A syntactic system comprises a *vocabulary* and a grammar. The latter is a specification of how the nouns and sentences are to be constructed from the vocabulary. We shall now make this somewhat more precise by using set-theoretical notions.

The vocabulary of a syntactic system is a nonempty set of elements called *words*. An *expression* is any finite sequence of words; the restriction to finite sequences is, however, only a convenience adopted by us for didactic purposes. In addition, we shall assume that there are at most denumerably many words, again for convenience; it follows then that there are exactly denumerably many expressions in the language.

If A is the expression $\langle e_1, \ldots, e_n \rangle$ we shall simply write it as $e_1 \cdots e_n$. In addition, we define the operation of *concatenation*: the concatenation AB of two expressions A and B is defined by

$$\langle e_1, \ldots, e_m \rangle \langle e_{m+1}, \ldots, e_n \rangle = \langle e_1, \ldots, e_m, e_{m+1}, \ldots, e_n \rangle.$$

With any syntactic system there is associated a well-ordering of the expressions, called the *alphabetical order*.

The grammar of the system consists in the division of the set of expressions into the class of nouns, the class of sentences, classes of functors of various kinds (and possibly a remainder of expressions that have no significant role at all). When a noun or sentence belongs to the vocabulary itself, it is generally called *atomic*; expressions that are not words are called *molecular*. When the system is defined, the grammatical division of the vocabulary may be given at once, and used to define the molecular nouns and sentences.

As an example, we take the language of the propositional calculus.

DEFINITION. A *propositional syntactic system* (PCS) is a triple $\langle \mathscr{A}, L, S \rangle$, where
(a) $\mathscr{A}$ is a set, at most denumerable (the *atomic sentences*);
(b) L is a set of four distinct elements $\{\&, \neg,), (\}$ (*logical signs*), disjoint from $\mathscr{A}$;
(c) S (the set of *sentences*) is the smallest set including $\mathscr{A}$ and such that if A, B are in S, so are $(\neg A)$ and $(A \,\&\, B)$.

We have here taken & and $\neg$ as primitive; the other familiar connectives may be defined in terms of them as usual. It is to be noted that here the vocabulary consists of $\mathscr{A}$ and L, and the grammar of the definition of S. Parentheses will be omitted where convenient.

A *syntactic transformation* is a mapping of (sets of) expressions into expressions. In the case of a PCS, we would only be interested in transformations that preserve the property of being a sentence. An example of such a transformation would be

$$f : f(A) = \neg A,$$

which transforms each sentence into its contradictory. Less trivial examples are the substitution transformations. There are several kinds; a well-known one is that of substitution of sentences A for atomic sentences p in a PCS:

DEFINITION. $S_p^A(B) =$
(a) B if B is an atomic sentence other than p;
(b) A if B is p;
(c) $(\neg S_p^A(C))$ if B is $\neg C$;
(d) $(S_p^A(C) \& S_p^A(D))$ if B is $(C \& D)$.

Another kind of substitution replaces all the atomic sentences by (other) sentences all at once:

DEFINITION.   If s is a mapping of atomic sentences into sentences and E is the expression $e_1 \cdots e_n (e_i, i = 1, \ldots, n$ belonging to the vocabulary), then $S^s(E) = e_1^* \cdots e_n^*$, where $e_i^* = s(e_i)$ if e_i is an atomic sentence, and $e_i^* = e_i$ otherwise.

In both cases the transformation preserves the property of being a sentence; this can be shown by an easy inductive argument.

We shall call the operation S_p^A *unary substitution*, and S^s *infinitary substitution*, and, if s is a mapping into atomic sentences only, *atomic infinitary substitution*. Note that infinitary substitution is a notion defined for any syntactic system with a class of atomic sentences, while unary substitution has been defined only for a PCS.

A generalization of unary substitution is *simultaneous* substitution, which can be characterized informally by

$S_{p_1 \cdots p_n}^{B_1 \cdots B_n}(A)$ is the expression that differs from A only in having B_i, where A has p_i, $i + 1, \ldots, n$; where $p_i \neq p_j$ if $i \neq j$.

This cannot be defined simply as an iteration of unary substitutions, since some of the p_i may occur in some of the B_i. For example, we cannot transform $(p \ \& \ q)$ into $(q \ \& \ p)$ by first substituting q for p [to get the result $(q \ \& \ q)$], and then substituting p for q—the final result would be $(p \ \& \ p)$. This difficulty is avoided by first replacing the atomic sentences in question by entirely new atomic sentences.

DEFINITION. $S_{p_1 \cdots p_n}^{B_1 \cdots B_n}(A) = S_{q_1}^{B_1} \cdots S_{q_n}^{B_n} S_{p_1}^{q_1} \cdots S_{p_n}^{q_n}(A)$, where $q_1, \ldots,$ q_n are alphabetically the first n atomic sentences not to occur in B_i, p_i, or A ($i = 1, \ldots, n$) and $p_i \neq p_j$ if $i \neq j$.

Unary substitution is a special case of simultaneous substitution; and any case of simultaneous substitution can be defined in terms of unary substitution. We now add that unary substitution can be defined in terms of infinitary substitution.

Theorem. $S_p^B(A) = S^s(A)$, *where for any atomic sentence q, $s(q) = q$ if $q \neq p$, and $s(p) = B$.*

Proof: Since unary substitution has a recursive definition, we can prove this by mathematical induction.

Hypothesis of Induction. *If C is of length less than A, $S_p^B(C) = S^s(C)$.*

  Case 1. A is p. Then $S_p^B(A) = B = S^s(A)$.
  Case 2. A is an atomic sentence $q \neq p$. Then $S_p^B(A) = q = S^s(A)$.
  Case 3. A is $(\neg C)$. Then $S_p^B(A) = (\neg S_p^B(C))$. By hypothesis, this is $(\neg S^s(C)) = S^s(A)$.
  Case 4. A is $(C \ \& \ D)$. Then $S_p^B(A) = (S_p^B(C) \ \& \ S_p^B(D))$. By hypothesis, this is $(S^s(C) \ \& \ S^s(D)) = S^s(C \ \& \ D)$.

3. Semantic Concepts

A *valuation* of a syntactic system is a function that assigns T (*true*) to some of its sentences, and/or F (*false*) to some of its sentences. We do not rule out that not all sentences are assigned T or F, nor that no sentence is assigned T (respectively, F), nor that some sentences are assigned something else. Precisely, a valuation maps a nonempty subset of the set of sentences into the set {T, F}. We call a valuation *bivalent* iff it maps all the sentences into {T, F}.

In general, some of the symbols have an intended meaning, and this leads to a distinction between admissible and inadmissible valuations. A *language* comprises exactly a syntactic system (its *syntax*) and non-empty class of valuations of that syntactic system (its *admissible valuations*). The expressions of the syntax of L are also called expressions of L. As an example we consider again the propositional calculus. In that subject, one is generally concerned with a kind of language that we shall call a *bivalent propositional language*.

> DEFINITION. L is a *bivalent propositional language* iff its syntax is a PCS and its admissible valuations are the functions v such that for all sentences A, B of L,
> (a) $v(A) \in \{T, F\}$;
> (b) $v(\neg A) = T$ iff $v(A) = F$;
> (c) $v(A \& B) = T$ iff $v(A) = v(B) = T$.

In terms of valuations we can define semantic properties of sentences and sets of sentences, and semantic relations among these.

The most important concept is that of satisfaction. A set X of sentences of L is *satisfied* by an admissible valuation v of L iff $v(A) = T$ for every member A of X. We shall also say "v satisfies A" when v satisfies $\{A\}$, and "X (respectively, A) is satisfiable (in L)" when some admissible valuation of L satisfies X (respectively, A).

> DEFINITION. A is a *valid sentence* (in symbols, $\Vdash A$) in L iff every admissible valuation of L satisfies A.

DEFINITION. X is an *unassailable* set of sentences of L iff X is (a set of sentences of L) such that every admissible valuation of L satisfies some member of X.

Thus A is valid iff $\{A\}$ is unassailable; unassailability is a generalization of validity. Note that "X is unassailable" is not the same, as "no admissible valuation assigns F to every member of X" unless all the admissible valuations are bivalent. (This is why we could not use "not falsifiable" instead of the contrived term "unassailable.")

DEFINITION. X *semantically entails* $A(X \Vdash A)$ in L iff every admissible valuation of L that satisfies X also satisfies A.

We write "$A \Vdash B$" for "$\{A\} \Vdash B$"; $\Vdash$ is called the (double) *turnstile*. It is fairly easy to see that $\Vdash A$ in L if and only if $\Lambda \Vdash A$ in L, because all admissible valuations of L satisfy all sentences in the empty set, vacuously.

Syntactic transformations may preserve certain semantic properties. We call a mapping f of sets of sentences to sentences *truth-preserving* in language L when

$$\text{if } v \text{ satisfies } X, \text{ then } v \text{ satisfies } f(X)$$

holds for all arguments X of f and all admissible valuations v of L. Similarly, we say that f *preserves validity* in L when

$$\text{if } \Vdash A \text{ for all sentences } A \text{ in } X, \text{ then}$$
$$\Vdash f(X), \text{ and if } \Vdash B, \text{ then } \Vdash f(B)$$

holds all arguments X, B of f and all admissible valuations v of L. The first part of the following theorem says that a truth-preserving transformation also preserves validity.

Theorem. (a) *If $X \Vdash f(X)$ for every argument X of f, then f preserves validity.*
(b) *If $A \in X$, then $X \Vdash A$.*
(c) *If $X \subseteq Y$ and $X \Vdash A$, then $Y \Vdash A$.*
(d) *If $X \Vdash A$ for every $A \in Y$, and $Y \Vdash B$, then $X \Vdash B$.*

The proof of this theorem is an elementary exercise in logic. For example, to prove clause (a) it suffices to show that a statement of the form

$$(x)(Fx \supset Gx) \supset \cdot (x)(Fx) \supset (x)(Gx)$$

is a theorem of quantification theory. [Let Fx stand for "x satisfies X," and Gx for "x satisfies $f(X)$," interpreting x to be a variable ranging over the admissible valuations of the language.] It is advisable, of course, to keep the proofs informal enough not to become excessively long.

The simplest kind of syntactic system is that whose vocabulary is exactly its set of sentences. The semantics of a language that has this kind of syntax can therefore hardly go far beyond a discussion of its valuations. The only complication possible here seems to be that the set of admissible valuations might be defined in terms of something else, for example, in terms of mappings of the sentences into some mathematical structure (a "logical matrix," for example). Be that as it may, a discussion of valuations is apparently the most general kind of concern within semantics. While we shall remain at this level of generality in this chapter, we wish to make some remarks about the semantic structure of languages with a more complex syntax.

We have not ruled out, in our definition of a valuation v of a syntactic system S, that v may be defined for expressions of S that are not sentences. Thus v might assign denotations to nouns; that is, there may be a domain of discourse D such that v maps the nouns of S into D. In addition, v might assign relations or functions to functors of S. And finally, the mapping by v of sentences into truth values might be partly or entirely determined by what v assigns to the elements of the vocabulary of S. In such a case it is more usual to call v an *interpretation* of S rather than a valuation of S; but as long as v maps some sentences into truth values, it is still a valuation by our definition.[5]

4. Valuation Space of a Language

The role of the geometric imagination in logic is no doubt best exemplified in the use of Venn diagrams. But it has many other instances; witness, for example, the spatial metaphor in such expressions as "the predicate is contained in the subject" or even "the extension of the predicate." In metalogic, too, geometry provides inspiration; especially influential here has been *topology*, a subject that deals with spaces, and relations on and among spaces, in a very abstract fashion. The concepts and methods introduced in this and some later sections represent, in effect, an application of topology to logic. We do not require the reader to be already familiar with topology; on the other hand, we shall not attempt to carry through too exact an analogy with the actual topological notions.

Let L be a language and VL the set of its admissible valuations. We shall think of the members of VL as the points in an abstract space, the "valuation space" of L. Regions in that space are just sets of these points, that is, subsets of VL. An important kind of region is that usually designated as "elementary class."

> DEFINITION. If A is a sentence of L and VL the set of admissible valuations of L, $H(A) = \{v \in VL : v(A) = T\}$; and a set of $X \subseteq VL$ is an *elementary class* iff there is a sentence A such that $X = H(A)$.

$H(A)$ may be called the *truth set* of A; if we were to discuss several languages at once, we would obviously use expressions such as "$H(A)$ in L."

> DEFINITION. The *valuation space* of L is $H = \langle VL, \{H(A) : A$ a sentence of $L\}\rangle$.

We call the members of VL the *points* in H, and write $x \in H$ when x is such a point, or $X \subseteq H$ when X is a class of such points (*region*). So the valuation space consists of a set of points, plus a family of regions that are singled out for special consideration. These regions, which we call the elementary classes, are also called "arithmetical classes" or "axiomatic model classes."[6] Sometimes infinite intersections

$$H(X) = \bigcap_{A \in X} H(A) = \text{the set of all admissible valuations that satisfy } X$$

are also called elementary classes. We shall accept this shorthand notation, but we shall not extend the term "elementary class" in this way. [Note that $H(\Lambda) = H$ by the above definition, and restricting the range of our variables to H.]

Before going on, let us take as an example a bivalent propositional language with just two atomic sentences, p and q. This language has just four admissible valuations, which are partially depicted by the following truth table:

	p	q	$\neg p$	$\neg q$	$(p \& q)$	$(p \& \neg p)$	$\cdots$
v_1	T	T	F	F	T	F	$\cdots$
v_2	T	F	F	T	F	F	$\cdots$
v_3	F	T	T	F	F	F	$\cdots$
v_4	F	F	T	T	F	F	$\cdots$

Here

$$H(p) = \{v_1, v_2\}, \qquad H(\neg p) = \{v_3, v_4\},$$
$$H(q) = \{v_1, v_3\}, \qquad H(p \& q) = \{v_1\},$$
$$H(p \& \neg p) = \Lambda.$$

We also say that $H = \{v_1, v_2, v_3, v_4\}$—although this is clearly an inaccurate way of speaking—hence H and Λ function as the universal and null set here. Note that just as Λ is the elementary class defined by a contradiction, so H is the elementary class defined by a tautology.

The basic semantic concepts are easily expressed in terms of the valuation space:

(a) A is a valid sentence iff $H(A) = H$.
(b) X is unassailable iff $\bigcup_{A \in X} H(A) = H$.
(c) X is satisfiable iff $\bigcap_{A \in X} H(A) \neq \Lambda$.
(d) B semantically entails A iff $H(B) \subseteq H(A)$.
(e) X semantically entails A iff $H(X) \subseteq H(A)$.

This is proved by inspecting the definitions.

A term that metalogic has taken over directly from topology is "compactness." In both subjects, the term has several definitions, which are equivalent relative to the usual assumptions. Because we shall not make all the usual assumptions, these definitions correspond to distinct concepts for us; we shall then investigate the conditions under which the equivalence obtains.

DEFINITION.   The language L (and its valuation space H) is *I-compact* iff for any set of sentences X of L, $\bigcap_{A \in X} H(A) = \Lambda$ only if $\bigcap_{A \in Y} H(A) = \Lambda$ for some finite subset Y of X.

This condition is clearly equivalent to: Any nonsatisfiable set has a finite nonsatisfiable subset; *or* a set of sentences is satisfiable iff all its finite subsets are satisfiable. (The I stands for "intersection.")

DEFINITION.   The language L (and its valuation space H) is *U-compact* iff for any set of sentences X of L, $\bigcup_{A \in X} H(A) = H$ only if $\bigcup_{A \in Y} H(A) = H$ for some finite subset Y of X.

This condition amounts to: Any unassailable set has a finite unassailable subset. A family of elementary classes whose union equals H is also said to *cover H*, or to be an *elementary cover* of H. Hence the condition for U-compactness can also be stated as: Any elementary cover of H contains a finite subcover of H. We shall call a language L (and its valuation space H) *compact* iff it is both I-compact and U-compact.[7]

We add finally a property of languages that is very similar to compactness; the relations between these notions are explored below.

DEFINITION.   A language L has *finitary semantic entailment* iff for any set of sentences X of L, and sentence A of L, $H(X) \subseteq H(A)$ only if $H(Y) \subseteq H(A)$ for some finite subset Y of X.

The condition amounts to: $X \Vdash A$ only if some finite subset of X semantically entails A.

In classical logic one is concerned only with languages that have both compactness and finitary entailment. But suppose we have a language containing the numerals $1, 2, 3, \ldots$ and in which $(x)Fx$ is to mean that all positive integers have the property F. Then the entailment

$$\{F(1), F(2), F(3), \ldots\} \Vdash (x)Fx$$

shows that this language does not have finitary entailment.

If, in addition, this language has the usual kind of negation, then the unassailability of

$$\{(x)Fx, \neg F(1), \neg F(2), \ldots\}$$

shows that it is not U-compact, and the unsatisfiability of

$$\{\neg(x)Fx, F(1), F(2), \ldots\}$$

shows that it is not I-compact. We shall now explore this subject in a more general way, beginning with a familiar case.

We say that a language L has *exclusion negation* iff for every sentence A of L there is a sentence A' of L such that $H(A') = H - H(A)$ in L. Clearly, a bivalent propositional language has exclusion negation, as has the language of quantification theory.[8]

Theorem. *For a language L with exclusion negation, the following conditions are all equivalent:*

(*a*) *L is I-compact.*
(*b*) *L is U-compact.*
(*c*) *L is compact.*
(*d*) *L has finitary semantic entailment.*

Proof: Since (c) is equivalent to the conjunction of (a) and (b), it suffices to show that (a) implies (b), (b) implies (d), and (d) implies (a).

First suppose that L is I-compact, and let X be such that

1. $\bigcup_{A \in X} H(A) = H$; hence
2. $H - \bigcup_{A \in X} H(A) = \Lambda$.

By the generalized laws of de Morgan and distribution, this yields

3. $\bigcap_{A \in X} (H - H(A')) = \Lambda$.

Using A' for the exclusion negation of A, this means that

4. $\bigcap_{A \in X} H(A') = \Lambda$,

which by I-compactness, has the consequence

5. $\bigcap_{A \in Y} H(A') = \Lambda$ for a finite subset Y of X.

Retracing our steps via de Morgan's laws, that implies that

6. $\bigcup_{A \in Y} H(A) = H$ for a finite subset Y of X.

Hence I-compactness implies U-compactness.

Now suppose that L is U-compact and that $X \Vdash A$. Then

7. $\bigcap_{B \in X} H(B) \subseteq H(A)$,

which, as one may check by Venn diagram, implies

8. $\overline{\bigcap_{B \in X} H(B)} \cup H(A) = H$,

where we use $\overline{K}$ for $H - K$ ("relative complement"). By de Morgan's laws, that is equivalent to

9. $(\bigcup_{B \in X} \overline{H(B)}) \cup H(A) = H$, or
10. $(\bigcup_{B \in X} H(B')) \cup H(A) = H$.

By U-compactness this elementary cover has a finite subcover:

11. $(\bigcup_{B \in Y} H(B')) \cup H(A) = H$ for a finite subset Y of X.

Retracing our steps once more, we conclude that

12. $\bigcap_{B \in Y} H(B) \subseteq H(A)$ for a finite subset Y of X.

Hence U-compactness implies finitary entailment in this case.

Finally, suppose that semantic entailment is finitary, and also that X is not satisfiable. Let A be any sentence in X (X cannot be nonempty; why?). Then we have

13. $\bigcap_{B \in X} H(B) = \Lambda$; hence
14. $\bigcap(X - \{A\}) \cap H(A) = \Lambda$; hence
15. $\bigcap(X - \{A\}) \subseteq H(A')$; that is,
16. $X - \{A\} \Vdash A'$.

By the finitary character of ⊩ we deduce that there is a finite subset Y of $X - \{A\}$ such that

17. $Y \Vdash A'$.
18. $\bigcap\{H(B): B \in Y\} \cap H(A) = \Lambda$.
19. $\bigcap\{H(B): B \in Y \cup \{A\}\} = \Lambda$.

Therefore, X has a finite subset $Y \cup \{A\}$ that is not satisfiable.

While compactness and finitary semantic entailment are thus equivalent in most familiar cases, it is important to note that they are not equivalent in general.

Theorem. *There is a language L that is compact and does not have finitary entailment.*

Proof: We prove this by constructing an example. Let L have denumerably many sentences $q, p_1, p_2, p_3, \ldots$, and let the admissible valuations of L be the mappings v of all these sentences into $\{T, F\}$ such that

$$v(q) = T \quad \text{iff } v(p_i) = T \qquad \text{for } i = 1, 2, 3, \ldots.$$

It is easy to see that L does not have finitary entailment, because $\{p_1, p_2, p_3, \ldots\} \Vdash q$ in L, but for any n, $\{p_1, \ldots, p_n\}$ does not semantically entail q because the valuation

$$v: v(p_i) = T \quad \text{iff } i \leq n; \qquad v(q) = F$$

is admissible. Hence no finite subset of $\{p_1, p_2, p_3, \ldots\}$ semantically entails q in L. But L is compact, as we can show in two steps.

First, the valuation

$$v_1: v_1(q) = F, v_1(p_i) = F \qquad \text{for } i = 1, 2, 3, \ldots$$

is an admissible valuation of L. Since v_1 does not satisfy any set of sentences, it follows that no set of sentences is unassailable; hence L is U-compact. Second, the valuation

$$v_2: v_2(q) = T, v_2(p_i) = T \qquad \text{for } i = i, 2, 3, \ldots$$

is also admissible; hence no set of sentences of L is unsatisfiable, so L is I-compact.

We shall also prove that I-compactness and U-compactness are not equivalent in general and that finitary entailment does not imply compactness, after we have introduced the notion of a filter.

5. Semantic Entailment and Axiomatizability

The familiar notion of a deductive theory is that a theory is given by specifying the language in which it is formulated, its axioms, and the rules whereby the complete set of theorems may be derived from the axioms. The rules are here required to be such that any valid argument whose premises are theorems must have a theorem as conclusion. In the terminology of formal semantics, this means that the set of theorems is a system ("deductive system" and "theory" are also used).

> DEFINITION. A *system* in a language L is a set X of sentences of L such that any sentence A of L semantically entailed by X in L belongs to X.

If X is a system, then we may call Y a set of *axioms* for X—or say that Y axiomatizes X—if all the members of X are semantically entailed by Y. Of special interest here is the case in which Y is finite, and in the remainder of this section we shall study this case.

We say that two sets of sentences of L, X and Y, are *semantically equivalent* in L if they are satisfied by exactly the same admissible valuations of L. It is easily shown then that X and Y are semantically equivalent in L if and only if for any sentence A of L, $X \Vdash A$ iff $Y \Vdash A$ in L.

> DEFINITION. A set X of sentences is *finitely axiomatizable* in L iff X is semantically equivalent to some finite set of sentences in L.

To prove our first theorem, we need the notion of a chain of sets of sentences in a language. A class of sets $Y_1, \ldots, Y_k, \ldots$ is called a *chain of increasing strength* in L if $Y_i \subseteq Y_{i+1}$ but Y_{i+1} has a member not semantically entailed by Y_i in L (that is, $H(Y_i) \nsubseteq H(Y_{i+1})$), for $i = 1, \ldots, k, \ldots$.

Theorem. *If a set X of sentences of L is not finitely axiomatizable, then X is the union of a chain of increasing strength in L.*

Proof: Suppose that X is not finitely axiomatizable. Since we have assumed from the beginning that a language has at most denumerably many sentences, the members of X can be arranged in a series

$$A_1, A_2, A_3, \ldots.$$

And X is the union of the sets $X_k = \{A_1, \ldots, A_k\}$ for the positive integers k. Let us now define the sets Y_i as follows:

$Y_1 = X_1,$
$Y_{m+1} =$ the smallest set X_n containing a member not semantically entailed by Y_m.

Since the sets X_n form a chain, Y_{m+1} is uniquely defined if Y_m does not axiomatize X. Since none of the sets X_n axiomatizes X, there will be for each set Y_i a next set Y_{i+1}, and these sets Y_i form a chain of increasing strength whose union is X.

Theorem. *If X is a system in L, and X is the union of a chain of increasing strength in L, then X is not finitely axiomatizable.*

Proof: If X is a system, then it is axiomatizable only by one of its own subsets.

Suppose that X is axiomatizable by its finite subset $\{A_1, \ldots, A_n\}$, and is the union of the infinite chain $Y_1, Y_2, \ldots$. Then for each A_j there is a set Y_{k_j} in the chain that contains A_j. Let m be the highest of these subscripts k_j. Then Y_m contains all the sentences $A_1, \ldots, A_n$ and therefore semantically entails every member of X—including every member of Y_{m+1}. Thus the chain is not one of increasing strength.

We can also use the assumptions of finitary semantic entailment to strengthen this result of finite axiomatizability.[9]

Theorem. *If L has finitary semantic entailment, and the set X of sentences of L is semantically equivalent to an infinite chain of increasing strength in L, then X is not finitely axiomatizable.*

Proof: Let X be semantically equivalent to the union U of a chain $Y_1, Y_2, \ldots$. Suppose that X is axiomatizable by the finite set $\{A_1, \ldots, A_n\}$. Then X, and hence U, semantically entails A_i, for $i = 1, \ldots, n$. Given that L has finitary entailment, we conclude that for each i there is an integer k_i such that $Y_{k_i} \Vdash A_i$. Let k be the largest of these integers. Then $Y_k \Vdash A_i$ for each i; hence $Y_k \Vdash A$ for each sentence A in X. But then $Y_k \Vdash A$ for each A in Y_{k+1}, so the sequence $Y_1, Y_2, \ldots$ is not a chain of increasing strength.

It is important to see how this theorem strengthens the earlier one: The difference is that here we do not require that X be a system, and we no longer require X to *be* the union of some infinite chain of increasing strength but only to be equivalent to such a union. But this makes it necessary to suppose semantic entailment to be finitary. An example of a language in which $\Vdash$ is not finitary is one that has a name for every natural number and in which the quantifiers range over the natural numbers. There the set

$$X = \{F(0), F(1), F(2), \ldots\}$$

is semantically equivalent to the set

$$Y = \{(n)F(n)\}.$$

Thus X is finitely axiomatizable; so, therefore, is the system

$$Z = \{A : X \Vdash A\}.$$

Yet Z is equivalent to X, which is the union of the infinite chain of increasing strength:

$$\{F(0)\}, \{F(0), F(1)\}, \{F(0), F(1), F(2)\}, \ldots.$$

But X is not closed under $\Vdash$, so the previous theorem does not apply to X. Z is not itself the union of such a chain [because if Y_m contains $(n)F(n)$, then Y_m axiomatizes Z], so the previous theorem does not apply to it. Finally, $\Vdash$ is here not finitary, so the present theorem does not apply to X or to Z.

6. Theory of Deductive Systems

The study of semantic entailment is of special importance in connection with the subject of deductive theories. The most obvious way to conceive of a theory is as a systematic body of assertions: The theory provides us with a list of sentences (*theorems*) asserted to be true. This is of course equivalent to: To hold a theory is to hold that the actual situation is correctly represented by some admissible valuation that satisfies all its theorems. So one can alternatively conceive of the theory as specifying a set of valuations, and the single assertion that one of these valuations is the correct one. If we call the theory K, we can choose to discuss either the set of *K-theorems* or the set of *K-valuations*, with the correspondence:

$$K\text{-theorem} = \text{sentence satisfied by all } K\text{-valuations}$$
$$K\text{-valuation} = \text{valuation that satisfies all } K\text{-theorems}$$

From this correspondence we see at once that the set of K-theorems is closed under semantic entailment, that is, a system. We shall now study the general relationships that obtain among systems.

Theorem.   *For all systems X, Y, $X \subseteq Y$ iff $H(Y) \subseteq H(X)$.*

Proof: Suppose $X \subseteq Y$. Then $Y \Vdash A$ for all $A \in X$. Hence $H(Y) \subseteq H(A)$ for all A in X, and so $H(Y) \subseteq H(X)$. Suppose second, that

$H(Y) \subseteq H(X)$. If $A \in X$, $H(X) \subseteq H(A)$, so then $H(Y) \subseteq H(A)$; that is, $Y \Vdash A$ for all A in X. But Y is a system; therefore, it follows that $A \in Y$ for A in X; that is, $X \subseteq Y$.

Theorem.   *For all systems, X, Y, $X \cap Y$ is a system and $H(X) \cup H(Y) \subseteq H(X \cap Y)$.*

Proof: If $X \cap Y \Vdash A$, then $X \Vdash A$ and $Y \Vdash A$ because X and Y are supersets of $X \cap Y$. But then $A \in X$ and $A \in Y$, so $A \in X \cap Y$. This establishes that $X \cap Y$ is a system.

Second, $X \cap Y \subseteq X$, so $H(X) \subseteq H(X \cap Y)$ by the preceding theorem. Similarly, $H(Y) \subseteq H(X \cap Y)$. Therefore, $H(X) \cup H(Y) \subseteq H(X \cap Y)$.

Corollary.   *For all systems X, Y,*
$$\begin{aligned}
X \cap Y &= \{A : X \Vdash A \text{ and } Y \Vdash A\} \\
&= \{A : X \cap Y \Vdash A\} \\
&= \{A : H(X \cap Y) \subseteq H(A)\} \\
&= \{A : H(X) \cup H(Y) \subseteq H(A)\}.
\end{aligned}$$

Proof: Only the last equality is not obvious, since we know that $H(X \cap Y) \supseteq H(X) \cup H(Y)$ but that the converse does not generally hold. However, suppose that $H(X) \cup H(Y) \subseteq H(A)$. Then certainly $H(X) \subseteq H(A)$ and $H(Y) \subseteq H(A)$. But then A belongs to both X and Y, and hence to $X \cap Y$.

These obvious results for intersection do not all hold for union (why?), but one may introduce an operation on sets of sentences that is *like* union and does preserve the property of being a system. This leads to a calculus of systems, the study of which was begun by Tarski.[10] To begin we note that the intersection $\bigcap F$ of a family of systems F is again a system: for $\bigcap F$ is part of every system in F, so that if $\bigcap F \Vdash A$, then A is a member of every system in F—and hence a member of $\bigcap F$. Thus it makes sense to speak of the smallest system that contains both of two given systems.

DEFINITION. If X and Y are sets of sentences of L, the *system union* $X \cup Y$ of X and Y is the smallest system containing both X and Y.

As usual, "smallest" does not mean of least cardinality: it means, in effect, the intersection of all systems containing both X and Y.

Theorem. *For all systems* X, Y,
(a) $X \cup Y = \{A : X \cup Y \Vdash A\} = \{A : H(X \cup Y) \subseteq H(A)\}$;
(b) $H(X \cup Y) = H(X) \cap H(Y)$.

Proof: (a) That $\{A : X \cup Y \Vdash A\}$ contains both X and Y is clear. That it is a system follows from the transitivity of semantic entailment (see the theorem at the end of Section 3). Moreover, it is the smallest system containing both X and Y, for *any* such system must contain whatever is semantically entailed by $X \cup Y$.

(b) Let v satisfy $X \cup Y$; then it satisfies X and also Y, which are subsets of $X \cup Y$. Hence $v \in H(X) \cap H(Y)$. On the other hand, if v satisfies X and also Y, it satisfies all the sentences in X and also those in Y, hence all those in $X \cup Y$, and hence all those in $\{A : X \cup Y \Vdash A\} = X \cup Y$.

If L is a language, let us denote as "$\underline{\text{SYST}}(L)$" the family of systems in L. Then $\underline{\text{SYST}}(L)$ is partially ordered by the set-inclusion relation, the intersection of X and Y in $\underline{\text{SYST}}(L)$ is the largest system in $\underline{\text{SYST}}(L)$ included in both X and Y, and the system union of X and Y in $\underline{\text{SYST}}(L)$ is the smallest system in $\underline{\text{SYST}}(L)$ that includes both X and Y. That is, the following principles hold for all X, Y, and Z in $\underline{\text{SYST}}(L)$.

(a) $X \subseteq X$.
(b) If $X \subseteq Y$ and $Y \subseteq Z$, then $X \subseteq Z$.
(c) If $X \subseteq Y$ and $Y \subseteq X$, then $X = Y$.
(d) $X \cap Y \subseteq X$; $X \cap Y \subseteq Y$.
(e) If $Z \subseteq X$ and $Z \subseteq Y$, then $Z \subseteq X \cap Y$.
(f) $X \subseteq X \cup Y$; $Y \subseteq X \cup Y$.
(g) If $X \subseteq Z$ and $Y \subseteq Z$, then $X \cup Y \subseteq Z$.

This can be summed up by saying that the calculus of systems in any given language is a *lattice* (under the relation $\subseteq$ and operations $\cap$ and $\cup$). The question is now whether the set of principles (a)–(g) is complete or whether there are additional principles that can be expressed in terms of $\subseteq$, $\cap$, and $\cup$ that characterize every calculus of systems. That the set (a)–(g) is complete in this sense is proved in Appendix I.

7. System Complementation and Axiomatizability

It is quite possible, of course, to define operations on systems other than intersection and system union, and the most obvious candidate would be some analogue to complementation. This is, in fact, an interesting case, for it will allow us to formulate some conditions related to finite axiomatizability.

To introduce an analogue to complementation, we must single out for special consideration the *smallest system* and the *largest system*, that is, the system O included in all other systems, and the system I, which contains all other systems. It is clear that these exist, and are, respectively, the set of all valid sentences and the set of all sentences (of the language in question).

The main condition we place on the system complement is analogous to the law of noncontradiction:

$$(g) \quad X \cap \dot{\bar{X}} = O$$

It is not easy to see what other conditions should be put on this operation, just because different logics disagree so much on the properties of negation, beyond the law of noncontradiction. However, there is one case where we can have little doubt, and that is when we have exclusion negation $\neg$, and $X = \{A : B \Vdash A\}$. Then $\dot{\bar{X}}$ should be $\{A : \neg B \Vdash A\}$. In that case $\dot{\bar{X}} = \{A : H - H(B) \subseteq H(A)\}$; and we generalize this to:

DEFINITION.   The system complement $\dot{\bar{X}}$ of X is the set $\{A : H - H(X) \subseteq H(A)\}$.

There is, of course, in general no set Y such that $(H - H(X)) = H(Y)$, so this definition cannot be further simplified. For example, it is *not* generally true that $H(\overset{\cdot}{X}) = H - H(X)$, although $H - H(X) \subseteq H(\overset{\cdot}{X})$.

Theorem. *For all systems X, Y,*

(a) $H(X) \cup H(\overset{\cdot}{X}) = H$;

(b) $X \cap \overset{\cdot}{X} = O$;

(c) *If $X \subseteq Y$, then $\overset{\cdot}{Y} \subseteq \overset{\cdot}{X}$.*

Proof: (a) If $v \notin H(X)$, then $v \in H - H(X)$, so v satisfies every sentence A such that $H - H(X) \subseteq H(A)$. Therefore, $v \in H(X)$ or $v \in H(\overset{\cdot}{X})$, for every point v on H. (b) Now suppose that $A \in X \cap \overset{\cdot}{X}$. Then $X \Vdash A$ and $\overset{\cdot}{X} \Vdash A$, so $H(X) \subseteq H(A)$ and $H(X) \subseteq H(A)$, and therefore $H(X) \cup H(\overset{\cdot}{X}) \subseteq H(A)$. By the first part of this theorem, $H \subseteq H(A)$, so A is valid; that is, $A \in O$. (c) Suppose that $X \subseteq Y$. Then $H(Y) \subseteq H(X)$, so $H - H(X) \subseteq H - H(Y)$. Therefore, if $A \in \overset{\cdot}{Y}$, then $H - H(Y) \subseteq H(A)$; hence $H - H(X) \subseteq H(A)$, and so $A \in \overset{\cdot}{X}$. Generalizing on this, we conclude that $\overset{\cdot}{Y} \subseteq \overset{\cdot}{X}$.

The next theorem uses system complementation to exhibit a relation between intersection and system union.

Theorem. $\overline{X \overset{\cdot}{\cup} Y} = \overset{\cdot}{X} \cap \overset{\cdot}{Y}$.

Proof:
$$\begin{aligned}
\overline{X \overset{\cdot}{\cup} Y} &= \{A : H - H(X \overset{\cdot}{\cup} Y) \subseteq H(A)\} \\
&= \{A : H - [H(X) \cap H(Y)] \subseteq H(A)\} \\
&= \{A : [H - H(X)] \cup [H - H(Y)] \subseteq H(A)\} \\
&= \{A : H - H(X) \subseteq H(A) \text{ and } H - H(Y) \subseteq H(A)\} \\
&= \{A : H - H(X) \subseteq H(A)\} \cap \{H - H(Y) \subseteq H(A)\} \\
&= \overset{\cdot}{X} \cap \overset{\cdot}{Y}.
\end{aligned}$$

These are familiar properties that make it appropriate to regard the operation as a kind of complementation. But we must be very careful not to assume that other familiar principles about complementation carry over. For example, might some valuation satisfy both X and $\overset{\cdot}{X}$? The answer is *yes* if the language is unusual enough. For example, if v satisfied all sentences, it would certainly satisfy both X and $\overset{\cdot}{X}$. Also, $\overset{\cdot}{X}$ might be O.

Let L_a have the sentences $p_1, p_2, p_3, \ldots$ and let its admissible valuations be the mappings $v : v(A) \in \{T, F\}$ for all sentences A. Let the system X be $\{A : p_1 \Vdash A\}$. Because all the sentences in this language are logically independent, $X = \{p_1\}$, and there are no valid sentences. Moreover, no sentence is such that it is satisfied by every member of $\{v : v(p_1) = F\}$. Hence $\dot{\overline{X}} = \Lambda$. By similar reasoning, $Y = \{p_2\}$ is also a system and $\dot{\overline{Y}} = \Lambda$.

This shows two curious features of system complementation:

$$\dot{\overline{\dot{\overline{X}}}} = X \text{ and } X \cup \dot{\overline{X}} = I$$

do not hold in general. For example, in the above language L_a,

$$\dot{\overline{X}} = \Lambda = \dot{\overline{Y}} \quad \text{but } X \neq Y; \qquad X \cup \dot{\overline{X}} = X \neq I.$$

These features are characteristic of *intuitionistic negation*.

In some cases, $X \cup \dot{\overline{X}} = I$ does hold: This is related to the question of whether X is finitely axiomatizable. We prove two theorems concerning this case.

Theorem. *If L is a bivalent propositional language, and X is a finitely axiomatizable system in L, then $X \cup \dot{\overline{X}} = I$.*

Proof: Let X be axiomatized by $\{A_1, \ldots, A_n\}$; then X is also axiomatized by the sentence B, which is the conjunction of $A_1, \ldots, A_n$. There is now a unique sentence satisfied exactly by all members of $H - H(B)$, namely, $\neg B$. Hence $\neg B$ axiomatizes $\dot{\overline{X}}$. Thus $X \cup \dot{\overline{X}}$ is equivalent to $\{B, \neg B\}$, which is equivalent to I. And when two *systems* are semantically equivalent, they are identical. Hence $X \cup \dot{\overline{X}} = I$.

Theorem. *If L has exclusion negation and finitary semantic entailment, then X is a finitely axiomatizable system in L if $X \cup \dot{\overline{X}} = I$.*

Proof: We shall use A' for the exclusion negation of a sentence A, and assume that L has exclusion negation, finitary semantic entailment, and that system X is such that $X \cup \dot{\overline{X}} = I$ in L.

Now suppose, per absurdum, that X is not finitely axiomatizable. Then, by a preceding theorem, X is the union of an infinite chain

$$Y_1 \subseteq Y_2 \subseteq Y_3 \subseteq \cdots$$

of increasing strength in L. Concerning $\dot{X}$ there are now two possibilities: It may be empty or nonempty.

If $\dot{X}$ is empty, then $X = I - \Lambda = I$; therefore, both A and A' are in X (for arbitrary A). By finitary entailment, $Y_m \Vdash A$ and $Y_n \Vdash A'$ for certain m and n. The larger of the two sets Y_m and Y_n semantically entails both A and A'. But then it is not satisfiable, hence entails all sentences in I: That is, it axiomatizes X.

On the other hand, if $\dot{X}$ is not empty, let it be the set $\{B_1, B_2, \ldots\}$—where $B_{n+m} = B_n$ for all m if X has only n sentences. We now form the chain

$$Y_1 \cup \{B_1\}, \ Y_2 \cup \{B_1, B_2\}, \ldots, \ Y_m \cup \{B_1, \ldots, B_m\}, \ldots.$$

The union of this chain equals I; hence it contains both A and A' (for arbitrary sentence A). By the finitary character of semantic entailment, we find an integer n such that

$$Z_n = Y_n \cup \{B_1, \ldots, B_n\}$$

semantically entails both A and A', as before. Now this set Z_n is not satisfiable.

$$H(Z_n) = H(Y_n \cup \{B_1, \ldots, B_n\}) = \Lambda = H(Y_n) \cap H(\{B_1, \ldots, B_n\}).$$

But on the other hand, every valuation satisfies either Y_n or $\{B_1, \ldots, B_n\}$. For suppose v does not satisfy Y_n. Then clearly it does not satisfy X (since $Y_n \subseteq X$); therefore, $v \in H - H(X)$, and so satisfies $\dot{X}$. Succinctly phrased:

$$H(Y_n) \cap \left(\bigcap_{i=1}^{n} H(B_i) \right) = \Lambda,$$

$$H(Y_n) \cup \left(\bigcap_{i=1}^{n} H(B_i) \right) = H.$$

From this we deduce that

$$H(Y_n) = H - \bigcap_{i=1}^{n} H(B_i)$$

$$= \bigcup_{i=1}^{n} (H - H(B_i))$$

$$= \bigcup_{i=1}^{n} H(B_i').$$

Moreover, this holds for all numbers $r \geq n$, since once we get a contradiction in the chain, every subsequent member is self-contradictory. Looking specifically at r and $r + 1$ we notice that we have the relations shown in Figure 2. Hence we deduce that all four sets are equal.

$$\boxed{\bigcap_{B \in Y_{r+1}} H(B)} = \boxed{H - \bigcap_{i=1}^{r+1} H(B_i)}$$

$$\cap \qquad \cup \qquad \text{for all } r \geq n$$

$$\boxed{\bigcap_{B \in Y_r} H(B)} = \boxed{H - \bigcap_{i=1}^{r} H(B_i)}$$

FIGURE 2

This means that, in particular, Y_n is semantically equivalent with Y_r for all $r \geq n$. Hence Y_n axiomatizes X, the union of these sets Y_r (since $\Vdash$ is finitary). By reductio ad absurdum we conclude that if $X \cup \bar{X} = I$, then X is finitely axiomatizable.

This proof was quite lengthy, so an example may be helpful. If L is a bivalent propositional language, then if X is axiomatized by the set of atomic sentences $\{p_1, p_2, p_3, \ldots, p_n\}$, $\dot{\bar{X}}$ is axiomatized by

$$\{\neg(p_1 \& \cdots \& p_n)\}.$$

But if X is axiomatized by $\{p_1, p_2, p_3, \ldots\}$—and hence is not finitely axiomatizable—then the valuations that satisfy X are all those belonging to

$$\bigcup_{i=1}^{\infty} H(\neg p_i).$$

It is easy to see that $\neg p_1$ does not belong to either X or $\dot{X}$, since a valuation v such that $v(p_1) = \mathrm{T}$, $v(p_2) = \mathrm{F}$ belongs to the infinite union indicated.

8. Filters and the Compactness Problem

The use of compactness theorems is mainly in proofs that semantic entailment is finitary. All their significant applications in metalogic appear to be via the connections with finitary entailment that we have shown in Section 4. Thus the emphasis in metalogic on compactness is partly due to the fact that classical logic has exclusion negation. It is also partly due, however, to the early translation of the compactness problem into a topological problem. We shall now develop methods for proving compactness and finitary semantic entailment.[11]

The basic notion that we shall need is the notion of a filter on a set X. In our applications in this section, X will be the valuation space of some language, but this is not essential to the notion of a filter.

DEFINITION.   A *filter on* a set X is a nonempty family $\mathscr{F}$ of subsets of X such that

(a) $\Lambda \notin \mathscr{F}$;
(b) if $Y \in \mathscr{F}$ and $Y \subseteq Z \subseteq X$, then $Z \in \mathscr{F}$;
(c) if $Y \in \mathscr{F}$ and $Z \in \mathscr{F}$, then $Y \cap Z \in \mathscr{F}$.

[Some authors omit clause (a), and then call a filter *proper* if it does not contain the null set, *improper* otherwise.] It is clear from clause (b) that X belongs to every filter on X. [For motivation, suppose $\mathscr{F}$ is a filter on valuation space H on language L. Then if $L(\mathscr{F}) = \{A : H(A) \in \mathscr{F}\}$ we find that if $A_1, \ldots, A_n \in L(\mathscr{F})$, and $\{A_1, \ldots, A_n\} \Vdash B$ in L, then $B \in L(\mathscr{F})$ So if L has finitary entailment, then $L(\mathscr{F})$ is a system.]

DEFINITION. A *filter base on* X is a nonempty family $\mathcal{B}$ of subsets of X such that if $Y_1, \ldots, Y_n \in \mathcal{B}$, then $\bigcap \{Y_1, \ldots, Y_n\} \neq \Lambda$.

Lemma 1. *Every filter base is contained in a filter.*

(One may also express this as "every filter base can be extended into a filter"; the smallest such filter is called the filter "generated by" the base.)

Proof: Let $\mathcal{B}$ be a filter base, and let $\mathcal{B}^*$ be the family of intersections of finite subfamilies of $\mathcal{B}$:

$$\mathcal{B}^* = \left\{ \bigcap \mathcal{B}' : \mathcal{B}' \subseteq \mathcal{B} \text{ and } \mathcal{B}' \text{ is finite} \right\}.$$

Furthermore, let

$$\mathcal{F} = \{Y : Z \subseteq Y \text{ for some } Z \in \mathcal{B}^*\}.$$

Then we maintain that $\mathcal{F}$ is a filter (in fact, the filter generated by $\mathcal{B}$).

For suppose that $\Lambda \in \mathcal{F}$. Then there is a member Z of $\mathcal{B}^*$ such that $Z \subseteq \Lambda$; that is, $Z = \Lambda$. But then there is a finite subfamily of $\mathcal{B}$ that has an empty intersection.

Second, suppose that Y and Y' belong to $\mathcal{F}$. Then there are $Z, Z' \in \mathcal{B}^*$ such that $Z \subseteq Y, Z' \subseteq Y'$, so

$$Z \cap Z' \subseteq Y \cap Y'.$$

But then $Z = \bigcap \{Z_1, \ldots, Z_n\}, Z' = \bigcap \{Z_{n+1}, \ldots, Z_{n+m}\}$ for members Z_i $(i = 1, \ldots, n + m)$ of $\mathcal{B}$. Hence

$$Z \cap Z' = \bigcap \{Z_1, \ldots, Z_n, Z_{n+1}, \ldots, Z_{n+m}\}$$

and also a member of $\mathcal{B}^*$. Hence $Y \cap Y' \in \mathcal{F}$. Finally that $\mathcal{F}$ is closed under superset formation is obvious.

As an example, consider (as in Section 4) the bivalent propositional language that has p and q as only atomic sentences. The space H has only four members—v_1, v_2, v_3, v_4—hence only $2^4 = 16$ subsets. As it happens, each of these subsets is an elementary class (why?). An example of a filter base would be

$$\mathscr{B} = \{\{v_1\}, \{v_1, v_2\}\} = \{H(p \ \& \ q), H(p)\}.$$

(This is a filter base just because $\{p \ \& \ q, p\}$ is a satisfiable set.) $\mathscr{B}$ generates the filter

$$\mathscr{F}(\mathscr{B}) = \{\{v_1\}, \{v_1, v_2\}, \{v_1, v_3\}, \{v_1, v_4\}, \{v_1, v_2, v_3\}, \{v_1, v_2, v_4\},$$
$$\{v_1, v_3, v_4\}, \{v_1, v_2, v_3, v_4\}\},$$

which is equivalently the family

$$\mathscr{F}(\mathscr{B}) = H(p \ \& \ q), H(p), H(q), H(p \ \& \ q \cdot \vee \cdot \neg p \ \& \ \neg q),$$
$$H(\neg(\neg p \ \& \ \neg q)), H(\neg(\neg p \ \& \ q)), H(\neg(p \ \& \ \neg q)),$$
$$H(p \ \vee \ \neg p)\}$$

where $\vee$ is defined in terms of $\&$ and $\neg$ as usual. In the case of a bivalent language with infinitely many atomic sentences, not every subset of H would be an elementary class. For example, let v then assign T to all atomic sentences; then $\{v\}$ is not an elementary class because we do not have infinite conjunctions (we do not then have a sentence A that is true if and only if all the infinitely many atomic sentences are true).

The following definition is easily illustrated with reference to the above example.

DEFINITION.   A filter $\mathscr{F}$ on X is an *ultrafilter on X* iff there is no filter $\mathscr{F}'$ on X such that $\mathscr{F} \subseteq \mathscr{F}'$ and $\mathscr{F} \neq \mathscr{F}'$.

The filter $\mathscr{F}(\mathscr{B})$ above is of course an ultrafilter. The following is not an ultrafilter:

$$\mathscr{G} = \{\{v_1, v_2\}, \{v_1, v_2, v_3\}, \{v_1, v_2, v_4\}, \{v_1, v_2, v_3, v_4\}\}.$$

However, $\mathscr{G}$ is a filter, and is contained in an ultrafilter, $\mathscr{F}(\mathscr{B})$.

Lemma 2. *The following conditions are equivalent if $\mathscr{F}$ is a filter on X:*
(a) *$\mathscr{F}$ is an ultrafilter on X.*
(b) *$Y \cup Z \in \mathscr{F}$ iff $Y \in \mathscr{F}$ or $Z \in \mathscr{F}$, for all $Y, Z \subseteq X$.*
(c) *For every $Y \subseteq X$, either $Y \in \mathscr{F}$ or $(X - Y) \in \mathscr{F}$.*

Proof: To establish this we should prove that (a) implies (b), (b) implies (c), and (c) implies (a). We shall do two of these and leave the other as exercise.

(a) *implies* (b): Let $\mathscr{F}$ be a filter, and suppose that $Z \cup Y \in \mathscr{F}$, but $Z \notin \mathscr{F}$ and $Y \notin \mathscr{F}$. We define:

$$\mathscr{G} = \{Z' : Z \cup Z' \in \mathscr{F}\}.$$

We are going to show that $\mathscr{G}$ is a filter, which contains $\mathscr{F}$ as a proper part.

First, since $Z \cup Y \in \mathscr{F}$, $Y \in \mathscr{G}$; hence $\mathscr{G}$ is nonempty. Second, $\mathscr{F}$ does not contain Z, hence not $Z \cup \Lambda$; so $\mathscr{G}$ does not contain Λ. Third, if $Z \cup Z' \in \mathscr{F}$, and $Z' \subseteq Z''$, then $Z \cup Z''$ is in $\mathscr{F}$; hence $\mathscr{G}$ is closed under superset formation. Finally, if $Z \cup Z'$ and $Z \cup Z''$ are in $\mathscr{F}$,

$$(Z \cup Z') \cap (Z \cup Z'') = Z \cup (Z' \cap Z'')$$

belongs to $\mathscr{F}$, so $\mathscr{G}$ is also closed under intersection. Thus $\mathscr{G}$ is a filter. Also $\mathscr{F} \subseteq \mathscr{G}$, because if $Z' \in \mathscr{F}$, then $Z \cup Z' \in \mathscr{F}$ (since $Z' \subseteq Z \cup Z'$), so $Z' \in \mathscr{G}$. But $Y \in \mathscr{G}$, and not in $\mathscr{F}$, so $\mathscr{F} \neq \mathscr{G}$. Thus $\mathscr{F}$ is not an ultrafilter.

(c) *implies* (a): Suppose that $\mathscr{F}$ is properly contained in a filter $\mathscr{G}$; let $Y \notin \mathscr{F}$ but $Y \in \mathscr{G}$. Suppose, per absurdum, that (c) holds. Then $X - Y \in \mathscr{F}$. Hence both Y and $X - Y$ belong to $\mathscr{G}$: $\mathscr{G}$ then contains $Y \cap (X - Y) = \Lambda$, which is not possible.

Probably the most important theorem about filters is the following:

Theorem. *Every filter on a set Z is contained in an ultrafilter on Z.*

Proof: The crucial point to notice is that ultrafilters are maximal elements among the filters. And we have a theorem concerning the existence of maximal elements: *Zorn's lemma* (Chapter 1, Section 3). This provides the strategy for our proof.

The partially ordered set under consideration is the family Σ of all filters on Z that contain a given filter $\mathscr{F}$. This family Σ is partially ordered by the relation $\subseteq$; if we can show it to have a maximal element, it will be a filter $\mathscr{G}$ containing $\mathscr{F}$, and it will also be an ultrafilter. For if $\mathscr{G}$ were included in $\mathscr{G}'$, then $\mathscr{G}'$ contains $\mathscr{F}$ also, hence belongs to Σ— and that means that either $\mathscr{G} = \mathscr{G}'$ or $\mathscr{G}$ is not maximal in Σ.

By Zorn's lemma, that Σ has a maximal element will follow if we can show that every chain in Σ has an upper bound in Σ. Let $\mathbf{C}$ be such a chain, and $\mathscr{G} = \bigcup \mathbf{C}$. Since every member of $\mathbf{C}$ contains $\mathscr{F}$, so does its union $\mathscr{G}$. Since no member of $\mathbf{C}$ contains the empty set, neither does $\mathscr{G}$. Since each member of $\mathbf{C}$ contains the supersets of all *its* members, $\mathscr{G}$ contains the supersets of all the members of $\mathscr{G}$. Finally, suppose X and Y to belong to $\mathscr{G}$. Let $\mathscr{F}_1$ and $\mathscr{F}_2$ be members of $\mathbf{C}$ to which X and Y belong, respectively. Since $\mathbf{C}$ is a chain, $\mathscr{F}_1 \subseteq \mathscr{F}_2$ or $\mathscr{F}_2 \subseteq \mathscr{F}_1$. In either case, X and Y both belong to the larger, and so does their intersection. Therefore, $X \cap Y$ belongs to $\mathscr{G}$. This establishes that $\mathscr{G}$ is a filter which contains $\mathscr{F}$. Therefore, $\mathscr{G}$ belongs to Σ; that is, each chain in Σ has an upper bound in Σ—its own union.

With these basic results concerning filters and ultrafilters, it is now fruitful to approach the subject of compactness by studying the filters on the valuation space.

DEFINITION. If $\mathscr{F}$ is a filter on a valuation space H, then $\mathscr{F}$ is

(a) *U-convergent* to v (in H) iff every elementary class containing v belongs to $\mathscr{F}$;

(b) *I-convergent* to v iff every elementary class in $\mathscr{F}$ contains v;

(c) *convergent* to v iff an elementary class belongs to $\mathscr{F}$ if and only if it contains v.

We also say that $\mathscr{F}$ *converges* or is *convergent* if it is convergent to some point on H, and so on. It is to be noted that convergence is not the conjunction of I- and U-convergence; *prima facie*, $\mathscr{F}$ might I-converge to one point, and U-converge to another.

Theorem.   *If every ultrafilter on a valuation space H is I-convergent (U-convergent), then H is I-compact (U-compact).*

Proof: Suppose first that H is not I-compact, so that there is a family of sentences X such that $H(X) = \Lambda$ and $H(Y) \neq \Lambda$ for any finite subset Y of X. This shows that the family

$$\mathscr{B} = \{H(B): B \in X\}$$

forms a filter base; $\mathscr{B}$ generates a filter that is in turn contained in an ultrafilter $\mathscr{F}$. Now if $\mathscr{F}$ is I-convergent to a valuation v, then $v \in \bigcap \{H(B): H(B) \in \mathscr{F}\}$. Since $\mathscr{B} \subseteq \mathscr{F}$, it follows that if $B \in X$, then $H(B) \in \mathscr{F}$, so

$$v \in \left(\bigcap_{B \in X} H(B)\right) = H(X),$$

but that intersection is empty. We conclude that $\mathscr{F}$ is not I-convergent.

Suppose, second, that H is not U-compact, so that there is a family X of sentences such that

$$\bigcup_{B \in X} H(B) = H; \qquad \bigcup_{B \in Y} H(B) \neq H \quad \text{for any finite } Y \subseteq X.$$

If we now consider the relative complements $H - H(B)$ of these elementary classes, we obtain

$$\bigcap_{B \in X} (H - H(B)) = \Lambda; \qquad \bigcap_{B \in Y} (H - H(B)) \neq \Lambda \quad \text{for any finite } Y \subseteq X.$$

So these complements form a filter base

$$B = \{H - H(B): B \in X\}$$

which is contained in an ultrafilter $\mathscr{F}$. If $\mathscr{F}$ were U-convergent to a valuation v, we would have

for all sentences A, if $v \in H(A)$, then $H(A) \in \mathscr{F}$.

Since the family X provides a cover for H, there is a sentence B such that

$$B \in X \quad \text{and} \quad v \in H(B);$$

hence also $H(B) \in \mathscr{F}$. But since $B \in X$, $H - H(B)$ is in $\mathscr{B}$ and hence in $\mathscr{F}$. Now we have deduced that if $\mathscr{F}$ is U-convergent, $\mathscr{F}$ contains both $H - H(B)$ and $H(B)$, and hence their intersection Λ, which is impossible. So if H is not U-compact, then not every ultrafilter on H is U-convergent.

Before considering the subject of finitary semantic entailment, we shall use the preceding result to show that I-compactness and U-compactness are not equivalent in general.

Theorem. *There is a language that has finitary entailment and is U-compact but is not I-compact.*

Proof: Let L have as sentences exactly the set $\{q, p_1, p_2, p_3, \ldots\}$ and as admissible valuations the functions v such that

$$v(q) = \text{T iff } v(p_i) \neq \text{T} \quad \text{for some } i = 1, 2, 3, \ldots;$$
$$v(A) \in \{\text{T, F}\} \quad \text{for all sentences } A.$$

We note that, for each i, $H - H(p_i) \subseteq H(q)$.

(a) L is not I-compact. For the set $K = \{q, p_1, p_2, p_3, \ldots\}$ is not satisfiable, but any finite subset K' of K is satisfiable, namely by the bivalent valuation v such that $v(q) = \text{T}$, $v(p_i) = \text{T iff } p_i \in K'$.

(b) L is U-compact. For let $\mathscr{F}$ be an ultrafilter on the valuation space H of L. Define

$$L(\mathscr{F}) = \{A : H(A) \in \mathscr{F}\}.$$

There are two possibilities.

1. $p_i \in L(\mathscr{F})$ for each $i = 1, 2, 3, \ldots$. Then the valuation v such that $v(p_i) = \text{T}$ for each $i = 1, 2, 3, \ldots$ and $v(q) = \text{F}$ is admissible, and

$\mathscr{F}$ U-converges to v, because $H(p_i)$ for each $i = 1, 2, 3, \ldots$ belong to $\mathscr{F}$. [Note that $H(q)$ *may* belong to $\mathscr{F}$ also.]

2. $p_i \notin L(\mathscr{F})$ for some index i. Then $H(p_i) \notin \mathscr{F}$, and $\mathscr{F}$ is an ultra-filter, so $H - H(p_i) \in \mathscr{F}$. But $H - H(p_i) \subseteq H(q)$; hence $H(q) \in \mathscr{F}$, and $q \in L(\mathscr{F})$. Therefore, the valuation v such that $v(A) = $ T iff $A \in L(\mathscr{F})$ and $v(A) = $ F otherwise is admissible, and $\mathscr{F}$ U-converges to v.

(c) L has finitary entailment. For suppose that X is infinite and $X \Vdash A$. Then we distinguish two cases.

1. $q \in X$. Then A must be a member of X, for if $A \notin X$, then $A = p_i$ for some index i, and the valuation that maps the members of X into T and the other sentences into F is an admissible valuation.

2. $q \notin X$. Then q cannot be A because the valuation which maps q into F and all other sentences into T is admissible. Second, suppose that $A = p_i$ for some index i. Then A must be in X, for the valuation that maps p_i into F and the other sentences into T is admissible.

We conclude therefore that X has a finite subset, $\{A\}$, which also semantically entails A in L.

We shall leave it to the reader to consider the question whether finitary entailment and/or I-compactness entails U-compactness. For we shall now use the notion of convergence of ultrafilters to provide a sufficient condition for finitary semantic entailment.

Theorem. *If every ultrafilter on a valuation space H of a language L converges, then L has finitary semantic entailment and is compact.*

Proof: Compactness follows from a previous theorem. Now suppose the antecedent and let X be a set of sentences of L and A a sentence of L such that $X_i \Vdash A$ does not hold for any finite subset X_i of X. Then the sets

$$I(X_i) = H(X_i) - H(A)$$

are nonempty and form a filter base, because $I(X_{i_1}) \cap \cdots \cap I(X_{i_n}) = I(X_j)$, where $X_j = X_{i_1} \cup \cdots \cup X_{i_n}$. This filter base is included in an ultrafilter $\mathscr{F}$ converging to a valuation v. Now if B is a member of X, then $I(\{B\}) = H(B) - H(A)$ is in $\mathscr{F}$, so $H(B) \in \mathscr{F}$; hence v satisfies any member B of X. But $H(A) \notin \mathscr{F}$, for then $H(A) \cap (H(B) - H(A)) = \Lambda$ would be in $\mathscr{F}$, which is impossible. Therefore, v does not satisfy A. So not all valuations that satisfy X satisfy A; that is, not $X \Vdash A$.

We can now prove theorems of compactness and finitary entailment for the classical propositional calculus by our preceding theorem and the following result.

Theorem. *If H is the valuation space of a bivalent propositional language L, then every ultrafilter on H is convergent.*

Proof: Let us first point out that the definition of admissible valuation for L has as immediate consequences:

1. $H(\neg A) = H - H(A)$.
2. $H(A \& B) = H(A) \cap H(B)$.

The definition of ultrafilter $\mathscr{F}$, on the other hand, has as immediate consequences

3. Exactly one of $H(A)$, $H - H(A)$ belongs to $\mathscr{F}$.
4. $H(A) \cap H(B) \in \mathscr{F}$ iff $H(A) \in \mathscr{F}$ and $H(B) \in \mathscr{F}$.

From these four propositions it follows that

5. $H(\neg A) \in \mathscr{F}$ iff $H(A) \notin \mathscr{F}$.
6. $H(A \& B) \in \mathscr{F}$ iff $H(A) \in \mathscr{F}$ and $H(B) \in \mathscr{F}$.

This suggests that all the sentences A such that $H(A) \in \mathscr{F}$ can be true together; that is, that there is an admissible valuation v that assigns T to all these sentences, and only these sentences.

We can define this valuation v in one of two ways:

D1. v is the function defined for all sentences A, such that $v(A) = $ T if $H(A) \in \mathscr{F}$, and $v(A) = $ F otherwise.

D2. v is the admissible valuation for L that assigns T to an atomic sentence p of L iff $H(p) \in \mathscr{F}$.

If we choose D2, we shall have to show that the defined admissible valuation v exists and is such that $v(A) = $ T iff $H(A) \in \mathscr{F}$. If we choose D1, we can see at once that $v(A) = $ T iff $H(A) \in \mathscr{F}$ but we need to show that this defined function v is an admissible valuation. Let us choose D1; the reader can explore the option of choosing D2.

The function v defined by D1 is an admissible valuation because

(a) v maps all sentences into $\{$T, F$\}$;
(b) $v(\neg A) = $ T iff $H(\neg A) \in \mathscr{F}$ iff $H(A) \notin \mathscr{F}$ (see 5) iff $v(A) = $ F.
(c) $v(A \ \& \ B) = $ T iff $H(A \ \& \ B) \in \mathscr{F}$ iff $H(A)$ and $H(B)$ are both in $\mathscr{F}$ (see 6) iff $v(A) = v(B) = $ T.

Now v belongs to an elementary class iff that class belongs to $\mathscr{F}$; hence $\mathscr{F}$ converges to v.

9. Ultraproducts and the Compactness Problem

The notion of ultraproduct is of quite recent origin, but it has already proved fruitful for many different purposes in formal semantics.[12] We shall here study it in a very general and abstract way, hoping thereby to shed some light on its specific applications. We introduce the notion of an *ultraproduct of valuations* (which is a generalization of the usual notion of an ultraproduct of models) and aim to show how this notion is related to the topological notions of the preceding sections, and how it leads to a method for proving that semantic entailment is finitary.

If X is a set with which we are concerned, we often order its members in some way, and then denote the ith member of X (by the ordering) as A_i. Here i is the *index* of some member of X; each distinct member of X receives a distinct index. The set I of all these indices is called, very appropriately, the *index set*. While the index set is usually the set of natural numbers, or one of the initial segments $(1, \ldots, n)$ of that set, it need not be; it could be any set whatever. When X has been indexed by I, we often write

$$X = \{A_i\}, \ i \in I.$$

This notion of index set will be used in the definition of ultraproduct.

The second notion we need is that of a valuation defined in terms of a family of valuations. As an illustration we define the *direct product* of a family of valuations. If $V = \{v_i\}$, $i \in I$ is a family of valuations on a syntax Syn, the *direct product* of V is the valuation $v\cdot$ such that (1) $v \cdot (A) = $ T iff $v_i(A) = $ T for all $i \in I$, (2) $v \cdot (A) = $ F otherwise.

It is easily seen that if L is a bivalent propositional language, the direct products of its admissible valuations are not generally admissible. whereas they are admissible if L is like a bivalent propositional language except for lacking negation. For let V be a family of admissible valuations for L. Then for either assumption about L we have

$$
\begin{aligned}
v \cdot (A \ \& \ B) = \text{T} \quad &\text{iff for all } v \in V, v(A \ \& \ B) = \text{T} \\
&\text{iff for all } v \in V, v(A) = v(B) = \text{T} \\
&\text{iff } v \cdot (A) = v \cdot (B) = \text{T},
\end{aligned}
$$

which is as it should be. But in the case of negation we find

$$
\begin{aligned}
v \cdot (\neg A) = \text{T} \quad &\text{iff for all } v \in V, v(\neg A) = \text{T} \\
&\text{iff for all } v \in V, v(A) = \text{F},
\end{aligned}
$$

while $v \cdot (A) = $ F iff for *some* $v \in V$, $v(A) = $ F. So if V contains two members v_1 and v_2 such that

$$v_1(A) = \text{T}; \qquad v_2(A) = \text{F},$$

hence
$$v_1(\neg A) = \text{F}; \qquad v_2(\neg A) = \text{T},$$

we find that $v \cdot (A) = v \cdot (\neg A) = $ F.

This shows at once how a new valuation may be defined in terms of a family of valuations, and why it is necessary to prove carefully that the defined valuation is admissible, if this be asserted.

We turn now to the basic notion of this section:

DEFINITION.   If $V = \{v_i\}$, $i \in I$ is a family of valuations on a syntax Syn, and $\mathcal{U}$ is an ultrafilter on I, then v is an *ultraproduct* of V (*generated by* $\mathcal{U}$) iff for all sentences A of Syn, $v(A) = \mathrm{T}$ iff $\{i \in I : v_i(A) = \mathrm{T}\} \in \mathcal{U}$.

As an illustration we consider ultraproducts in bivalent propositional languages.

Theorem.   *If $V = \{v_i\}$, $i \in I$ is a family of admissible valuations for a bivalent propositional language L, and $\mathcal{U}$ an ultrafilter on I, there is an ultraproduct of V generated by $\mathcal{U}$ which is an admissible valuation for L.*

Proof: We define:

$$v(A) = \mathrm{T} \text{ iff } \{i \in I : v_i(A) = \mathrm{T}\} \in \mathcal{U},$$
$$v(A) = \mathrm{F} \text{ otherwise, for all sentences } A \text{ of } L.$$

That v is an ultraproduct of V generated by $\mathcal{U}$ is obvious. To show that v is admissible, we note that

(a) $v(A) \in \{\mathrm{T}, \mathrm{F}\}$ for all sentences A of L.

(b) $v(A \ \& \ B) = \mathrm{T}$ iff $\{i \in I : v_i(A \ \& \ B) = \mathrm{T}\} \in \mathcal{U}$
                    iff $\{i \in I : v_i(A) = \mathrm{T} \text{ and } v_i(B) = \mathrm{T}\} \in \mathcal{U}$
                    iff $\{i \in I : v_i(A) = \mathrm{T}\} \cap \{i \in I : v_i(B) = \mathrm{T}\} \in \mathcal{U}$
                    iff $\{i \in I : v_i(A) = \mathrm{T}\}$ and
                        $\{i \in I : v_i(B) = \mathrm{T}\}$ are both in $\mathcal{U}$
                    iff $v(A) = v(B) = \mathrm{T}$.

(c) $v(\neg A) = \mathrm{T}$ iff $\{i \in I : v_i(\neg A) = \mathrm{T}\} \in \mathcal{U}$
                iff $I - \{i \in I : v_i(A) = \mathrm{T}\} \in \mathcal{U}$
                iff $\{i \in I : v_i(A) = \mathrm{T}\} \notin \mathcal{U}$
                iff $v(A) = \mathrm{F}$.

From now on we use the following terminology:

DEFINITION.   A valuation space H *admits all ultraproducts* iff for every subset $V = \{v_i\}$, $i \in I$ of H, and ultrafilter $\mathcal{U}$ on I, some member of H is an ultraproduct of V generated by $\mathcal{U}$.

We shall now show how the existence of ultraproducts can be used to demonstrate that semantic entailment is finitary.

Theorem. *If the valuation space H of a language L admits all ultraproducts, then L has finitary semantic entailment.*

Proof: Let A be a sentence and X a set of sentences of L, and let us index the finite subsets of X as $\{X_i\}$, $i \in I$. Suppose that no finite subset X_i of X semantically entails A. We intend to show that $X \Vdash A$ does not hold then, given that H admits all ultraproducts.

For each $i \in I$ there is a valuation v_i such that v_i satisfies X_i but not A; otherwise, $X_i \Vdash A$ would hold. Define, for each finite $X_m \subseteq X$:

$$J_m = \{i \in I : v_i \text{ satisfies } X_m\},$$

where $V = \{v_i\}$, $i \in I$ is the indicated class of valuations.

The family $\mathscr{J} = \{J_m\}$, $m \in I$ is a filter base on I, for no member is empty, and

$$J_{m_1} \cap \cdots \cap J_{m_n} = J_m \in \mathscr{J},$$

where

$$J_m = \{i : v_i \text{ satisfies } X_{m_1} \cup \cdots \cup X_{m_n}\}.$$

This filter base can be extended to an ultrafilter $\mathscr{U}$ on I, $\mathscr{J} \subseteq \mathscr{U}$. If H admits all ultraproducts, then it has a member v such that, for all sentences B,

$$v(B) = \text{T} \quad \text{iff } \{i : v_i(B) = \text{T}\} \in \mathscr{U}.$$

If $B \in X$, there is a $J_m \in \mathscr{J}$ such that

$$J_m = \{i : v_i \text{ satisfies } B\}, \qquad J_m \in \mathscr{U};$$

hence this ultraproduct satisfies every sentence in X. But we chose $V = \{v_i\}$, $i \in I$ such that for each $i \in I$, $v_i(A) \neq \text{T}$. Hence

$$\{i : v_i(A) = \text{T}\} = \Lambda \notin \mathscr{U},$$

so the ultraproduct v does not satisfy A. This shows that $X \Vdash A$ does not hold, as was required.

We have established along the way that in a bivalent propositional language, semantic entailment is finitary; however, we knew this already. We shall now connect the existence of ultraproducts with the convergence of ultrafilters. Note first that ultrafilters on the index set I correspond in a one-to-one fashion to ultrafilters on the indexed set $V = \{v_i\}, i \in I$. The one-to-one mapping involved is just the function that assigns a distinct index to each member of V:

$$v_i \leftrightarrow i,$$
$$X \subseteq V \leftrightarrow \{i : v_i \in X\} \subseteq I.$$

So to an ultrafilter $\mathscr{U}$ on I corresponds an ultrafilter $\mathscr{U}'$ on V defined by

$$X \subseteq V \text{ belongs to } \mathscr{U}' \quad \text{iff } \{i : v_i \in X\} \in \mathscr{U}.$$

Suppose now that v is an ultraproduct of V generated by $\mathscr{U}$; then we have for any sentence A:

$$v(A) = \text{T} \quad \text{iff } \{i \in I : v_i(A) = \text{T}\} \in \mathscr{U},$$
$$v(A) = \text{T} \quad \text{iff } \{v_i : v_i(A) = \text{T}\} \in \mathscr{U}',$$
$$v \in H(A) \quad \text{iff } \{v_i \in V : v_i(A) = \text{T}\} \in \mathscr{U}',$$
$$v \in H(A) \quad \text{iff } H(A) \cap V \in \mathscr{U}'.$$

If V is the whole of H this means simply that

$$\text{For all sentences } A, \, v \in H(A) \text{ iff } H(A) \in \mathscr{U}';$$

that is, $\mathscr{U}'$ converges to the ultraproduct v. This essentially proves one part of the next theorem.

Theorem.   *A valuation space H admits all ultraproducts iff every ultra-filter on H converges.*

Proof: Suppose first that H admits all ultraproducts, and let $\mathscr{U}$ be an ultrafilter on H. We shall first index every member of H, so that we can write, for some I:

$$H = \{v_i\}, \, i \in I.$$

To do this most simply, let $I = H$, and let the mapping that assigns each member v of H an index i be $f:f(v) = v$. That is, $v = v_v$ and $H = \{v_v\}$, $v \in H$. Now $\mathcal{U}$ is also an ultrafilter on I, and generates an ultraproduct $v \in H$ such that

$$
\begin{aligned}
v \in H(A) \quad &\text{iff } \{v \in I : v_v(A) = \mathrm{T}\} \in \mathcal{U} \\
&\text{iff } \{v_v : v_v(A) = \mathrm{T}\} \in \mathcal{U} \\
&\text{iff } \{v : v(A) = \mathrm{T}\} \in \mathcal{U} \\
&\text{iff } H(A) \in \mathcal{U}.
\end{aligned}
$$

That is, $\mathcal{U}$ converges to v.

Suppose, second, that all ultrafilters of H converge, and let $V = \{v_i\}$, $i \in I$ be a subset of H, $\mathcal{U}$ an ultrafilter on I. We define the family $\mathcal{B}$ of subsets of V:

$$
X \in \mathcal{B} \quad \text{iff } \{i : v_i \in X\} \in \mathcal{U};
$$

clearly $\mathcal{B}$ is a filter base in H and can be extended to an ultrafilter $\mathcal{U}'$ on H. We show now that for any elementary class $H(A)$,

$$
H(A) \in \mathcal{U}' \quad \text{iff } V \cap H(A) \in \mathcal{B}.
$$

From this it follows readily that if $\mathcal{U}'$ converges to v, then v is an ultraproduct of V generated by $\mathcal{U}$; for then $v \in H(A)$ iff $V \cap H(A) \in \mathcal{B}$, iff $\{i : v_i(A) = \mathrm{T}\} \in \mathcal{U}$.

(a) Suppose $V \cap H(A) \in \mathcal{B}$. Then $V \cap H(A) \in \mathcal{U}'$. Hence $H(A)$—as well as V—belongs to $\mathcal{U}'$.

(b) Suppose $H(A) \in \mathcal{U}'$. Since $V \in \mathcal{B}$, $V \in \mathcal{U}'$. Hence $V \cap H(A) \in \mathcal{U}'$. Because $\mathcal{U}$ is an ultrafilter on I, either $\{i : v_i \in V \cap H(A)\} \in \mathcal{U}$ or $\{i : v_i \notin V \cap H(A)\} \in \mathcal{U}$. Hence either $V \cap H(A)$ or $V - H(A)$ belongs to $\mathcal{B}$. Were $V - H(A)$ to belong to $\mathcal{B}$, it would also belong to $\mathcal{U}'$. But then $V \cap H(A)$ and $V - H(A)$, and so $V \cap \overline{H(A)} \cap H(A) = \Lambda$ would belong to $\mathcal{U}'$, which is impossible. It follows, therefore, that $V \cap H(A) \in \mathcal{B}$.

10. Partial Valuations and the Compactness Problem

The methods of ultrafilters and of ultraproducts for proving compactness may appropriately be called *topological* methods. In this section we shall discuss a different kind of method, introduced by Henkin for propositional logic and adapted by Robinson to quantificational logic and by P. Woodruff and my student Bruce Myers to many-valued logic.[13]

If f is a binary function and Y a set, then we define the *restriction of f to Y* to be the function f' defined by

$$f' = \{\langle x, y\rangle : x \in Y \text{ and } f(x) = y\}.$$

In addition, we call f an *extension* of all its restrictions. If L and L' are languages such that all sentences of L' are sentences of L, and the admissible valuations of L' are the restrictions of the admissible valuations of L to the sentences of L', we call L' a *fragment* of L. The admissible valuations of any fragment of L are called *partial valuations* of L.

Theorem. *If L is I-compact (U-compact, compact) so are all its fragments.*

For let L' be a fragment of L, let L be I-compact and let X be a set of sentences of L' that is not satisfiable in L'. Then X is not satisfiable in L, for if v satisfies X, so does its restriction to L'. So X has a finite subset Y that is not satisfiable in L. Then Y is not satisfiable in L', since if v satisfies Y, so do all its extensions. The cases of U-compactness and compactness are similar.

Theorem. *If L has finitary entailment, so do all its fragments.*

The proof is as for the preceding theorem: If X is a set of sentences of L' and A a sentence of L', then v satisfies X but not A iff the restriction of v to L' does so, and iff all the extensions of v do so, when v is an admissible valuation for L'.

These theorems may provide an easy method for compactness proofs, when one language can be shown to be a fragment of another language for which we already have such proofs. For example, the languages of modal logic can be construed as fragments of the language of quantificational logic. But such construal may not be easy; in general, compactness proofs require work, if not in one place then in another.

Henkin showed how to use partial valuations in compactness proofs without relying on previous compactness results. Let us call a language L' *finitary* iff it has only finitely many distinct admissible valuations. Let us call the sequence $L_1, L_2, L_3, \ldots$ a *chain* of languages iff L_i is a fragment of L_{i+1}, for $i = 1, 2, 3, \ldots$.

> DEFINITION. L is the *union* of the chain $L_1, L_2, \ldots$ if and only if
> (a) L_i is a fragment of L, for $i = 1, 2, \ldots$;
> (b) each sentence of L is a sentence of L_i for some i;
> (c) if $v_1, v_2, \ldots$ is such that v_i is an admissible valuation for L_i and $v_i \subseteq v_{i+1}$ for $i = 1, 2, \ldots$, then the union of this series is an admissible valuation for L.

Then we have the following general result.

Theorem. *If a language L is the union of a chain of its finitary fragments, then L has finitary semantic entailment.*

Proof: Let L be the union of a chain $L_1, L_2, \ldots$ of its finitary fragments, and let no finite subset of X semantically entail the sentence A of L. Now X is the union of a series of sets of sentences

$$X_1 \subseteq X_2 \subseteq X_3 \subseteq \cdots$$

such that for $i = 1, 2, \ldots$, X_i is the largest of these sets whose sentences all belong to L_i. Since L_i is finitary, X_i must be semantically equivalent to one of its finite subsets. For if a set $X = \{B_1, \ldots, B_j, \ldots\}$ is not equivalent to any of its finite subsets, then there must be valuations $v_1, \ldots, v_j \ldots$ such that v_j satisfies $\{B_1, \ldots, B_j\}$ but does not satisfy X. Some of these valuations may not be distinct, but there can be no integer m such that $v_m = v_n$ for all $n \geq m$, or v_m would satisfy X. Thus there would have to be infinitely many distinct valuations.

Let V_i be the set of admissible valuations of L_i which satisfy X_i but do not satisfy (or are not defined for) A, for $i = 1, 2, 3, \ldots$. We know that each set V_i is nonempty, for if L_i provides no counterexample to $X_i \Vdash A$, then neither does L. Also, each set V_i is finite, because each language L_i is finitary. Now consider the relation R:

$\mathrm{R}vv'$ iff $v' \in V_{i+1}$ and $v \in V_i$, and v is the restriction of v' to L_i, for $i = 1, 2, 3, \ldots$, or v' belongs to V_1 and v is the set Λ.

Then for each v' in each set V_i there is a unique v such that $\mathrm{R}vv'$. In the case $i = 1$ this is obvious; in the case $i > 1$, suppose v' satisfies X_i but not A; then v' satisfies X_{i-1} but not A. Now, X_{i-1} is a set of sentences of L_{i-1}; hence the restriction of v' to L_{i-1}, call it v, satisfies X_{i-1} but not A, and hence belongs to V_{i-1}. Moreover, restrictions are unique.

We have now shown that we have here a finitely branching tree, with Λ and the members of all the sets V_i as nodes, Λ as origin, and R as immediate descendant relation. By Koenig's lemma, this tree has an infinite branch Λ, v_1, v_2, v_3, $\ldots$. This branch has as union an admissible valuation for L, which clearly satisfies X but not A.

The proof for I-compactness results if we simply delete all reference to the sentence A in the above proof; the question of U-compactness is left to the reader. As illustration we prove:

Theorem.   *If L is bivalent propositional language, then L is the union of a chain of its finitary fragments.*

Proof: Let the atomic sentences of L be $p_1, p_2, p_3, \ldots$ and let L_i be the bivalent propositional language whose only atomic sentences are $p_1, \ldots, p_i$, for $i = 1, 2, \ldots$. Then each sentence A of L belongs to a finitary fragment L_j of L; that is, j is the highest index of A's atomic constituents. Second, let $v_1 \subseteq v_2 \subseteq \cdots$ be a series of admissible valuations for $L_1, L_2, \ldots$, respectively, and let v be the union of this series. Then for any sentence A of L_i and B of L_j, for $i, j = 1, 2, 3, \ldots$, with $j \geq i$, we have

$v(A) \in \{T, F\}$ because $v_i(A) \in \{T, F\}$,

$v(\neg A) = v_i(\neg A) = T$ iff $v_i(A) = F = v(A)$,

$v(A \,\&\, B) = v_j(A \,\&\, B) = T$ iff $v_j(A) = v_j(B) = T$ iff $v(A) = v(B) = T$.

Hence v is an admissible valuation for L.

NOTES

1. See I. M. Bochenski, *A History of Formal Logic*, I. Thomas, trans. (Notre Dame, Ind.: University of Notre Dame Press, 1961), pp. 159–162.

2. J. Richardson, ed., *Kant's Philosophy*, Vol. 3, Part 1 (London: Simpkin and Marshall, 1819).

3. Cf. I. M. Bochenski, "On the Syntactical Categories," *Logico-Philosophical Studies*, A. Menne, ed. (Dordrecht, Holland: Reidel, 1962), pp. 67–87, and H. B. Curry, *Foundations of Mathematical Logic* (New York: McGraw-Hill, 1963), chap. 2, sec. A3–4, pp. 32–37.

4. See Curry, *Foundations*, chap. 2, secs. A1–2, pp. 28–32; secs. C1–2, pp. 50–51; sec. C6, pp. 61–62; sec. S, pp. 89–91.

5. Cf. Curry, *Foundations*, chap. 2, sec. C5, pp. 59–60.

6. Cf. E. W. Beth, *The Foundations of Mathematics* (Amsterdam: North-Holland, 1965), sec. 188, p. 534; A. Mostowski, *Thirty Years of Foundational Studies* (New York: Barnes & Noble, 1966), p. 129. Note that the latter, but not the former, calls $H(X)$ an elementary class even in cases in which X is a set of sentences. Also, our usage of this term for arbitrary languages constitutes an extension of common usage. See further P. M. Cohn, *Universal Algebra* (New York: Harper & Row, 1965), pp. 205–209, 213–219.

7. The theorem that the language of classical logic is (U-)compact is known as *Maltsev's theorem*, after the Soviet mathematician A. I. Maltsev; for an exposition see P. S. Novikov, *Elements of Mathematical Logic* (Edinburgh: Oliver & Boyd, 1964), chap. IV, sec. 16, pp. 184–189. In this case, as we shall see, U-compactness is equivalent to compactness.

8. The terms "exclusion negation" and its contrary "choice negation" were introduced by the Dutch mathematician and philosopher Gerrit

Mannoury, and after often employed in philosophy of mathematics; see E. W. Beth, *Mathematical Thought* (Dordrecht, Holland: Reidel, 1965), pp. 20–21.

9. See, e.g., Beth, *Foundations*, p. 544, and A. Robinson, *Introduction to Model Theory and to the Metamathematics of Algebra* (Amsterdam: North-Holland, 1965), p. 36.

10. See A. Tarski, *Logic, Semantics, Metamathematics*, J. H. Woodger, trans. (Oxford: Clarendon, 1956), chaps. V and XII; Beth, *Foundations*, chap. 19.

11. The theory of filters is developed in many texts on topology; see, e.g., S. A. Gaal, *Point Set Topology* (New York: Academic Press, 1964), chap. V. The dual of a filter is an *ideal*, and some authors prefer to deal with ideals. For a compactness proof for bivalent propositional languages that relies on certain facts concerning propositional logic and the theory of ideals see Beth, *Foundations*, sec. 183, pp. 523–525.

12. The classical paper is T. Frayne, A. C. Morel, and D. S. Scott, "Reduced Direct Products," *Fundamenta Mathematicae, 51* (1962), 195–228. Elementary expositions of the subject of ultraproducts of models may be found in Mostowski, *Thirty Years*, pp. 150–156, and in Robinson, *Model Theory*, pp. 238–244. See further Cohn, *Algebra*, pp. 209–213.

13. L. Henkin, "Fragments of the Propositional Calculus," *Journal of Symbolic Logic, 14* (1949), pp. 42–48; Robinson, *Model Theory*, sec. 1.5; B. Myers, "A Compactness Theorem for Languages with Finite Matrix," forthcoming; P. Woodruff, "Compactness in N-Valued Logic," forthcoming. See also G. Kreisel and J. Krivine, *Elements of Mathematical Logic* (Amsterdam: North-Holland, 1967), p. 7; the proofs by Robinson and Kreisel and Krivine are essentially applications of a more general result due to R. Rado, "Axiomatic Treatment of Rank in Infinite Sets," *Canadian Journal of Mathematics, 1* (1949), pp. 337–343 (especially pp. 337–339).

CHAPTER III

APPRAISAL
OF
LOGICAL
SYSTEMS

In this chapter we attempt to construct a general concept of logical systems and provide general criteria for their appraisal. In addition, we consider the possibility of diverse interpretations with respect to which a given logical system is equally adequate. As before, classical propositional logic provides the main illustration for the concepts and methods developed.

1. Logical Systems

The best known characterization of logical systems is probably the one given by Carnap, which says that a logical system is described by stating its *formation rules* and its *transformation rules*.[1] We may take this as the starting point of our discussion.

The formation rules describe the class of expressions that are *grammatically well-formed*. The transformation rules are simply some syntactic transformations, and if A can be produced by applying a finite sequence of these transformations to a class of expressions X, we say that A is *deducible from* X in the logical system. All transformation rules preserve well-formedness.

This suggests that a logical system can be identified with a syntactic system together with a set of syntactic transformations (preserving the property of being a sentence, and perhaps some wider syntactic property, depending on the usage of "well-formed formula" and "sentence"). But that is not quite accurate because a given logical system will pertain to a variety of languages, which need not have the same syntax. For example, the propositional calculus can be applied in any language with a PCS for syntax—the choice of the exact set of expressions regarded as sentences is clearly not important. The propositional calculus applies as well to the language of quantification theory, of modal logic, of set theory, and so on. So the formation rules are not to specify a single syntactic system, but a *kind* of syntactic system.

And this is to be very general. Consider again the propositional calculus with & and $\neg$ as primitive. All that is needed for the propositional calculus to be applicable (correctly or incorrectly, of course) is that the language L in question have some binary sentential connective $\&_L$ and some unary sentential connective $\neg_L$. (L might be the language of intuitionistic logic with $\rightarrow$ as $\&_L$ and $\neg\neg$ as $\neg_L$.) Only after we have explained how we shall apply the logical system to the language can questions of correctness even arise.

Turning now to the transformation rules, we find that a good deal more can be said about them, too. Their first job is to specify the class of *theorems* of the system. If we insist on giving a basic role to transformations, we can define theorems as those sentences into which any set of sentences (or the null set) can be transformed. A more familiar procedure is simply to list a basic set of theorems, the *axioms*, and define the theorems as the sentences deducible from the axioms. So beside the axioms, one would have a set of *theoremhood-preserving rules*. We shall write "$\vdash A$" for "A is a theorem."

The second job of the transformation rules is to specify the class of *valid deductions* or *validated arguments*. We shall write "$X \vdash A$" for "A may be deduced from X" or "the argument from X to A is validated (by the system in question)." The rules that validate arguments are not just the theoremhood-preserving rules. For example, in the propositional calculus *substitution* is one of the latter; if $\vdash A$, then $\vdash S_p^B(A)$. But of course $A \vdash S_p^B(A)$ does not hold. So some rules simply say of a certain transformation f that $X \vdash f(X)$, while others say of a certain transformation g that if $\vdash A$ then $\vdash g(A)$. Finally there are rules, to be found in Gentzen and natural deduction systems, which say of some transformations f and g that if $X_1 \vdash A_1, \ldots, X_k \vdash A_k$, then $f(X_1, \ldots, X_k, A_1, \ldots, A_k) \vdash g(X_1, \ldots, X_k, A_1, \ldots, A_k)$. An example of this would be

$$\frac{X \vdash A \qquad X \vdash B}{X \vdash A \ \& \ B}.$$

So we would expect to find the following kinds of transformation rules in a logical system:

I. If A has such and such a syntactic form, then $\vdash A$. (AXIOMS)

II. If A is gotten from X in such and such a way, and $\vdash B$ for every member B of X, then $\vdash A$.

III. If A is gotten from X in such and such a way, then $X \vdash A$.

IV. If X and A are gotten from $X_1, \ldots, X_i, \ldots$ and $A_1, \ldots, A_i, \ldots$ in such and such a way, then

$$\frac{X_1 \vdash A_1; \ldots; X_i \vdash A_i; \ldots}{X \vdash A}.$$

There are actually still further kinds of transformation rules, but these are the most common.

Turning now to metalogical appraisal, we note that the usual intention behind constructing such a logical system is that under the intended interpretation, $\vdash$ coincide with $\Vdash$. That is, the theorems ought to be exactly the valid sentences, and the validated arguments exactly the semantic entailments. When that is not the case, one may yet ask whether any part of this intention is fulfilled, for example, whether at least the theorems are all valid sentences. Or one may ask whether there be not *some* (interesting) interpretation or other under which (part of) the intention is fulfilled. The general problem is that of finding an adequate syntactic description of a semantically defined class, or of finding an adequate semantic description of a syntactically defined class. The aim of a logical system is to provide us with a syntactic characterization of semantic notions, and the aim of metalogic to appraise such attempts.

For convenience, we shall identify a logical system with the ordered triple of (a) a representative syntactic system to which it pertains, (b) the class of its theorems in this syntactic system, and (c) the class of its validated arguments in this syntactic system. We arrive therefore at the following characterization.

DEFINITION. A *logical system* is a triple $LS = \langle \text{Syn, Th}, \vdash \rangle$, where

(a) Syn is a syntactic system (to which LS is said to *pertain*);

(b) $\vdash$ is a relation from sets of sentences of Syn to sentences of Syn (the *consequence* relation);

(c) $\text{Th} = \{A : \Lambda \vdash A\}$ (the set of *theorems*).

We shall also write $\vdash A$ for "$\Lambda \vdash A$."

While a logical system may in principle be used to characterize any relation from sets of sentences to sentences, and may itself be specified in any way whatsoever, there are also more restricted concepts. From the point of view of proof theory, specifically, it would not make much sense to call LS a logical system unless the consequence relation or the set of theorems can be specified in a more of less constructive manner.[2] More important from our point of view is that the main use of logical systems is to characterize the relation of semantic entailment in some (kind of) language. When that is the case, the consequence relation must have certain properties, which we shall now discuss.

In any language L, the relation of semantic entailment satisfies the principles

(a) $X \Vdash A$ if $A \in X$.
(b) If $X \Vdash A$ for all A in Y, and $Y \Vdash B$, then $X \Vdash B$.
(c) If $X \subseteq Y$ and $X \Vdash A$ then $Y \Vdash A$.

If the relation $\vdash$ in a logical system LS pertaining to the syntax of L is to coincide with the relation $\Vdash$ in L, it must accordingly satisfy analogous principles. This can be stated in a convenient manner by looking at the *consequence operator* of LS,

$$\mathrm{Cn}(X) = \{A : X \vdash A\}.$$

This operator on sets of sentences is called a *closure operator* if it satisfies

I. $X \subseteq \mathrm{Cn}(X)$.
II. $\mathrm{Cn}(\mathrm{Cn}(X)) \subseteq \mathrm{Cn}(X)$.
III. If $X \subseteq Y$, then $\mathrm{Cn}(X) \subseteq \mathrm{Cn}(Y)$.

And this must be the case if $\vdash$ is to conincide with $\Vdash$. Hence we shall call a logical system *normal* if its consequence operator is a closure operator. In the remainder of this section we shall only be concerned with normal systems.

The appraisal of a logical system thus concerns the correspondence between its theorems and the set of valid sentences of the language, and the correspondence between its consequence relation and semantic entailment. (When the system has rules of type IV, its appraisal may involve further criteria, but this we shall disregard for now; see, however, Chapter V, Section 3c.) The basic concepts used in this appraisal are *soundness* and *completeness*. These must be related both to theorems and to deductions.

> DEFINITION.   *LS* is *sound* for *L*
> (a) *with respect to statements* iff all theorems of *LS* are valid in *L*;
> (b) *with respect to arguments* iff $X \Vdash A$ in *L* whenever $X \vdash A$ in *LS*.

We shall use "statement sound" for property (a), "argument sound" for property (b), and "sound" for the conjunction of both.

> DEFINITION.   *LS* is *statement complete* for *L* iff $\vdash A$ in *LS* whenever $\Vdash A$ in *L*.
>
> DEFINITION.   *LS* has (*weak*) *argument completeness* for *L* iff $X \vdash A$ in *LS* for every finite set *X* and sentence *A* such that $X \Vdash A$ in *L*.
>
> DEFINITION.   *LS* has *strong* (*argument*) *completeness* for *L* iff $X \vdash A$ in *LS* whenever $X \Vdash A$ in *L*.

The indicated use of "strong completeness" is common; hence we can safely abbreviate "weak argument completeness" to "argument completeness." We shall use "weak completeness" for "statement and argument completeness." The reason for the weak/strong distinction is partly that proofs concerning infinite sets of sentences require more powerful methods, and partly because there are some important cases in which a system has weak but not strong completeness under an interesting interpretation.[3]

The distinctions between statement and argument soundness and completeness also correspond to a substantial difference. The best known example of this is a result due to Gödel that the $\&\text{-}\neg$ fragments of classical and intuitionistic logic are the same as far as theorems are concerned. Since the other classical connectives are definable in terms of

& and $\neg$, one may state this result in the form: All the classical theorems are intuitionistically valid. But the same does not hold for arguments; for example, $\neg\neg A \vdash A$ holds in classical but not in intuitionistic logic.

There are, however, also a number of important relations among these concepts, depending largely on the structure of the language under discussion.

Theorem. *If LS is argument sound (complete) for L, then LS is statement sound (complete) for L.*

This is so simply because $\Vdash A$ iff $\Lambda \Vdash A$ and $\vdash A$ iff $\Lambda \vdash A$.

Theorem. *If L has a connector $\rightarrow$ such that $A_1, \ldots, A_n \Vdash B$ iff $A_1, \ldots, A_{n-1} \Vdash A_n \rightarrow B$, the statement soundness (completeness) of a system LS for L implies its argument soundness (completeness), provided, $A_1, \ldots, A_n \vdash B$ iff $A_1, \ldots, A_{n-1} \vdash A_n \rightarrow B$ in LS.*

Finally, we note that if L has finitary semantic entailment, then argument completeness for L implies strong completeness for L. Conversely, if the consequence relation of LS is finitary, and LS is strongly complete for L, then L has finitary semantic entailment. If L has exclusion negation, these connections hold for compactness as well as for finitary semantic entailment. Indeed, compactness results most usually appear as corollaries to strong completeness proofs, notwithstanding their purely semantic character, which makes them essentially independent of the properties of any logical system.

We shall devote the next two sections to the formulation and appraisal of the most familiar logical system, the classical propositional calculus.

2. Classical Propositional Logic: Axiomatics

The most familiar early formulations of the propositional calculus (including the one in Whitehead and Russell's *Principia Mathematica*) consist of a set of axioms with the rules of *modus ponens* and *substitution*. Let us to begin take these rules to have the form

(MP)   If ⊢A and ⊢$A \supset B$, then ⊢B.

(Sub.)   If ⊢A, then ⊢$S_p^B(A)$.

The axioms were then formulated using specific atomic sentences $p, q, \ldots$; for example,

$$⊢p \supset (p \,\&\, p).$$

This was simplified by eliminating the rule Sub. and using axiom schemes rather than axioms:

Any sentence of form $A \supset (A \,\&\, A)$ is a theorem,

which for brevity is just expressed by

$$⊢A \supset (A \,\&\, A).$$

A complete formulation of the propositional calculus with & and $\neg$ as primitive, and the other connectors defined as usual, was first given by Sobocinski.[4] Using axiom schemes and rule MP, it has:

A1. ⊢$A \supset (A \,\&\, A)$.
A2. ⊢$(A \,\&\, B) \supset A$.
A3. ⊢$\neg(A \,\&\, B) \supset \neg(B \,\&\, A)$.
A4. ⊢$A \supset B \cdot \supset : \neg(C \,\&\, B) \supset \neg(C \,\&\, A)$.

A difficulty with such formulations, both from a practical and a meta-logical point of view, is that they do not provide one with a definite method of proving any particular theorem (although they provide, in effect, a method for churning out all theorems in the fullness of time).

For this reason, we turn to the subject of algorithms. What we should like to have is an algorithm that, when applied to a sentence, produces a certain kind of resultant expression if and only if that sentence is a theorem. One such algorithm was introduced by Beth: It transforms the negation of a theorem into a disjunction of explicit contradictions.[5] To describe it, we must introduce some conventions.

> CONVENTIONS.   (a) We use X, Y, Z to stand for conjunctions of sentences, possibly empty, with qualification that X is not of the form $\neg\neg A$ or $\neg(A \,\&\, B)$.
>
> (b) We use $A_1 \,\&\, \cdots \,\&\, A_n$ to stand for any sentence resulting from this expression by replacing A_i by a sentence ($i = 1, \ldots, n$) and a judicious addition of parentheses. The expression $A_1 \vee \cdots \vee A_n$ abbreviates $\neg(\neg A_1 \,\&\, \cdots \,\&\, \neg A_n)$.

When the algorithm is applied to an expression A, it produces a sequence of expressions $B_1, \ldots, B_k, \ldots$ with $B_1 = \neg A$. This sequence is called the *tableau sequence* for A. Each expression B_i is a disjunction $B_i^1 \vee \cdots \vee B_i^n$, $n \geq 1$; we call B_i^j a *disjunctive part* of B_i.

Let B_i be $K \vee B \vee M$, where K and M are themselves multiple disjunctions (possibly empty), and B is the leftmost disjunctive part of B_i to which any of the rules below are applicable; then B_{i+1} is

$$K \vee M \vee B',$$

where B' is the result of applying the first applicable rule to B. The rules are

(DN) $X \,\&\, \neg\neg A \,\&\, Y \rightarrow X \,\&\, A \,\&\, Y.$

(NK) $X \,\&\, \neg(A \,\&\, B) \,\&\, Y \rightarrow (X \,\&\, \neg A \,\&\, Y) \vee (X \,\&\, \neg B \,\&\, Y).$

> CLOSURE RULE.   If a disjunct in B_k has the form $X \,\&\, A \,\&\, Y \,\&\, \neg A \,\&\, Z$ or $X \,\&\, \neg A \,\&\, Y \,\&\, A \,\&\, Z$ it is underlined.

Note that CN and NK are not applicable to underlined expressions. An underlined expression is said to be *closed*. If some member B_k of the tableau sequence consists entirely of closed disjuncts, it is clearly the last member; in this case the sequence is said to *terminate*.

Theorem.   *The tableau sequence of a sentence A terminates iff A is a theorem of the propositional calculus.*

The proof is left to the reader; the reader may prefer to leave it, too. As an example we apply the algorithm to Peirce's law, $\vdash[(p \supset q) \supset p] \supset p$. This must first be stated with & and $\neg$ as only logical symbols; then $\neg$ must be prefixed.

B_1 $\neg\neg\{\neg[\neg(p \ \& \ \neg q) \ \& \ \neg p] \ \& \ \neg p\}$

B_2 $\neg[\neg(p \ \& \ \neg q) \ \& \ \neg p] \ \& \ \neg p$ DN

B_3 $\neg\neg(p \ \& \ \neg q) \ \& \ \neg p$ $\cdot \vee \cdot$ $\neg\neg p \ \& \ \neg p$ NK

B_4 $\neg\neg p \ \& \ \neg p$ $\cdot \vee \cdot$ $(p \ \& \ \neg q) \ \& \ \neg p$ DN

B_5 $p \ \& \ \neg q \ \& \ \neg p$ $\cdot \vee \cdot$ $p \ \& \ \neg p$ DN

B_6 $p \ \& \ \neg p$ $\cdot \vee \cdot$ $\underline{p \ \& \ \neg q \ \& \ \neg p}$ C1

B_7 $\underline{p \ \& \ \neg q \ \& \ \neg p}$ $\cdot \vee \cdot$ $\underline{p \ \& \ \neg p}$ C1

This tableau sequence has the structure of a tree, if we leave out the disjunction signs, and write the results of applying a rule under the disjunct to which the rule was applied, Figure 3. Thus, thinking of the

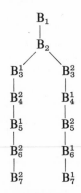

FIGURE 3

disjunction as indicating a branching, the tableau sequence has the structure of a tree. And this tree terminates exactly when each of its branches ends in an explicit contradiction (let us say then that those branches *terminate*). The idea is that a terminating tree provides us with a proof of the formula, but a nonterminating branch provides us with a counterexample to the formula. This is the pattern of many statement soundness and completeness proofs.

In this case, our job is made easier because the tree is always finite.

Theorem.   *For any sentence A, the tableau sequence for A is finite.*

Proof: Let the tableau sequence be $B_1, B_2, B_3, \ldots$ with $B_1 = \neg A$. Each application of DN reduces the number of symbols. Each application of NK replaces a disjunct C_i by two disjuncts C_i^1 and C_i^2, but then there is one fewer symbol in C_i^j than in C_i. So going down the branches we find that the number of symbols does not increase, until closure occurs (if it does).

Now suppose that one of the rules DN or NK is applicable to a disjunct C. Then that rule will eventually be applied. For we have insisted that the immediate result of any application of a rule be placed at the far right so that each disjunct is eventually considered.

So in any given branch, the number of symbols decreases until no further rule is applicable (perhaps because of closure). Hence for each branch B_i there is a rank m_i beyond which all its members (if any) are the same as its member of rank $m_i - 1$. Let us lop off all those excess members. Then we have a tree T, with the finite branching property, and each branch finite. So by Koenig's lemma, T is finite.

Let n be the maximum length of branches of T. Then the tableau sequence has at most n members; for the algorithm would not be applicable to (any part of) member B_n. So the tableau sequence is finite.

That the tableau sequences are finite means that the algorithm gives us a *decision procedure*: for any sentence A, we can tell in finitely many steps whether or not A is a theorem. This feature will make the proof of completeness considerably easier.

It will be clear that the algorithm, as well as the axiomatic system, specifies *only* the class of theorems, and does not tell us which arguments are valid. To extend the propositional calculus to the validation of inferences, we add the rule

(ARG)   If $\vdash \neg(A_1 \& \cdots \& A_n \& \neg B)$, then $A_1, \ldots, A_n \vdash B$.

where we write "$A_1, \ldots, A_n \vdash B$" as short for "$\{A_1, \ldots, A_n\} \vdash B$." The relation $\vdash$ can now be defined inductively: For all sentences $A, A_1, \ldots, A_n, B$ of Syn, and sets X, Y of sentences of Syn:

(a) If the tableau sequence of A terminates, then $\langle \Lambda, A \rangle \in \vdash$.
(b) If $\langle \Lambda, \neg(A_1 \& \cdots \& A_n \& \neg B) \rangle \in \vdash$, then $\langle \{A_1, \ldots, A_n\}, B \rangle \in \vdash$.
(c) If $\langle X, A \rangle \in \vdash$ and $X \subseteq Y$, then $\langle Y, A \rangle \in \vdash$.
(d) Nothing belongs to $\vdash$ except by virtue of clauses (a)–(c).

Propositional logic may then be identified with a triple $\langle \text{Syn}, \text{Th}, \vdash \rangle$ such that Syn is a PCS, $\vdash$ the relation from sets of sentences to sentences of Syn defined by clauses (a)–(d), and $\text{Th} = \{A : \Lambda \vdash A\}$. It can be verified that this is a normal logical system.

A good question at this point is whether the rule (ARG) is really needed, or whether it is somehow derivable from the original system. The derivation could not be in any sense a straightforward one, since in the original system nothing is said about validity of arguments. The other possibility is that one might be able to show that the argument from $A_1, \ldots, A_n$ to B is valid iff $\vdash \neg(A_1, \& \cdots \& A_n \& \neg B)$ is a theorem, under any interpretation of the syntax for which the logical system is statement sound and complete. In Section 1 we said that this is not so, referring to the $\&$-$\neg$ fragment of intuitionistic logic. In Section 5 we shall present other interpretations, which can be used to show this. For the logical appraisal of reasoning it is not enough to consider only the question of which sentences are valid.

3. Classical Propositional Logic: Soundness and Completeness

Everyone is, of course, already familiar with the standard interpretation of propositional logic: the proximate subject matter of this logical system is validity in a bivalent propositional language. Before turning to the soundness and completeness proofs, we state a lemma.

Lemma 1.   *If $A_1, \ldots, A_n$ are sentences of a bivalent propositional language L, and v an admissible valuation for L, then*
(a) $v(A_1 \& \cdots \& A_n) = T$ iff $v(A_1) = \cdots = v(A_n) = T$.
(b) $v(A_1 \lor \cdots \lor A_n) = F$ iff $v(A_1) = \cdots = v(A_n) = F$.

Proof: It is important to note that this cannot be proved at once by natural induction since the sentence denoted as $A_1 \& \cdots \& A_n$ may not have the form $(A_1 \& \cdots \& A_{n-1}) \& A_n$ or the form $A_1 \& (A_2 \& \cdots \& A_n)$ but the form $(A_1 \& \cdots \& A_i) \& (A_{i+1} \& \cdots \& A_n)$, where $2 < i < n - 1$, in which case it does not have a conjunct of $(n - 1)$ of the sentences in question. (It can be proved by natural induction if we first prove associativity.) We prove it therefore by strong induction.

Hypothesis of Strong Induction.   *For any multiple conjunction $B_1 \& \cdots \& B_m$ of length less than $A_1 \& \cdots \& A_n$, $v(B_1 \& \cdots \& B_m) = T$ iff $v(B_1) = \cdots = v(B_m) = T$.*

 Case 1. $A_1 \& \cdots \& A_n$ does not have the form $B \& C$; that is, $n = 1$. In that case the required conclusion is simply $v(A_1) = v(A_1)$.
 Case 2. $A_1 \& \cdots \& A_n$ does have the form $B \& C$; let $B = (A_1 \& \cdots \& A_i)$ and $C = (A_{i+1} \& \cdots \& A_n)$. By the definition of admissible valuation, $v(A_1 \& \cdots \& A_n) = T$ iff $v(B) = v(C) = T$. By the hypothesis of induction this is the same as $v(A_1) = \cdots = v(A_i) = v(A_{i+1}) = \cdots = v(A_n) = T$.

These are all possible cases, so proposition (a) is proved. The proof of (b) is left as an exercise.

Theorem.   (Statement soundness)   *If A is a sentence of a bivalent propositional language L, and the tableau sequence for A terminates, then A is a valid sentence of L.*

Proof: That the tableau sequence $A = B_1, B_2, \ldots$ terminates means that it has a last member B_k, which is a multiple disjunction of closed expressions. We shall show that $v(B_k) = F$ for each admissible valuation

v, and that if $v(B_{i+1}) = F$, then $v(B_i) = F$ for $i \geq 1$. By induction it follows that $v(B_1) = v(\neg A) = F$, hence that $v(A) = T$, for each admissible valuation v.

First, let $B_k = C_1 \vee \cdots \vee C_m$. Then $v(B_k) = F$ if $v(C_1) = \cdots = v(C_m) = F$ (Lemma 1). But C_i is closed; let $C_i = D_1 \& \cdots \& D_n$, where $D_j = \neg D_l$. Then $v(C_i) = F$; for if $v(C_i) = T$, then $v(D_j) = v(D_l) = T$; that is, $v(\neg D_l) = v(D_l) = T$, which is impossible. Hence the value of C_i, for $i = 1, \ldots, m$, is indeed F.

Second, let $i \geq 1$ and $v(B_{i+1}) = F$. Then B_{i+1} comes from B_i by an application of C1 or DN or NK, which replaces some disjunct of B_i by another expression. What we need to show is that when the replacement is false, so is the original expression—the conclusion then follows again by Lemma 1.

There are here two important cases. The first is that a disjunct $(X \& \neg\neg A \& Y)$ is replaced by $(X \& A \& Y)$. If $v(X \& A \& Y) = F$, then, by Lemma 1, $v(X)$ or $v(A)$ or $v(Y)$ equals F. Well, $v(\neg\neg A) = v(A)$; hence $v(X)$ or $v(\neg\neg A)$ or $v(Y)$ equals F. Hence $v(X \& \neg\neg A \& Y) = F$. The second case is that a disjunct $D = (X \& \neg(A \& B) \& Y)$ is replaced by the expression

$$D' = (X \& \neg A \& Y) \vee (X \& \neg B \& Y).$$

If $v(D') = F$, then $v(X \& \neg A \& Y) = v(X \& \neg B \& Y) = F$, by Lemma 1. Hence either $v(X)$ or $v(Y)$ or $v(\neg A)$ equals F, *and* either $v(X)$ or $v(Y)$ or $v(\neg B)$ equals F. If either $v(X)$ or $v(Y)$ equals F, then surely $v(D) = F$. If neither $v(X)$ nor $v(Y)$ equals F, then $v(\neg A) = v(\neg B) = F$. Hence $v(A) = v(B) = T$; therefore, $v(A \& B) = T$; therefore, $v(\neg(A \& B)) = F$. So in this case also, $v(D) = F$.

Theorem. (Statement completeness) *If A is a valid sentence of a bivalent language L, then the tableau sequence for A terminates.*

Proof: Recall from the previous section that a tableau sequence is always finite. This means that it has a last member B_k. If the sequence does not terminate, B_k is a multiple disjunction $C_1 \vee \cdots \vee C_m$ such that for some i $(1 \leq i \leq m)$, C_i is not closed. C_i is itself a multiple conjunction of *atomic sentences and negations of atomic sentences.* (For if it were not, then either DN or NK would be applicable, contrary to our assumption that B_k is the last member of our sequence.) We define an admissible valuation v, by the condition that for any atomic sentence p

$$v(p) = T \quad \text{iff } p \text{ is a conjunct in } C_i.$$

Hence if $\neg p$ is a conjunct in C_i, $v(p) = F$, so $v(\neg p) = T$. All the conjuncts of C_i receiving the value T, it follows by Lemma 1 that $v(C_i) = T$. By the other part of Lemma 1 (concerning disjunctions) it now follows that $v(B_k) = T$.

To complete the proof by mathematical induction we must now show that if $v(B_{i+1}) = T$, then $v(B_i) = T$ for $i \geq 1$. Then $v(B_i) = v(\neg A) = T$, so that $v(A) = F$; and this will show that a sentence A with nonterminating tableau sequence is not valid.

If $i \geq 1$, then B_{i+1} comes from B_i either by DN or by Cl or by NK, so we have three cases.

Case 1. One of the disjuncts C of B_{i+1} which is also a disjunct of B_i is such that $v(C) = T$. Then clearly $v(B_i) = T$.

Case 2. B_{i+1} is essentially[6] like B_i except for having the disjunct $C' = (X \ \& \ A \ \& \ Y)$, where B_i has $C = (X \ \& \ \neg\neg A \ \& \ Y)$, and $v(C') = T$. It clearly follows that $v(C) = T$, hence $v(B_i) = T$.

Case 3. B_{i+1} is essentially like B_i except for having

$$C' = (X \ \& \ \neg A \ \& \ Y) \lor (X \ \& \ \neg B \ \& \ Y),$$

where B_i has $C = (X \ \& \ \neg(A \ \& \ B) \ \& \ Y)$, and $v(C') = T$. Then $v(X \ \& \ \neg A \ \& \ Y) = T$ or $v(X \ \& \ \neg B \ \& \ Y) = T$. This means that

(a) $v(X) = v(Y) = T$;

(b) $v(\neg A) = T$ or $v(\neg B) = T$.

From (b) it follows that $v(A) = F$ or $v(B) = F$, so $v(A \ \& \ B) = F$, so

(c) $v(\neg(A \ \& \ B)) = T$.

By Lemma 1 and (a) and (c) we deduce that $v(C) = T$; hence $v(B_i) = T$ in this case also.

Turning now to argument completeness, we recall that $A_1, \ldots, A_n \vdash B$ iff $\vdash \neg(A_1 \,\&\, \cdots \,\&\, A_n \,\&\, \neg B)$. We prove

Theorem.   *In a bivalent propositional language* L, $A_1, \ldots, A_n \Vdash B$ *iff* $\Vdash \neg(A_1 \,\&\, \cdots \,\&\, \neg B)$.

Proof: We first note that by Lemma 1, $v(A_1) = \cdots = v(A_n) = \mathrm{T}$ iff $v(A_1 \,\&\, \cdots \,\&\, A_n) = \mathrm{T}$. Hence the case of more than one premise is reducible to the case of a single premise. We must show then that

$$A \Vdash B \text{ iff } \Vdash \neg(A \,\&\, \neg B).$$

Suppose that $v(\neg(A \,\&\, B)) = \mathrm{F}$. Then $v(A \,\&\, \neg B) = \mathrm{T}$, so $v(A) = \mathrm{T}$ and $v(B) = \mathrm{F}$. This shows at once that if $\neg(A \,\&\, \neg B)$ is not valid, A does not semantically entail B. On the other hand, if $v(\neg(A \,\&\, \neg B)) = \mathrm{T}$ and $v(A) = \mathrm{T}$, then $v(B) = \mathrm{T}$.

Defining $(A \to B)$ as $\neg(A \,\&\, \neg B)$, we find that the conditions of the last theorem of Section 1 are satisfied. Since we have just proved statement soundness and completeness, we conclude

Theorem.   *The propositional calculus is sound and has weak completeness for a bivalent propositional language.*

Second, we may recall that a bivalent propositional language has finitary semantic entailment. From this and the preceding theorem we may conclude that propositional logic is strongly complete with respect to a bivalent propositional language.

It is worthwhile to point out here that the tableau method may be adapted to provide a strong completeness proof directly.[7] Let $X = \{A_1, \ldots, A_i, \ldots\}$ be a consistent set of sentences, and let us start the procedure of the Beth algorithm on sentence A_1, thereafter adding the expression A_{i+1} on the right-hand side of each disjunct at the $(i + 1)$th step, $i = 1, 2, 3, \ldots$. The result will be a tree with at least one non-terminating branch, and this branch contains among its conjuncts all members of X. The proof of our weak completeness theorem carries over to this case and shows the satisfiability of the set X. So every consistent set is satisfiable—and from this the strong completeness property follows.

But to this we must add that it is *crucial* to this method of proving strong completeness that there are only denumerably many sentences in the language. That this is so we have assumed throughout; however, this assumption plays no essential role in topological compactness proofs. For this reason, a strong completeness theorem deduced from a weak completeness theorem proved by the use of tableau sequences plus a semantic compactness theorem proved by the use of ultrafilters generalizes easily to noncountable languages. There are, however, also other methods of proving strong completeness directly which are equally capable of such generalization. Our most important reason for proving compactness independently of completeness theorems is, of course, our aim to answer purely semantical questions in purely semantical terms, that is, without recourse to the properties of logical systems.

4. Interpretations of Logical Systems

The appraisal of a logic is always with respect to a given language. And a logical system is entirely adequate with respect to a given language if the system is argument sound and strongly complete with respect to that language. We must here reckon with the possibility, however, that the system may be entirely adequate, in this sense, with respect to more than one language.

This possibility makes such phrases as "the language of propositional logic" ambiguous. For if we know the syntax of a language, and we know what arguments are valid in that language, we cannot deduce from this the truth conditions for the sentences of that language. And we are going to show, by concrete examples, that it is not even possible to decide on this basis such fundamental questions as whether the language is or is not bivalent.

Before turning to specific examples, we shall make our terminology somewhat more precise. We have identified logical systems with triples, of which the first member is a syntactic system. Now the most basic use of "interpretation" is that noted in Chapter II, Section 3: An interpretation of a syntactic system is a function that is a valuation of the system but is also defined for some nouns and/or functors of the system. In a second usage, to give the semantics of a language is to interpret its syntax. For the specification of the set of admissible valuations is to set limits to the interpretations, in the first sense, of its syntax. Specifically, the semantics of a bivalent propositional language consists in defining the truth conditions for longer sentences in terms of those for shorter sentences, so that any latitude in interpretation is limited to the assignments of truth values to the atomic sentences.

We now wish to introduce a third sense of "interpretation": If $LS = \langle \text{Syn, Th}, \vdash \rangle$, and L is a language with syntax Syn, then the semantics of L is an *interpretation* of LS. (If the reader finds "the semantics of L" too imprecise, he may read it as "the set of admissible valuations of L.") In other words, an interpretation in the second sense of the syntax of LS is a candidate for an interpretation of LS and is successful if the criteria of soundness and completeness are met. I do not think this is too novel a sense of "interpretation"; Lewis and Langford apparently used the word in this sense when they talked of the extensional and intensional interpretations of the Boole–Schröder algebra (essentially, propositional logic).[8]

In the remaining sections of this chapter we shall introduce two devices for constructing nonbivalent interpretations of propositional logic: matrices and supervaluations. These will themselves be investigated further in Chapter V, and the discussions in the present chapter provide a somewhat more elementary introduction to those subjects.

5. Interpretation Through Matrices

The most familiar example of a logical matrix is the two-valued truth table. Abstractly speaking, this consists of a set of elements {T, F}, a subset of designated elements {T}, a binary and unary operation on those elements (correlated with & and ¬). Generalizing this concept, we obtain:

DEFINITION. $M = \langle E, D, \cdot, - \rangle$ is a *logical matrix* iff E is a set (the *elements* of M), D a nonempty subset of E (the *designated* elements), $\cdot$ a binary operation on E, and $-$ a unary operation on E.

For convenience we shall often write "$(x \cdot y)$" for "$\cdot (x, y)$" and "$\bar{x}$" for "$-x$." The limitation to two operations is not essential.

DEFINITION. If $M = \langle E, D, \cdot, - \rangle$ is a logical matrix, then a function d is an *M-assignment* to a PCS iff
(a) d maps the sentences of the PCS into E;
(b) $d(A \& B) = d(A) \cdot d(B)$;
(c) $d(\neg A) = \overline{d(A)}$.

DEFINITION. If $M = \langle E, D, \cdot, - \rangle$ is a logical matrix and d an M-assignment to a PCS, then an *M-valuation* on that PCS *induced by d* is any valuation v on that PCS such that $v(A) = $ T iff $d(A) \in D$.

Various motives induce us to let d induce a unique valuation; for example, by adding $v(A) = $ F iff $d(A) \notin D$. Another possibility is to say that $v(A) = $ F iff $d(\neg A) \in D$, in which case bivalence does not generally hold. In the latter case, we must stipulate that x and $\bar{x}$ are not both designated. In the present context, however, nothing would be affected by such a choice.

If M is a logical matrix, then L is an *M-propositional language* if the syntax of L is a PCS and the admissible valuations of L are the M-valuations on that PCS. We call L a *matrix propositional language* iff L is an M-propositional language for some logical matrix M.

The familiar truth table is a matrix, a two-element Boolean algebra.[9]

DEFINITION. A logical matrix $M = \langle E, D, \cdot, - \rangle$ is a *two-element Boolean algebra* iff E contains exactly two elements, D contains exactly one element, and for all x, y in E:
(a) $\bar{x} \neq x$;
(b) $(x \cdot y) \in D$ iff $x, y \in D$.

Using "1" to denote the designated element and "0" for the other element, operations of this algebra are conveniently defined by the *operator diagrams*

$\cdot$	1	0		$-$	
1	1	0		1	0
0	0	0		0	1

An *M*-assignment correlates $\cdot$ with & and $-$ with $\neg$; thus the following *interpretation diagram* also defines the matrix:

p	q	$p\,\&\,q$	$\neg p$
1	1	1	0
1	0	0	
0	1	0	1
0	0	0	

If a system *LS* is statement sound and complete for an *M*-propositional language, we shall call *M* an *adequate matrix* for *LS*. So the two-element Boolean algebra is an adequate matrix for the classical propositional calculus.

This raises the question of what general conditions a matrix must satisfy to be adequate for the classical propositional logic. The following theorems provide a partial answer.

DEFINITION.   A mapping f of E into E' is a *homomorphism* from $M = \langle E, D, \cdot, - \rangle$ to $M' = \langle E', D', \wedge, \sim \rangle$ if and only if
(a) $f(b \cdot c) = f(b) \wedge f(c)$;
(b) $f(-b) = \sim f(b)$

Theorem. *If there is a homomorphism f from M to M' that maps undesignated elements of M into undesignated elements of M', then all the sentences that are valid in M' are valid in M.*

Proof: Suppose A is not valid in M; let d be an *M*-assignment such that $d(A)$ is not designated. Assuming the antecedent of the theorem,

$f(d(A))$ is not designated in M'. But the function d' such that $d'(A) = f(d(A))$ for all sentences A (of the PCS in question) is an M' assignment when f is an homomorphism:

$$d'(A \& B) = f(d(A \& B)) = f(d(A) \cdot d(B))$$
$$= f(d(A)) \wedge f(d(B)) = d'(A) \wedge d'(B),$$
$$d'(\neg A) = f(d(\neg A)) = f(-d(A)) = \sim f(d(A)) = \sim d'(A).$$

This theorem allows us to show of other matrices than B_2 that they are also sound and/or complete for the propositional calculus. An obvious example is the four-element Boolean algebra with two designated elements $B_4 = \langle \{1, b, a, 0\}, \{1, b\}, \cdot, - \rangle$ with operator diagrams

$\cdot$	1	b	a	0		$-$	
1	1	b	a	0		1	0
b	b	b	0	0		b	a
a	a	0	a	0		a	b
0	0	0	0	0		0	1

The mapping f from B_2 into B_4 defined by

$$f(1) = 1,$$
$$f(0) = 0$$

satisfies the conditions of the previous theorem, so all the sentences valid in B_4 are valid in B_2. Therefore, the propositional calculus is statement complete for a B_4-propositional language. That it is also statement sound for such a language follows from the fact that the function g from B_4 into B_2 defined below also satisfies the conditions of the above theorem:

$$g(1) = 1,$$
$$g(b) = 1,$$
$$g(a) = 0,$$
$$g(0) = 0.$$

That g preserves the property of not being designated is obvious, that it is a homomorphism is easily seen by replacing b and a by 1 and 0 in the operator diagrams:

$\cdot$	1	1	0	0		$-$	
1	1	1	0	0		1	0
1	1	1	0	0		1	0
0	0	0	0	0		0	1
0	0	0	0	0		0	1

which simply yields redundant operator diagrams for B_2. Our conclusion is that B_4 is also an adequate matrix for classical propositional logic.

So far we have only talked about statement soundness and completeness. We leave it to the reader to worry about whether the theorem concerning homomorphisms extends to valid arguments as well as valid sentences.[10]

If the classical propositional calculus has an adequate matrix M, but is not argument sound for an M-propositional language, M is called a *nonnormal matrix*.[11] Clearly M is *normal* iff M is adequate for propositional calculus, and when $d(A)$ and $d(A \supset B)$ are designated, then $d(B)$ is designated. A very simple nonnormal matrix can be constructed with just three elements:

$$M_3 = \langle \{1, b, 0\}, \{1\}, \cdot, - \rangle$$

$\cdot$	1	b	0		$-$	
1	1	1	0		1	0
b	1	1	0		b	0
0	0	0	0		0	1

Theorem. *M_3 is an adequate matrix for the classical propositional calculus, but this calculus is not argument sound for an M_3-propositional language.*

Proof: Starting with the easy part, let us observe that the argument from $\neg\neg A$ to A is not valid in an M_3-propositional language because if $d(A) = b$, then $d(\neg\neg A) = 1$ also. So we do not have argument soundness.

The mapping $f\!:\!f(1) = 1, f(0) = 0$ is a homomorphism from B_2 to M_3, and it takes 0 into an undesignated element. Hence all the sentences valid in M_3 are valid in B_2, by our theorem. So if a sentence is valid in M_3, it is demonstrable in classical propositional logic (statement completeness).

Second, suppose that A is a theorem of classical propositional logic. Then A has a terminating tableau sequence. Now it is easy to see that $\cdot$ is an associative operation:

$$x \cdot (y \cdot z) = (x \cdot y) \cdot z \qquad \text{for all } x, y, z \text{ in } \{1, b, 0\}.$$

(For in this matrix, either side equals zero if and only if either x, or y, or z equals zero.) Second, $d(B \,\&\, \neg B) = 0$ in all cases; thus every tip of a terminating branch has the value 0 under every M_3-assignment.

Third, when $d(B) = 0$, then $d(\neg\neg B) = 0$, and when both $d(\neg B) = 0$ and $d(\neg C) = 0$, then neither $d(B)$ nor $d(C)$ equals zero, so $d(B) \cdot d(C) = 1$, so $d(\neg(B \,\&\, C)) = 0$. Thus we see that as we go up the branches, all disjunctive parts have the value zero; therefore, the first member of the tableau sequence, $\neg A$, always has the value zero. It follows that A is valid in M_3 (statement soundness), since A must be complex if the tableau sequence terminates.

In the exercises, the reader is asked to prove that argument soundness and completeness does hold in the case of another three-valued matrix M_3^*, which is rather like M_3. The peculiarity of these matrices is that $(A \,\&\, B)$ is true when A and B are not both false (in the sense of being assigned value 0). We conclude this section by investigating the matrix M_3^{**} in which $(A \,\&\, B)$ is true when A and B are both true, and $(\neg A)$ is true when A is not true[12]:

$$M_3^{**} = \langle \{1, b, 0\}, \{1\}, \cdot, - \rangle$$

·	1	b	0		−	
1	1	0	0		1	0
b	0	0	0		b	1
0	0	0	0		0	1

The interpretation diagram for $(A \supset B)$, that is, $\neg(A \,\&\, \neg B)$, is such that $(A \supset B)$ receives the value 0 if and only if A receives 1 and B receives 0 or b. So this is a normal matrix. In addition, it follows that $A \Vdash B$ in an M_3^{**}-propositional language if and only if $\Vdash A \supset B$ in that language.

Second, the mapping $f(1) = 1$ and $f(0) = 0$ is a homomorphism of B_2 into M_3^{**}, so that propositional logic is statement complete for an M_3^{**}-propositional logic. On the other hand, the mapping $g(1) = 1$, $g(b) = 0$, $g(0) = 0$ is a homomorphism from M_3^{**} to B_2, as can be seen by replacing b by 0 in the operator diagrams. Therefore, we also have statement soundness: M_3^{**} is an adequate matrix for propositional logic.

Thus we have found that propositional logic is entirely adequate with respect to an M_3^{**}-propositional language (except that we have not proved compactness; but see Chapter V, Section 1b). We must be careful, however, not to conclude that M_3^{**} is in some important sense "the natural" three-valued matrix. There is first of all the adequacy of M_3^{*}. But more important is the fact that, although $\&$ and $\neg$ receive an "intuitive" interpretation in M_3^{**}, the nonprimitive connectives do not. For example, if $\equiv$ is defined as usual, then $(A \equiv B)$ is true when A has value b and B has value 0.

6. Interpretation Through Supervaluations

The original motivation for the introduction of logical matrices seems to have been philosophical. Under the standard interpretation, classical logic pertains to bivalent languages, but philosophers argued that the law of bivalence is itself not universally valid. Matrices appeared to provide an easy way to construct perfectly intelligible nonbivalent languages. However, the use of matrices also introduces various complexities, and philosophers did not rush to embrace this method with which the logicians so agreeably provided them. This may have been due in part, however, to the fact that it seems not to have been widely noticed (a) that most concepts in the semantic analysis of logic can be defined in terms of truth, without use of the notion of falsity, or (b) that there are adequate matrices for classical propositional logic for which it is not the case that every element or its complement is designated. Nevertheless, the use of matrices is hardly ever intuitively motivated to any great extent.

For this reason we shall here describe the method of *supervaluations*, which is intuitively very simple.[13] It also has the advantage that it can be applied independently of the syntactic structure of the language, so that we do not have the problem (as with matrices) of having to start again from the beginning if the syntax is not a PCS. We begin by supposing that in any situation, certain sentences are true and others are false. If L is a language in which these sentences occur, let us say that an admissible valuation of L *reflects* that situation if it assigns T to the sentences true in that situation and F to those false in that situation. In general, many valuations admissible for L may reflect the same situation—but they are correct with respect to that situation at most to the extent to which they agree upon assignments of truth and falsity. (For if v and v' both reflect a given situation, and $v(A) \neq v'(A)$, then A is neither true nor false in that situation, given our usage of "reflect.") The common assignment of T and F to sentences upon which they agree, by the set of valuations reflecting the same situation, we call a *supervaluation*.

DEFINITION. A valuation s is a *supervaluation* for a language L iff there is a nonempty set K of admissible valuations for L such that, for all sentences A of L,

$s(A) = $ T iff $v(A) = $ T for all $v \in K$,

$s(A) = $ F iff $v(A) = $ F for all $v \in K$,

$s(A)$ is not defined otherwise.

In general, a supervaluation for L is not an admissible valuation for L. (We may also note that supervaluations are rather like direct products—the difference concerns the assignment of falsity.)

Theorem. *Let L and L^* have the same syntax, and be such that the admissible valuations for L^* are the supervaluations for L; then $X \Vdash A$ in L^* iff $X \Vdash A$ in L, for all sentences A and sets of sentences X of L.*

Proof: Suppose $X \Vdash A$ in L, and let s be a supervaluation for L such that $s(B) = T$ iff $v(B) = T$ for all $v \in K$. Then if s satisfies X, so does each member of K. But then each member of K satisfies A; hence so does s.

Suppose not $X \Vdash A$ in L; let v' satisfy X but not A. Then if s is the supervaluation such that $s(B) = T$ iff $v(B) = T$ for all $v \in \{v'\}$, we find that s satisfies X but not A.

Corollary. *If L is a bivalent propositional language, and L^* is such that the syntax of L^* is that of L, and the admissible valuations for L^* are the supervaluations for L, then the classical propositional calculus is argument sound and strongly complete for L^*.*

The proof is immediate from the preceding theorem; this is simply an example of how the theorem can be applied. In applications, however, one may also have reason to take only *some* of the supervaluations as admissible for the new language. In that case, the soundness results still carry over automatically, but not the completeness results.

NOTES

1. R. Carnap, *The Logical Syntax of Language*, A. Smeaton, trans. (Paterson, N. J.: Littlefield, Adams & Co., 1959), sec. 1, pp. 1–4, and secs. 46–48, pp. 167–175.
2. Cf., e.g., W. V. O. Quine, *Mathematical Logic*, rev. ed. (Cambridge, Mass.: Harvard University Press, 1958), chap. 7, sec. 55, pp. 291–292.

3. The term "statement complete" is from N. D. Belnap, Jr., and R. H. Thomason, "A Rule-Completeness Theorem," *Notre Dame Journal of Formal Logic, 4* (1963), pp. 39–43.

4. For an informative discussion of alternative formulations of the propositional calculus, see H. B. Curry, *Foundations of Mathematical Logic* (New York: McGraw-Hill, 1963), chap. 6, sec. D2, pp. 292–296.

5. E. W. Beth, *Foundations of Mathematics* (Amsterdam: North-Holland, 1959), sec. 67, pp. 186–189; sec. 70, pp. 196–200. An algorithm exactly dual to this, turning theorems into conjunctions of excluded middles, was constructed by A. R. Anderson and N. D. Belnap, Jr., "A Simple Treatment of Truth Functions," *Journal of Symbolic Logic, 24* (1959), pp. 301–302, and "A Simple Proof of Gödel's Completeness Theorem" (abstract), *Journal of Symbolic Logic, 24* (1959), pp. 320–321.

6. That is, B_{i+1} is a permutation of the disjuncts of sentence B_i' which is like B_i except....

7. This was first pointed out to me by N. Cocchiarella. Proofs of compactness for propositional logic and of the compactness and Löwenheim–Skolem theorems for quantificational logic by this method are given explicitly by R. M. Smullyan, *First-Order Logic* (New York: Springer-Verlag, 1968), pp. 32–33, 64–65.

8. C. I. Lewis and C. H. Langford, *Symbolic Logic*, 2nd ed. (New York: Dover, 1959), p. 50 ("this interpretation of the algebra"); see also pp. 79, 91.

9. Strictly speaking we should say that this is a two-element Boolean algebra *with the unit element designated.*

10. Cf. J. Łoś and R. Suszko, "Remarks on Sentential Logics," *Indagationes Mathematicae, 20* (1958), pp. 177–183, esp. sec. II.

11. Cf. A. Church, "Non-Normal Truth-Tables for the Propositional Calculus," *Boletin de la Sociedad Matematica Mexicana, 10* (1953), pp. 41–52. Compare also the discussion of "weak models" by R. Harrop, "Some Structure Results for Propositional Calculi," *Journal of Symbolic Logic, 30* (1965), pp. 271–292.

12. Compare, e.g., E. Sosa, "Presupposition, the Aristotelian Square, and the Theory of Descriptions," mimeographed, University of Western Ontario, 1966.

13. Supervaluations were first introduced in B. van Fraassen, "Singular Terms, Truth-Value Gaps, and Free Logic," *Journal of Philosophy, 63* (1966), pp. 481–495; additional references will be given in chap. V, secs. 3 and 4.

CHAPTER IV

CLASSICAL QUANTIFICATION AND IDENTITY THEORY

In this chapter we shall study a familiar logical system, somewhat grandiloquently called classical quantification and identity theory; for convenience we shall also refer to it, somewhat less precisely, as *quantificational logic*. This system is an extension of classical propositional logic, and we can give an algorithm to define the class of theorems by extending the Beth algorithm described in Chapter III.

The appraisal of this system will proceed with respect to two kinds of languages, here called *referential quantifier languages* and *substitutional quantifier languages*. We shall also be interested in studying semantic aspects of these languages, especially semantic relations invariant under certain substitution operations, compactness, and semantic properties of deductive theories.

The referential quantifier languages are the more important since they provide the usual semantics for quantificational logic. In the discussion of these languages, the previously central notion of valuation tends to become somewhat subordinate to the notion of *model* (just as the notion of valuation tended to become subordinate to that of matrix in Section 5 of Chapter III). This is not necessary, of course, and it is not the case in all sections in this chapter.[1] But there may be some gain in intuitive understanding if we regard referential quantifier languages from the outset as languages for the description of relational structures. The substitutional quantifier languages will be shown to be definable in two ways: in terms of referential quantifier languages, and independently. Finally, we shall discuss certain extensions of quantificational logic to richer languages.

1. Syntax of Quantifier Languages

We are now going to enrich the syntactic resources of propositional logic in three ways: by regarding even atomic propositions as complex ("*x* is *F*," "*x* bears *R* to *y*"), by a special predicate for identity (which for convenience is listed among the logical signs), and by a universal quantifier. To begin, therefore, we define the requisite kind of syntactic system, a quantificational syntax (QCS).

DEFINITION. A QCS is a quadruple $\langle \mathscr{P}, V, \mathscr{L}, S \rangle$ where $\mathscr{P}$ is a set, nonempty and at most denumerable, (*the predicates*) of which each member has associated with it a positive integer (its *degree*); V is a set, denumerable (the *variables*), disjoint of $\mathscr{P}$;

$\mathscr{L}$ is a set with exactly five members (the *logical signs*) denoted as &, ¬, =,), (, disjoint of $\mathscr{P}$ and V;

S is the least set (the *sentences*) such that

(a) if P^n is a predicate of degree n and $x_1, \ldots, x_n$ are variables, then $P^n x_1 \ldots x_n$ and $x_1 = x_2$ belong to S;

(b) if x is a variable and A, B belong to S, so do $(\neg A)$, $(A \ \& \ B)$, and $(x)(A)$.

We shall use P^n, Q^n to stand for predicates of degree n; x, y, z for variables; A, B, C for sentences; all with or without accents or subscripts. We shall call a sentence A a *statement* if all occurrences of any variable x in A lie within parts of A that are themselves sentences of the form $(x)B$. (That is, all variables in A are *bound*, or *not free*; note that as usual we omit parentheses in our notation when that can cause no confusion.) Members of S in virtue of clause (a) are called *atomic sentences*.

The terminological distinction between "sentence" and "statement" is not uniform in the literature. Some authors use, for example, not "sentence" but "well-formed formula" [to be abbreviated as "wff" (pronounced "woof-ef") or as "wef," depending on one's preferred style of barking]. In that case "closed (well-formed) formula" is used for our "statement." In still different usages, "formula" and "sentence." or "formula" and "statement," are used for our "sentence" and "statement," respectively.[2] These suggest that expressions in which variables occur free (Quine calls them "matrices") do not enjoy the degree of grammatical significance conveyed by the term "sentence." And this suggestion is not altogether misleading; we shall find, however, that it makes very little difference for the appraisal of quantificational logic, whether what we call sentences or what we call statements are regarded as the sentences of the language.

There is a very important kind of syntactic transformation that can be defined for a QCS: substitution of variables for variables. This kind comprises several (sub-)kinds. The most common kind has the following general form:

If A is a sentence, then $(x/y)A$ is a sentence that results from replacing each[3] free occurrence of y in A by an occurrence of x, but only after A has been rewritten so as to avoid confusion of bound variables (*unary variable substitution*).

The problem of confusion of bound variables occurs when y occurs free in a part of A of the form $(x)B$. For example, $(x/y) \neg (x = y)$ cannot be $\neg(x)(x = x)$. [Or, $(Ex)(x \neq y)$ cannot be transformed into $(Ex)(x \neq x)$ by substitution of x for y. We shall henceforth use $x \neq y$ for $\neg(x = y)$, $(Ex)A$ for $\neg(x)\neg A$, and also the usual truth-functional connectives $\vee$, $\equiv$, $\supset$ with their usual (contextual) definitions in terms of & and $\neg$.]

A particular recipe for avoiding this kind of confusion is adopted in the following definition.

DEFINITION. $(x/y)A$, the result of *unary variable substitution of x for y in A*, is the result of replacing each free occurrence of y by an occurrence of x in the sentence A', which is formed as follows: Replace each part of A of the form $(x)B$ in which y occurs free, by the result of replacing each occurrence of x in that part by an occurrence of a distinct variable not in A.

This is rather a complex substitution operation, but happily it can be analyzed as a sequence of simpler operations. These simpler operations we shall call *proper substitution* and *alphabetic variance*.[4]

First, we shall call $(y/x)A$ the result of a *proper substitution of y for x in A* if y does not occur free in any part of A that has the form $(x)B$. Note that in this case, the substitution is simple replacement: No rewriting of bound variables is necessary. So we can also characterize the relation as follows: B comes from A by proper substitution of y for x if B is like A except for having free occurrences of y wherever A has free occurrences of x. The definition of alphabetic variance is somewhat more complex.

DEFINITION.   If A has the form $(x)B$, then A' is an *immediate alphabetic variant* of A if and only if A' has the form $(y)B'$, where $B' = (y/x)B$ and $B = (x/y)B'$ and the substitutions are proper in both cases.

Note that this cannot be the case unless y is not free in A and x not free in A'. In fact, the *same* variables are free in A as in A'.

DEFINITION. A' is an *alphabetic variant* of A if and only if A' differs from A only in having, for certain sentences $B_1, \ldots, B_n$, occurrences of immediate alphabetic variants of $B_1, \ldots, B_n$, where A has occurrences of $B_1, \ldots, B_n$, respectively.

Now we can see that a unary substitution is in general the result of an alphabetic variance followed by a proper substitution.

The proofs of the following theorems are immediate.

Theorem.   *If $(y/x)A$ is the result of a proper substitution of y for x in A, then*

(a) *if A is $\neg B$, $(y/x)A$ is $\neg(y/x)B$;*

(b) *if A is $(B \mathbin{\&} C)$, $(y/x)A$ is $((y/x)B \mathbin{\&} (y/x)C)$;*

(c) *if A is $(x)B$, $(y/x)A$ is A;*

(d) *if A is $(z)B$, and z is not x or y, then $(y/x)A$ is $(z)(y/x)B$, provided z occurs in B.*

Theorem.   *If B' and C' are alphabetic variants of B and C, respectively, then*

(a) *$\neg B'$ is an alphabetic variant of $\neg B$;*

(b) *$(B' \mathbin{\&} C')$ is an alphabetic variant of $(B \mathbin{\&} C)$;*

(c) *$(x)B'$ is an alphabetic variant of $(x)B$.*

There are no equally elegant results for unary variable substitution in general, owing to the necessity of using a recipe (for preceding a proper substitution by an alphabetic variation) that depends on which variables occur in the expression being transformed.

We turn now to another kind of substitution, related to the infinitary substitution described in Section 2 of Chapter II. Let us call a *substitution function* for QCS any mapping of the set of variables of that QCS into itself. Then if f is a substitution function for QCS and A a sentence of that QCS, let us define

$$S^f(A) = e_1^* \cdots e_n^*, \qquad \text{where } A \text{ is the expression } e_1 \cdots e_n$$

$$e_i^* = \begin{cases} f(e_i) & \text{if } e_i \text{ is a variable,} \\ e_i & \text{otherwise.} \end{cases}$$

The operation S^f we shall call an *infinitary variable substitution* (*by* the substitution function f). For brevity and convenience we write

$$\text{``} f(A) \text{''} \quad \text{for} \quad \text{``} S^f(A), \text{''}$$
$$\text{``} f(X) \text{''} \quad \text{for} \quad \text{``} \{f(A) : A \in X\}, \text{''}$$

when A is a sentence and X a set of sentences of the relevant QCS. It is easily seen that this kind of substitution does not result in the confusion of bound variables if the substitution function is one-to-one. And we also have

$$f((\neg A)) = (\neg f(A)),$$
$$f((A \ \& \ B)) = (f(A) \ \& \ f(B)),$$
$$f((x)A) = (f(x))(f(A)),$$

for any substitution function for a QCS and sentences A, B of that QCS.

2. Axiomatics of Quantificational Logic

Systems of quantificational logic can be divided into those which concern themselves only with statements (*bound variable systems*) and those which concern themselves with all sentences (*free variable systems*). Each bound variable system LS_b can be associated with a unique free variable system LS_f, by the stipulation that the theorems of LS_b are also theorems of LS_f, and that in LS_f we have

$$\vdash A \text{ if and only if } \vdash (x_1) \cdots (x_n)A,$$

where $x_1, \ldots, x_n$ are all the variables free in A (*quantificational closure of A*). Hence it does not matter very much, from the point of view of axiomatics, which kind of system we consider. We choose a free variable system. A convenient axiomatic formulation[5] specifies as axioms:

A1. All sentences that are theorems of the propositional calculus.
A2. All sentences that have the form
    (a) $(x)(A \supset B) \supset \cdot A \supset (x)B$, x not free in A;
    (b) $(x)A \supset (y/x)A$;
    (c) $x = x$;
    (d) $x = y \supset \cdot A \supset (y/x)A$;

and as rules of inference

R1. If A and $A \supset B$ are theorems, so is B (*modus ponens*).
R2. If $(y/x)A$ is a theorem, and y is x or y is not free in A, then $(x)A$ is a theorem (*generalization*).

[Note that in A1 we are momentarily regarding the QCS as a PCS with all sentences not of the form $(A \And B)$ or $(\neg A)$ as atomic.] The reason for the restriction in rule **R2** is that in inference by generalization upon a variable y, all free instances of y in $(y/x)A$ should become bound instances of x in $(x)A$. Thus it would be incorrect to infer $\vdash (x)(x = y)$ from $\vdash (y = y)$ by generalization, although $(y = y) = (y/x)(x = y)$, just because y is free in $(x = y)$.

Again we can simplify many of our problems by constructing an algorithm for the theorems.[6] To extend the Beth algorithm to quantificational logic, we must add three rules to be placed after the rule NK, and amend the closure rule.

Ur. $X \And \neg(x)A \And Y \rightarrow X \And \neg(y/x)A \And Y$, where y is the first variable that does not occur in $X \And \neg(x)A \And Y$.

I. $X \& x = y \& Y \rightarrow (y/x)(X \& Y)$.

UI. $X \& (x)A \& Y \rightarrow X \& (y_1/x)A \& \cdots \& (y_n/x)A \& Y \& (x)A$,
where $y_1, \ldots, y_n$ are the variables free in $X \& (x)A \& Y$; if there
are none free, then $n = 1$ and y_1 is the first variable that does not
occur free in $X \& (x)A \& Y$.

Closure Rule. *If a disjunct has any of the forms*

$X \& A \& Y \& \neg A \& Z$,
$X \& \neg A \& Y \& A \& Z$,
$X \& (\neg x = x) \& Y$,
it is underlined.

All conventions for the Beth algorithm for the propositional calculus
remain in force, except that convention (a) is amended to read: (a) We
use X, Y, Z to stand for possibly empty conjunctions of sentences,
where X does not have the form $\neg\neg A$ or $\neg(A \& B)$ or $(x)A$ or $\neg(x)A$
or $x = y$ (x and y distinct).

The following theorem follows immediately from the construction of
the algorithm and the definitions of *branch* and *conjunct in a branch*.

> DEFINITION. Let $\mathscr{T} = D_1, D_2, \ldots, D_k, \ldots$ be the tableau se-
> quence (generated by the above algorithm) for a sentence A of a QCS.
> Then $\mathscr{B} = C_1, C_2, \ldots, C_k, \ldots$ is a *branch* of $\mathscr{T}$ iff, for $i = 1, 2, \ldots,$
> $k, \ldots$:
> (a) C_i is a disjunct of D_i;
> (b) if in the formation of D_{i+1}, C_i is not replaced in accordance with
> a rule, then $C_i = C_{i+1}$ or C_i is the last member of $\mathscr{B}$;
> (c) if in the formation of D_{i+1}, C_i is replaced in accordance with a
> rule by one or two disjuncts (of D_{i+1}), then C_{i+1} is one of those
> disjuncts.

If $\mathscr{B} = C_1, \ldots, C_k, \ldots$ is a branch of a tableau sequence $\mathscr{T}$, then we
call A a *conjunct in $\mathscr{B}$* (and *in $\mathscr{T}$*) iff for some $i = 1, \ldots, k, \ldots, C_i$ has the
form $X \& A \& Y$.

Theorem. (Closure property for branches) *If $\mathscr{B}$ is a nonterminating
branch of the tableau sequence for some sentence of a QCS, then*

(a) if $\neg\neg A$ is a conjunct in $\mathscr{B}$, so is A;

(b) if $\neg(A \ \& \ B)$ is a conjunct in $\mathscr{B}$, so is $\neg A$ or $\neg B$;

(c) if $(x)A$ is a conjunct in $\mathscr{B}$, and y is a variable free in some conjunct in $\mathscr{B}$, then $(y/x)A$ is a conjunct in $\mathscr{B}$; there is at least one variable y such that $(y/x)A$ is a conjunct in $\mathscr{B}$;

(d) if $\neg(x)A$ is a conjunct in $\mathscr{B}$, then there is a variable y such that $\neg(y/x)A$ is a conjunct in $\mathscr{B}$;

(e) if $x = y$ is a conjunct in $\mathscr{B}$, then at some point, x is eliminated in favor of y by rule I.

The following theorem is a basic proof-theoretic result.

Theorem. *The tableau sequence of a sentence A of a QCS terminates iff A is a theorem of quantificational logic.*

This theorem is proved in part by doing the exercises for this section and the next.

So far we have only been concerned to define the set of theorems rather than the relation $\vdash$ as a whole. We complete the definition of $\vdash$ exactly as in Chapter III, Section 2, essentially by adding the rule (ARG): If $\vdash \neg(A_1 \ \& \ \cdots \ \& \ A_n \ \& \ \neg B)$, then $A_1, \ldots, A_n \vdash B$.

3. Referential Interpretation: Models

The best known interpretation of the quantifiers is what we shall call the *referential interpretation*, in which $(x)A$ is taken to be true if A is true of all members of a certain set, the *domain of discourse*. Our purpose here is to state this interpretation in a precise form.

A factual situation comprises a set of individuals bearing certain relations to each other. Hence a situation can be represented by a relational structure $\langle D, R_1, \ldots, R_i, \ldots \rangle$, where D is the set of individuals in question and $R_1, \ldots, R_i, \ldots$ certain relations on D. If we wish to describe this relational structure in a language with a quantificational syntax, we assign some member of D to each variable as its denotation, and some n-ary relation on D to each n-ary predicate as its extension. The function used to make the assignment to the predicates is called an *interpretation function*, and the set D a *domain of discourse*. Together they make up a *model* for the syntax. We can specify the model either by specifying a domain D and interpretation function f, or by specifying a domain and a sequence of relations on that domain, the ith relation in the sequence being $f(P_i)$, the extension of alphabetically the ith predicate P_i. These procedures are clearly equivalent; we begin by following the former.

DEFINITION. A *model for* a QCS is a couple $M = \langle f, D \rangle$, where D is a nonempty set (the *domain* of M); f is a function (the *interpretation function* of M) defined for each predicate of the QCS, and such that if P^n is an n-ary predicate, then $f(P^n) \subseteq D^n$.

A mapping d of the variables of a QCS into the domain D of the model $M = \langle f, D \rangle$ for that QCS is called an *assignment function* (*for M*, or *for D and for* that QCS).

Truth of a sentence A in a model M is relative to an assignment d of values to the variables; we shall say that d *satisfies A in M* (briefly, $M \vDash A[d]$), and define this relation inductively below. We shall write $M \vDash A$ for the assertion that $M \vDash A[d]$ holds for all assignment functions d for M ($M \vDash A$ to be read as A *is true in M*) and $\sim M \vDash A[d]$, $\sim M \vDash A$ for the denials of $M \vDash A[d]$ and $M \vDash A$, respectively.

DEFINITION. If $M = \langle f, D \rangle$ is a model for a QCS and d an assignment function for M, then $\vDash$ is the least relation such that
(a) $M \vDash (x_1 = x_2)[d]$ iff $d(x_1) = d(x_2)$;
(b) $M \vDash (P^n x_1 \cdots x_n)[d]$ iff $\langle d(x_1), \ldots, d(x_n) \rangle \in f(P^n)$;
(c) $M \vDash (A \ \& \ B)[d]$ iff $M \vDash A[d]$ and $M \vDash B[d]$;
(d) $M \vDash (\neg A)[d]$ iff $\sim M \vDash A[d]$;
(e) $M \vDash (x_1)A[d]$ iff $M \vDash A[d']$ for all assignments d' for M which are like d except perhaps at x_1 (symbolically, $d' =_{x_1} d$)
for all sentences A, B, variables $x_1, \ldots, x_n$, and n-ary predicates P^n of that QCS.

If M is a model for QCS and d an assignment function for M, then a *valuation of* that QCS *induced by M and d* is a valuation v of that QCS such that

$$v(A) \in \{\text{T, F}\},$$
$$v(A) = \text{T} \quad \text{iff } M \vDash A[d]$$

for all sentences A of that QCS (we also call v a valuation *over M*).

DEFINITION. L is a *referential quantifier language* iff the syntax of L is a QCS and the admissible valuations of L are the valuations induced by the models for that QCS and the assignment functions for these models.

As a preliminary to our main metatheorems, we shall prove some theorems on our substitution operations. Each of these theorems applies to any referential quantifier language L, but the reference to L will be left tacit.

Lemma.   *For any assignment functions d and d' for a model M, if $d(x) = d'(x)$ for each variable x that occurs (free) in sentence A, then $M \vDash A[d]$ iff $M \vDash A[d']$.*

Proof: We prove this in the strong form, supposing only agreement between d and d' with respect to variables *free* in A. Let this be the case for all sentences of length less than A.

  (a) A is atomic: obvious.
  (b) A is $\neg B$, A is $(B \& C)$: obvious.
  (c) A is $(x)B$. Suppose $\sim M \vDash A[d]$. Then for some $d'' =_x d$, $\sim M \vDash B[d'']$. Let $d''' =_x d'$ and $d'''(x) = d''(x)$. By hypothesis, $\sim M \vDash B[d''']$ because $\sim M \vDash B(d'')$, so $\sim M \vDash (x)B[d']$. Mutatis mutandis if $\sim M \vDash A[d']$. Therefore, $M \vDash A[d]$ iff $M \vDash A[d']$.

Theorem (Unary Substitution Theorem).   *For any variable, y, sentence A, model M, and assignment function d for M, if $d' =_x d$ and $d'(x) = d(y)$, then $M \vDash A[d']$ iff $M \vDash (y/x)A[d]$.*

Proof: Suppose that for all sentences B of length less than A, and all assignments d for $M = \langle f, D \rangle$, if $d' =_x d$ and $d'(x) = d(y)$, then $M \vDash B[d']$ iff $M \vDash (y/x)B[d]$. We now consider the various possible cases for A.

Case 1. A is $Px_1 \cdots x \cdots x_n$. Then $\langle d'(x_1), \ldots, d'(x), \ldots, d'(x_n) \rangle \in f(P)$ iff $\langle d(x_1), \ldots, d(y), \ldots, d(x_n) \rangle \in f(P)$, and similarly if x has more than one occurrence in A.

Case 2. A is $x = x'$. Then $d'(x) = d'(x')$ iff $d(y) = d(x')$; similarly for $x' = x$, $x' = x''$.

Case 3. A is $\neg B$; A is $(B \,\&\, C)$; obvious.

Case 4. A is $(z)B$. If z does not occur in B, then $M \vDash B[d'']$ iff $M \vDash (z)B[d'']$, for any assignment d'' for M; this follows from our lemma. If z does occur in B, we have several subcases.

(a) If z is x, then $(y/x)A$ is just A, so the result follows again by our lemma.

(b) If z is neither x nor y, then $(y/x)(z)B = (z)(y/x)B$. Suppose $\sim M \vDash A[d']$. There is then an assignment $d'' =_z d'$ such that $\sim M \vDash B[d'']$. Let $d''' =_z d$, and $d'''(z) = d''(z)$. We note that $d'' =_x d'''$, and $d''(x) = d'''(y)$, so by the hypothesis of induction, $\sim M \vDash (y/x)B[d''']$. This shows that $\sim M \vDash (z)(y/x)B[d]$.

The diagram below should help to see these relations among the assignment functions.

	d'	d''	d	d'''
x	1	1	4	4
y	1	1	1	1
z	2	3	2	3

The converse can be proved similarly: suppose $\sim M \vDash (z)(y/x)B[d]$. Then there is a $d''' =_z d$ such that $\sim M \vDash (y/x)B[d''']$. Let d'' be such that $d''(z) = d'''(z)$ and $d'' =_z d'$. We can see from the next diagram that d'' is so related to d''' that the hypothesis of induction implies that $\sim M \vDash B[d'']$. But then $\sim M \vDash (z)B[d']$.

	d	d'	d''	d''
x	1	2	1	2
y	2	2	2	2
z	3	3	4	4

(c) Finally, suppose that z is not x but z is y; then there are two subsubcases. (1) If x is not free in A, the result follows by our lemma. (2) If x is free in A, then $(y/x)A$ is $(y/x)(z')B'$, where $(z')B'$ is an alphabetic variant of $(z)B$ and z' is neither y nor x; hence this reduces to case (b).

Theorem. *If A' is an alphabetic variant of A, then $M \vDash A'[d]$ iff $M \vDash A[d]$, for all models M and assignment functions d for their domains.*

Proof: If we can prove this for immediate alphabetic variants, the rest will follow by an easy induction.

Suppose then that $B' = (y/x)B$ and $B = (x/y)B'$. Then x does not occur free in B', nor y in B. Suppose now that $\sim M \vDash (y)B'[d]$, so that for some $d' =_y d$, $\sim M \vDash B'[d']$; that is, $\sim M \vDash (y/x)B[d']$. Let $d'' =_x d'$, and $d''(x) = d'(y)$. By the preceding theorem, $M \vDash B[d'']$ iff $M \vDash (y/x)B[d']$; therefore, $\sim M \vDash B[d'']$. But d'' is like d except at x and y; let $d''' =_y d''$ and $d'''(y) = d(y)$, so that $d''' =_y d''$ and $d''' =_x d$. Since y does not occur free in B, the value of B in M relative to d''' and relative to d'' must be the same (lemma). So $\sim M \vDash B[d''']$, and hence $\sim M \vDash (x)B[d]$. The converse follows by parity of reasoning.

To follow this proof, the reader may find it helpful to draw diagrams such as we used in the preceding proof. And after seeing these proofs, it will occasion no surprise that most authors prefer not to enquire too deeply into substitution. But the above theorems are needed in the soundness and completeness proofs for quantificational logic.

4. Soundness and Completeness Theorems

We can now turn to the soundness and completeness proofs for quantificational logic under the present interpretation.

Theorem. *If the tableau sequence of a sentence A terminates, then A is valid.*

Proof: Let A have a terminating tableau sequence $D_1, \ldots, D_k$. We prove that for an arbitrary model $M = \langle f, D \rangle$,
 (a) $\sim M \vDash D_k[d]$, for all d;
 (b) if $\sim M \vDash D_{i+1}[d]$ for all d, then $\sim M \vDash D_i[d]$ for all d, $i > 0$.

Since $D_1 = \neg A$, this shows that A is true in all models (and hence satisfied by all admissible valuations). In what follows we omit parts of the proof already encountered in the case of classical propositional logic, and use some further shortcuts suggested by our experience there.

 ad a. $\sim M \vDash (x \neq x)[d]$ for all d, and any variable x.
 ad. b. Here we consider each added rule.
  Ul. If $\sim M \vDash (y/x)A[d]$, then by our theorem on unary substitution, there is a $d' =_x d$ such that $\sim M \vDash A[d']$. Hence $\sim M \vDash (x)A[d]$.
  Ur. Suppose that $\sim M \vDash \neg(y/x)A[d]$ for any d, where y is a new variable not in D_i. Then $M \vDash (y/x)A$. A fortiori, $M \vDash (y/x)A[d']$ for all $d' =_y d$, for any given d. Hence $M \vDash (y)(y/x)A$. But since y is a new variable, $(y)(y/x)A$ is an alphabetic variant of $(x)A$. Hence by our theorem on alphabetic variance, $M \vDash (x)A$. Therefore, for all d,

$$\sim M \vDash \neg(x)A[d].$$

  I. It will suffice to show that if $M \vDash (x = y)[d]$, then $M \vDash A[d]$ iff $M \vDash (y/x)A[d]$, for any d, and any sentence A. That this is so for atomic sentences A is clear. Suppose it is the case for all sentences B of length less than A. Then if A is

$\neg B$, it holds for A because it holds for B and $(y/x)A = \neg(y/x)B$. If A is $(B \& C)$, then $(y/x)A$ is an alphabetic variant of $((y/x)B \& (y/x)C)$, so it holds for A because it holds for B and C. Finally, if A is $(z)B$, we have three cases.

Case 1. z is x. Then $(y/x)A = A$.

Case 2. z is neither x nor y. By hypothesis, $M \vDash B[d]$ iff $M \vDash (y/x)B[d]$ for any d such that $M \vDash (x = y)[d]$. A fortiori, this is so for any $d' =_z d$, for any given d, for in that case $d'(y) = d'(x) = d(x)$. But then, for any such d, $M \vDash (z)B[d]$ iff $M \vDash (z)(y/x)B[d]$. This establishes the conclusion, for in this case, $(z)(y/x)B$ is $(y/x)(z)B$, if z occurs in B; if not, the case is obvious.

Case 3. z is y, z is not x. Then $(y/x)A$ is $(y/x)A'$, where A' is an alphabetic variant $(z')B'$ of A, where z' is neither y nor x. Therefore, this case reduces to the previous one.

Theorem. *If the tableau sequence of a sentence A does not terminate, then A is not valid.*

Proof: If the tableau sequence of A does not terminate, then it has a nonterminating branch $\mathscr{B}$. We now show how to define a model $M = \langle f, D \rangle$ and assignment d such that $M \vDash B[d]$ for every conjunct B in that branch. Since $\neg A$ is the first member of $\mathscr{B}$, it follows that $M \vDash \neg A[d]$, hence that A is not valid.

Before we can construct this model, we need to define a subsidiary notion. If $x = y$ occurs as a conjunct in the nonterminating branch $\mathscr{B}$, then one of x, y at least will disappear at some stage, owing to an application of rule I. For example, as the tableau is being constructed, x may be eliminated in favor of x_1, x_1 in favor of $x_2, \ldots$, and x_{n-1} in favor of y, so that we see successively the conjuncts $x = y$, $x_1 = y$, $x_2 = y, \ldots, x_n = y, y = y$. In that case we call $\langle x, x_1, \ldots, x_n, y \rangle$ an *elimination string* in $\mathscr{B}$. Some elimination strings are contained in others in the sense that $\langle x, x_1 \rangle$ is contained in $\langle x, x_1, \ldots, x_n, y \rangle$; let us call an elimination string *prime* if it is not contained in any other elimination string, and let us call any singleton $\{x\}$ also an elimination string in $\mathscr{B}$. Then every variable x belongs to exactly one prime elimination string in $\mathscr{B}$. Define $ev(x)$ to be the first variable in the prime elimination string to which x belongs that is free in (some conjunct in) $\mathscr{B}$.

Now we define the model $M = \langle f, D \rangle$:
1. $D = \{ev(x) : x \text{ is free in } \mathscr{B}\}$
2. $f(P^n) = \{\langle ev(x_1), \ldots, ev(x_n) \rangle : P^n x_1 \cdots x_n \text{ is a conjunct in } \mathscr{B}\}$

That there is exactly one model $M = \langle f, D \rangle$ that satisfies 1 and 2 is an immediate consequence of the definition of model, and the fact that the rule **UI** guarantees that at least one variable is free in $\mathscr{B}$.

3. We define the assignment function d to be the mapping of the variables into D such that $d(y) = ev(y)$ when y is free in $\mathscr{B}$, and otherwise $d(y)$ is alphabetically the first variable in D.

Hypothesis of Induction. *If C is a conjunct in $\mathscr{B}$, then $M \vDash C[d]$, for all sentences C of length less than B.*

We now prove that if B is a conjunct in $\mathscr{B}$, then $M \vDash B[d]$.

(a) If B is $P^n y_1 \cdots y_n$ this follows from 2 and 3 above.
(b) If B is $x = y$, this follows from 3 above, because then x and y belong to an elimination string in $\mathscr{B}$.
(c) If B is $\neg P^n y_1 \cdots y_n$, this follows from 2 and 3 above, for then $\langle ev(y_1), \ldots, ev(y_n) \rangle$ cannot belong to $f(P^n)$. For if two conjuncts in B, say C and $\neg C'$, are such that C' differs from C only in that some variables in C are replaced by other members of their respective elimination strings, then there will be a member of $\mathscr{B}$ containing two conjuncts C'' and $\neg C''$ which have been formed by elimination of variables through rule **I**.[7]
(d) If B is $\neg(x = y)$, this follows from 3, for then x and y are free variables in $\mathscr{B}$, so that $ev(x)$ and $ev(y)$ belong to D, but x and y cannot belong to the same elimination string, so $ev(x) \neq ev(y)$.
(e) B is $\neg C$, $(C \& D)$, or $\neg(C \& D)$; these cases are familiar from propositional logic.

(f) B is $(x)C$. By the closure property for branches, $(y/x)C$ is a conjunct in B for every variable y in D. By hypothesis and our theorem on unary substitution, $M \vDash C(d')$ for all $d' =_x d$. Hence $M \vDash B[d]$.

(g) B is $\neg(x)C$. Then for some y free in $\mathscr{B}$, $\neg(y/x)C$ is a conjunct. By hypothesis, $M \vDash \neg(y/x)C[d]$. By the theorem of unary substitution it follows that $\sim M \vDash C[d']$ for some $d' =_x d$; hence $M \vDash \neg(x)C[d]$.

We have now established statement soundness and statement completeness for quantificational logic with respect to referential quantifier languages. (We retain these terms, although we are now using "statement" to refer only to a special kind of sentence, since, as we have remarked, it is only convenience that led us to concentrate on a free variable system of quantificational logic.) The extension to argument soundness and completeness is exactly as in Section 3 of Chapter III, and similar remarks concerning strong completeness and compactness apply.

5. Compactness and Countable Models

We shall now investigate the compactness problem for referential quantifier languages directly. Since these languages have exclusion negation, it is sufficient to consider I-compactness; the results for compactness and finitary semantic entailment follow then. We shall prove I-compactness in a strong form: If every finite subset of a set of sentences is satisfiable, then the set is itself satisfiable in a model with at most countable domain. The proof will be by the method of ultrafilters.

There is one obstacle to the proof which presents itself immediately: No less complex sentence, or set of such, semantically entails $(x)Fx$. Thus if $\mathscr{U}$ is an ultrafilter, on the valuation space H, it may contain $H((Ex)Fx)$ and also $H(\neg Fy)$ for every variable y. To bypass this difficulty, we prove compactness for the space of "regular valuations" which are such that for some specific variable y, they assign T to Fy if and only if they assign T to $(x)Fx$. This proof would be very uninterest-ing if we could not show, by a judicious use of theorems on substitution, that the regular valuations are really all that matter.

From Section 1 we recall the notion of a substitution function f, and the notation $f(A), f(X)$. If M is a model with domain D, and d an assignment function for M, then we use "v_d" to refer to the valuation v induced by M and d, when only the model M is referred to in the context. From here on we consider only one-to-one substitution functions, and if only one substitution function f is discussed in the context, we write E^* rather than $f(E)$, X^* rather than $f(X)$.

Theorem. *For any one-to-one substitution function f, model M, and set K of sentences, K is satisfied by a valuation over M if and only if $f(K)$ is satisfied by a valuation over M.*

This theorem follows from two lemmas, which follow.

Lemma 1. *If d, d' are assignment functions for the same model and $d'(y^*) = d(y)$ for all variables y, then $M \vDash A[d]$ iff $M \vDash A^*[d']$.*

Proof: We prove this by strong induction on the hypothesis that for any two assignment functions d_1, d_2 for the same model such that $d_2(y^*) = d_1(y)$ for all variables y, if B is any sentence of length less than A, then $v_{d_1}(A) = v_{d_2}(A^*)$. Let d, d' be as specified in the antecedent of the theorem.

(a) A is $x_1 = x_2$ and A^* is $x_1^* = x_2^*$, or A is $P^n x_1 \cdots x_n$ and A^* is $P^n x_1^* \cdots x_n^*$; obvious.

(b) A is $\neg B$ or A is $(B \,\&\, C)$; obvious.

(c) A is $(x)B$, and A^* is $(x^*)B^*$. Suppose first that $\sim M \vDash A[d]$, so that we have an assignment function $d_1 =_x d$ such that $\sim M \vDash B[d_1]$. Now let $d_2(y^*) = d_1(y)$ for all variables y, and let $d_2(z) = d'(z)$ for any variable z such that $z \neq y^*$ for any variable y. Then by hypothesis of induction, $\sim M \vDash B^*[d_2]$. But also $d_2 =_{x^*} d'$, so $\sim M \vDash (x^*)B^*[d']$. Second, suppose $\sim M \vDash A^*[d']$. Then there is a $d_2 =_{x^*} d'$ such that $\sim M \vDash B^*[d_2]$. Define $d_1(y) = d_2(y^*)$ for all variables y. By hypothesis, $\sim M \vDash B[d_1]$. But, in addition, $d_1 =_x d$; hence $\sim M \vDash (x)B[d]$.

The proof of the second lemma is similar and will be omitted.

We shall use the following notation: If d is an assignment function for model M, d^* is the assignment function $d^*(x) = d(x^*)$ for M, and if $v = v_d$, then $v^* = v_{d^*}$ over the same model.

Lemma 2. *For any valuation v over M and any sentence A, $v(A^*) = v^*(A)$.*

From now on we need consider only a single substitution function f: Let $f(x_i) = x_{2i}$, where x_j is alphabetically the jth variable. Then if X is a set of sentences, $f(X)$ contains no odd variables (x_j such that j is odd), whether bound or free. A set of sentences in which no odd variables occur will be called a *regular set*. We now introduce the notion of *regular valuation* in two steps, modifying this device due to Beth and Hasenjaeger only by concentrating on the odd variables.[8]

DEFINITION.   For each natural number m, the *variable y_m associated with m* is defined by:

(a) y_1 is the first *odd* variable that does not occur in alphabetically the first sentence that begins with a universal quantifier;

(b) y_{n+1} is the first *odd* variable after y_n that does not occur in alphabetically the first $(n + 1)$ sentences that begin with a universal quantifier.

DEFINITION.   A valuation v is *regular* iff $v((x)A) = F$ only if $v((y_k/x)A) = F$, where $(x)A$ is alphabetically the kth sentence that begins with a universal quantifier and y_k the variable associated with k.

The first obvious result to be proved is that, to regular sets, only regular valuations are relevant.

Theorem.   *A regular set is satisfied by a valuation over a model M if and only if it is satisfied by a regular valuation over M.*

Proof: The "if" part is obvious. To prove the "only if" part, assume that X is a regular set and that $v = v_d$ is a valuation that satisfies X.

Let us define a new assignment d' as follows:

(a) $d'(x_{2i}) = d(x_{2i})$ for all i.

(b) $d'(x_i) = d(x_i)$ if i is odd, but x_i is not y_k for any integer k (see the definition of "regular valuation" above).

(c) We define $d'(y_k)$ inductively. Suppose that $(x)A$ is the kth universally quantified sentence, and that $d'(z)$ has been defined for all variables z alphabetically before y_k. Then $d'(z)$ is defined for every variable z that occurs in $(x)A$. By the lemma proved in Section 3, this determines the value of $(x)A$ in M relative to d' (and is the same value relative to every assignment d'' which agrees with d' on the variables prior to y_k). If that value is T, let $d'(y_k) = d(y_k)$. If that value is F, let $d'(y_k) = b$, where b is some element $d''(x)$, where d'' is like d' with respect to all variables prior to y_k except perhaps x, and $v_{d''}(A) = $ F.

Now we maintain that $v_{d'}$ is regular and satisfies X. The latter follows from the same lemma to which we appealed above, since d and d' agree on all variables that occur in X. To show the former, we must show that if $v_{d'}((x)A) = $ F, then $v_{d'}((y_k/x)A) = $ F. Well, from (c) we know that if $v_{d'}((x)A) = $ F, then $d'(y_k) = d''(x)$, where d'' is some assignment which is like d' for all variables, except perhaps x, prior to y_k, and $v_{d''}(A) = $ F. Let $d''' =_x d'$, and $d'''(x) = d''(x)$. Then by that same lemma to which we already appealed twice above, $v_{d'''}(A) = v_{d''}(A) = $ F. Moreover, d' and d''' are related by $d''' =_x d'$, $d'''(x) = d'(y_k)$. By the unary substitution theorem it now follows that $v_{d'}((y_k/x)A) = v_{d'''}(A) = $ F.

The following diagram may help to follow the last few steps in this proof:

	d''	d'	d'''
	agreement		
x	2	1	2
	agreement		
y_k	3	2	2
		agreement	

In the diagram d'', d', and d''' all agree on all the variables prior to y_k except x; in addition, d''' and d' agree on all variables after y_k.

Now let R be the set of regular valuations and H the space of all valuations; we call

$$H_R = \langle R, \{H(B) \cap R : B \text{ a sentence of } L\}\rangle$$

the *regular valuation space* of the referential quantifier language L under consideration. We shall write $R(B)$ for $H(B) \cap R$.

Theorem. *If H_R is the regular valuation space of a referential quantifier language L, then every ultrafilter on H_R converges to a regular valuation over a model with a domain that is at most denumerable.*

Proof: Let $\mathscr{U}$ be an ultrafilter on H_R. We define a model $M = \langle f, D\rangle$ and assignment function d in terms of $\mathscr{U}$ as follows.

First, let $\mathrm{ev}(x)$ be alphabetically the first variable y such that $R(x = y) \in \mathscr{U}$. Clearly $\mathrm{ev}(x)$ exists for each variable x [since $R(x = x) \in \mathscr{U}$] and is unique. The domain D of M is defined by

$$D = \{y : y = \mathrm{ev}(x) \text{ for some variable } x\}.$$

Since there are at most denumerably many variables, D is denumerable.[9] We define the function f by

$$f(P^n) = \{\langle y_1, \ldots, y_n\rangle : R(P^n y_1 \cdots y_n) \in \mathscr{U} \quad \text{and} \quad y_1, \ldots, y_n \in D\}.$$

Finally, we define the assignment function d by $d(x) = \mathrm{ev}(x)$.

We now define

$$v(A) = \begin{cases} \mathrm{T} & \text{iff } R(A) \in \mathscr{U}, \\ \mathrm{F} & \text{otherwise.} \end{cases}$$

and maintain that v is the valuation induced by M and d, and is regular. That v is regular follows at once because $R(y_k/x)A \subseteq R((x)A)$; this is immediate from the definition of R. The following remarks show that v is the valuation induced by M and d.

(a) $v(A) \in \{T, F\}$; immediate.

(b) $v(x = y) = T$ iff $R(x = y) \in \mathscr{U}$ iff $\mathrm{ev}(x) = \mathrm{ev}(y)$ iff $d(x) = d(y)$.

(c) $v(P^n x_1 \cdots x_n) = T$ iff $R(P^n x_1 \cdots x_n) \in \mathscr{U}$ iff $R(P^n \mathrm{ev}(x_1) \cdots \mathrm{ev}(x_n)) \in \mathscr{U}$ (because $R(x = y) \cap R(A) \subseteq R((y/x)A)$) iff $\langle \mathrm{ev}(x_1) \ldots, \mathrm{ev}(x_n) \rangle \in f(P^n)$ iff $\langle d(x_1), \ldots, d(x_n) \rangle \in f(P^n)$.

(d) $v(A \mathrel{\&} B) = T$ iff $R(A \mathrel{\&} B) \in \mathscr{U}$ iff $R(A) \cap R(B) \in \mathscr{U}$ iff $R(A)$, $R(B) \in \mathscr{U}$ iff $v(A) = v(B) = T$.

(e) $v(\neg A) = T$ iff $R(\neg A) \in \mathscr{U}$ iff $R - R(A) \in \mathscr{U}$ iff $R(A) \notin \mathscr{U}$ iff $v(A) = F$.

(f) If $v((x)A) = T$, then $R((x)A) \in \mathscr{U}$; but $R((x)A) \subseteq R((y/x)A)$ for each variable y; hence $v((y/x)A) = T$ for each variable y. If $d' =_x d$, then $d'(x) = y$ for some variable y; but then $v_d((y/x)A) = v_{d'}(A)$; hence $v_{d'}(A) = T$ (see the theorem on unary substitution in Section 3).

On the other hand, if $v((x)A) = F$, then $v((y_k/x)A) = F$, because v is a regular valuation (see above). But then if $d' =_x d$ and $d'(x) = d(y_k)$, $v_{d'}(A) = F$ also (by the same unary-substitution theorem).

Now we are in a position to prove the compactness and theorem for the referential interpretation of the quantifiers.

Theorem.   *If every finite subset of a set X of sentences (of a referential quantifier language) is satisfiable, then X is satisfied by a valuation over a model with at most denumerable domain.*

Proof: Let the finite subsets of X be $\{X_i\}$, $i \in I$, and let each be satisfiable. Then each set $f(X_i)$, $i \in I$ is satisfiable by a regular valuation. Therefore, the family

$$\{R(B) : B \in f(X)\}$$

forms a filter base on H_R and is contained in an ultrafilter $\mathscr{U}$ on H_R. This ultrafilter converges to a regular valuation v over a model with at most denumerable domain which satisfies $f(X)$; therefore, X is satisfied by a valuation over the same model.

6. Elementary Relations Among Models

The study of the models of, and deductive systems in, referential quantifier languages is now known as *model theory*. In this section and the next two, we explore some of the basic methods and results of model theory. Our exposition is limited by our decision to consider only the models of a single, denumerable (but otherwise arbitrary) referential quantifier language L.

Some new notation will be convenient. When the predicates of L are, in alphabetic order, $P_1, P_2, \ldots$, and $f(P_1) = R_1, f(P_2) = R_2, \ldots$, then we also identify the model $M = \langle f, D \rangle$ as

$$M = \langle D, R_1, R_2, \ldots \rangle.$$

We speak of the members of D as members of M, of subsets of D as subsets of M, and of the cardinality of D as the cardinality of M. If d is an assignment function into D, it can be regarded as an infinite sequence in D (in M) with $d(x_i)$ as its ith member. We shall call such a sequence d (*essentially*) *finite* if for some m, its $(m + i)$th members are all the same, for all i.

If one model $M = \langle D, R_1, R_2, \ldots \rangle$ results from another model $M' = \langle D', R'_1, R'_2, \ldots \rangle$ by discarding some of the elements of M' [that is, $D \subseteq D'$ and $R_i = D^n \cap R'_i$, for $i = 1, 2, \ldots$ and n the degree of R_i], then we say that M is a *submodel* of M', and M' an *extension* of M. We say that M' is an *elementary extension* of M if M is a submodel of M' and, for all sequences d in the domain of M and all sentences A, $M \vDash A[d]$ iff $M' \vDash A[d]$. Finally, we say that M and M' are *elementarily equivalent* if $M \vDash A$ iff $M' \vDash A$ for all statements A. (Recall that statements are sentences in which no variables occur free.)

Theorem. *If M' is an elementary extension of M, then M and M' are elementarily equivalent.*

Proof: Let A be a statement. Then for any model M, the following are equivalent.

(a) $M \vDash A$.

(b) $M \vDash A[d]$ for all sequences d in M.

(c) $M \vDash A[d]$ for some sequence d in M.

Now suppose that M_2 is an elementary extension of M_1. Then we prove, for any statement A:

1. If $M_2 \vDash A$, then $M_2 \vDash A[d]$ for all sequences d in M_2. Hence $M_2 \vDash A[d]$ for all sequences d in M_1 because sequences in M_1 *are also sequences* in M_2. But then $M_1 \vDash A[d]$ for all sequences d in M_1. Therefore, $M_1 \vDash A$.

2. If $M_1 \vDash A$, then $M_1 \vDash A[d]$ for some sequence d in M_1, so $M_2 \vDash A[d]$ for some sequence d in M_1. And since d is also a sequence in M_2, $M_2 \vDash A[d]$ for some sequence d in M_2. Hence $M_2 \vDash A$.

7. Löwenheim–Skolem Theorem

In 1915 Löwenheim proved that any satisfiable sentence is satisfied in some model that is at most denumerable. A few years later, Skolem extended this result to sets of sentences.[10] An inspection of the proof of our weak completeness theorem will show that Löwenheim's theorem was proved along the way. For let A be satisfiable; then $\Vdash \neg A$ does not hold, so the tableau sequence of $\neg A$ (the first member of which is $\neg \neg A$) has a nonterminating branch. And we constructed there a model, with at most countable domain, in which all the conjuncts in that branch are satisfied. The general Löwenheim–Skolem result is an immediate corollary to our version of the compactness proof. For if a set of sentences is satisfiable, so is each of its finite subsets—hence the set is satisfiable in a model with at most countable domain.

But these proofs are such that one might still hold that some sets of sentences are satisfiable in countable or finite models only if the terms in them are given a rather peculiar interpretation. After all, in the proofs of the above theorems, the models constructed had sets of variables as their domain. Some philosophical mileage has been derived from this reaction in philosophy of mathematics. Set theory can be formulated in a quantificational syntax, with say the first binary predicate interpreted as the set-membership predicate. Now set theory has as one of its theorems that there are uncountable sets—yet the Löwenheim–Skolem theorem says that the theory can be satisfied in a countable model. This application of the theorem is sometimes referred to as the Löwenheim–Skolem paradox. And one reaction to this paradox is to say that under a countable interpretation, the set-membership predicate no longer denotes set membership.[11] Well, in any correct interpretation (in any model) the predicate denotes the relation of set membership among elements in the domain in question. And we shall now give a proof that takes the wind out of the sails of the above "resolution" of the paradox: If set theory has any models at all in which the set-membership predicate denotes the set-membership relation, it has such models with at most denumerable domains. This proof of the Löwenheim–Skolem theorem is due to Tarski and Vaught.[12] A lemma on elementary extensions will be useful.[13]

Lemma. *M' is an elementary extension of M if and only if (a) M' is an extension of M, and (b) for each sentence A, each variable x, and each sequence d in M, if $M' \vDash \neg(x)A[d]$, then there is a sequence $d' =_x d$ in M such that $M' \vDash \neg A[d']$.*

Proof: Suppose first that M' is an elementary extension of M. Then if $M' \vDash \neg(x)A[d]$, d a sequence in M, then $M \vDash \neg(x)A[d]$. But then for some $d' =_x d$ in M, $M \vDash \neg A[d']$, and hence $M' \vDash \neg A[d']$.

Suppose, second, that the stated conditions are met, and let us prove that M' is an elementary extension of M. Let it be the case for all sequences d in M, and all sentences B of length less than A, that $M \vDash B[d]$ iff $M' \vDash B[d]$. By strong induction we prove this to be the case for A. Let d range over sequences in M.

(a) A is atomic. Then $M \vDash A[d]$ iff $M' \vDash A[d]$; immediate.

(b) A is $\neg B$. Then $M \vDash B[d]$ iff $M' \vDash B[d]$; hence not $M \vDash B[d]$ iff not $M' \vDash B[d]$; hence $M \vDash \neg B[d]$ iff $M' \vDash \neg B[d]$.

(c) A is $(B \;\&\; D)$; equally obvious.

(d) A is $(x)B$. (a) $M' \vDash (x)B[d]$. Then $M' \vDash B[d']$ for all $d' =_x d$ in M'; hence $M' \vDash B[d']$ for all $d' =_x d$ in M. By hypothesis, $M \vDash B[d']$ for all $d' =_x d$ in M; hence $M \vDash (x)B[d]$. (b) Not $M' \vDash (x)B[d]$. Then $M' \vDash \neg(x)B[d]$, so by the stated conditions

$M' \vDash \neg B[d]$ for some $d' =_x d$ in M. But then $M \vDash \neg B[d']$, by hypothesis, so not $M \vDash B[d']$, so not $M \vDash (x)B[d]$.

Theorem. *If M is a model of cardinality higher than the denumerable, then M has an elementary submodel that is denumerable.*

Proof: Let $M = \langle D, R_1, R_2, \ldots \rangle$, and assume that D is well-ordered in some way, so that we can always speak of "the first member of D such that . . . ." We define a sequence of subsets of D:

D_1 is some denumerable subset of D

$D_{n+1} = \{b \in D$: for some sentence A, some essentially finite sequence d in D_n, and some variable x, b is the first element in D such that $M \vDash A[d']$, where $d' =_x d$, $d'(x) = b\}$

By considering the sentence $x = y$ for A in the definition of D_{n+1}, we see that $D_n \subseteq D_{n+1}$ for all n. For let A be $x = y$, let $d(y) = b \in D_n$. Then we have $M \vDash A[d']$ for $d' =_x d$ if and only if $d'(x) = d(y) = b$, so that then $b \in D_{n+1}$.

Second, D_1 is denumerable; let us assume that D_n is denumerable and prove that D_{n+1} is denumerable. There are only denumerably many finite sequences in D_n, only denumerably many variables, and only denumerably many sentences. Therefore, as the definition of D_{n+1} shows, the number of elements added to D_n in the formation of D_{n+1} can at most be denumerable infinity to the power three, which is denumerable infinity. So D_{n+1} is also denumerable. By induction, each set D_i is denumerable.

Now define $D_\infty = \bigcup_{i=1}^{\infty} D_i$. Then D_∞ is still only denumerable. Furthermore, let R_i' be $R_i \cap D_\infty^n$, where R_i has degree n, for all i. Then $M' = \langle D_\infty, R_1', R_2', \ldots \rangle$ is clearly a denumerable submodel of M. To finish the proof, we must show that the second condition of the preceding lemma holds, so that M' is an elementary submodel.

Let d be a sequence in M', and $M \vDash \neg(x)B[d]$. If x_k is alphabetically the first variable that does not occur in $\neg(x)B$, we may take $d(x_m) = d(x_k)$ for $m \geq k$, without loss of generality. It follows that for some n, d is a sequence in D_n.

Since $M \vDash \neg (x) B[d]$ there must be an element b of M such that $M \vDash \neg B[d']$, where $d' =_x d$ and $d'(x) = b$. Let b_0 be the first such element in D. Then b_0 belongs to D_{n+1}, hence to M'. Therefore, such an assignment d' is a sequence in the submodel M'; this is what was to be demonstrated.

8. Deductive Theories

In this section we shall study systems, that is, sets closed under semantic entailment. But it will now be convenient to concentrate on statements rather than sentences in general. We shall use the term "(deductive) theory" to refer to a system of statements. So we can define a *theory* either as the set of statements belonging to a given system of sentences, or as a set of statements X such that $A \in X$ if $X \vDash A$, for all statements A (in a given referential quantifier language L). A model of the language will be called a *model of the theory* if all statements in the theory are true in that model. In addition, we call a theory T (*negation-*) *complete* if for each statement A, either A or $\neg A$ belongs to T.

Lemma.   *A theory is complete if and only if any two of its models are elementarily equivalent.*

Proof: Note that elementary equivalence concerns only statements.

If T is complete, M and M' are models of T, and A is a statement, then either $A \in T$ or $\neg A \in T$: in the first case $M \vDash A$ and $M' \vDash A$, in the second case $\sim M \vDash A$ and $\sim M' \vDash A$. Hence $M \vDash A$ iff $M' \vDash A$.

If T is not complete, and A is a statement such that neither A nor $\neg A$ is in T, then neither $T \vDash A$ nor $T \vDash \neg A$ holds. Hence T has models M and M' such that $\sim M \vDash A$ and $\sim M' \vDash \neg A$. Therefore, $M \vDash \neg A$ and $\sim M' \vDash \neg A$, so M and M' are not elementarily equivalent.

DEFINITION.   Models $M = \langle D, R_1, R_2, \ldots \rangle$ and $M' = \langle D', R'_1, R'_2 \ldots \rangle$ are *isomorphic* if and only if there is a one-to-one function g from D onto D' such that $\langle b_1, \ldots, b_n \rangle \in R_i$ iff $\langle g(b_1), \ldots, g(b_n) \rangle \in R'_i$ for all members $b_1, \ldots, b_n$ of D.

Theorem. *If two models are isomorphic, they are elementarily equivalent.*

Proof: Let M and M' be isomorphic by the one-to-one function g, and let A be any sentence. We intend to prove that $M \vDash A$ iff $M' \vDash A$, and do so by induction on the length of A.

Hypothesis of Induction *For all sentences B of length less than A, $M \vDash B$ iff $M' \vDash B$. Recall that any one-to-one function has an inverse.*

Case 1. A is $P_i x_1 \cdots x_n$. Suppose that $\langle b_1, \ldots, b_n \rangle \in R_i$; then $\langle g(b_1), \ldots, g(b_n) \rangle \in R_i'$; conversely, if $\langle b_1', \ldots, b_n' \rangle \in R_i'$, then $\langle g^{-1}(b_1'), \ldots, g^{-1}(b_n') \rangle \in R_i$.

Case 2. A is $x = y$. Then if $b_1 \neq b_2$, $g(b_1) \neq g(b_2)$; conversely, if $b_i' \neq b_2'$, then $g^{-1}(b_1') \neq g^{-1}(b_2')$.

Case 3. A is $\neg B$. Then $M \vDash B$ iff $M' \vDash B$, so $\sim M \vDash B$ iff $\sim M' \vDash B$, so $M \vDash A$ iff $M' \vDash A$.

Case 4. A is $(B \& C)$. Then $M \vDash A$ iff $M \vDash B$ and $M \vDash C$, iff $M' \vDash B$ and $M' \vDash C$, iff $M' \vDash A$.

Case 5. A is $(x)B$. Then $M \vDash A$ iff $M \vDash B$ iff $M' \vDash B$ iff $M' \vDash A$.

When any two models of a theory are isomorphic, the theory is called *categorical*. By the above two theorems it follows that *a theory is categorical only if it is negation-complete*. But the converse does not hold: if two models have different cardinalities, then they are not isomorphic, and we know from the Löwenheim–Skolem theorem that *any* theory with nondenumerable models also has denumerable models (and is therefore not categorical). It seems reasonable therefore to consider a somewhat weaker condition than categoricity.

DEFINITION. *A theory is* categorical in power *m if and only if any two of its models of cardinality m are isomorphic.*

The cardinal number of a denumerable set is denoted as $\aleph_0$ (aleph null), and the condition which we wish to consider specifically now is that of categoricity in power $\aleph_0$. (The following theorem is a special case of *Vaught's test*.[14])

Theorem.   *If T is a satisfiable theory that has only infinite models and is categorical in power* $\aleph_0$, *then T is (negation)-complete.*

Proof: Let the antecedent of the theorem hold. If T is not complete, then for some statement A, neither A nor $\neg A$ belongs to T. So T has models M_1 and M_2 such that $M_1 \vDash \neg A$ and $M_2 \vDash A$. By the Löwenheim–Skolem theorem, M_1 and M_2 are respectively elementarily equivalent to certain denumerable models M_1' and M_2'. Clearly M_1' and M_2' are not elementarily equivalent to each other. By the preceding theorem, it follows that they are not isomorphic, so T is not categorical in power $\aleph_0$.

9. Substitution Interpretation

The intuitive idea of the substitution interpretation is that $(x)Fx$ is true iff Fx is true *whatever name x be*.[15] This clearly coincides with the referential interpretation exactly when (1) everything is designated by some name, and (2) every name designates something. These assumptions are not always satisfied (not every real number has a name; *Pegasus* does not designate anything). But the coincidence can be used to ferret out exactly the logic of the substitution interpretation, if we assume[16] that the names are meant to be the names in the language in question: We simply treat the variables as names, and supply them with designations (for example, themselves) solely to determine the truth values of the atomic sentences. Formally speaking, therefore, we begin by treating the substitution interpretation as a restricted referential interpretation. Then we shall show how it may be treated independently of the referential interpretation.

Let L' be a referential quantifier language and M a model for L'. We say that d is a *canonical assignment* for M iff d maps the variables onto the domain of M. (This is, of course, possible only if M is at most denumerable.) We call a valuation for L' *canonical* iff it is induced by a model and a canonical assignment for that model.

DEFINITION. L is a *substitutional quantifier language* iff there is a referential quantifier language L' such that L has the same syntax as L' and the admissible valuations of L are exactly the canonical valuations of L.

We call L and L' *corresponding languages* in this case.

Canonical valuations can be defined without recourse to models, as the following theorem shows.

Theorem. v *is a canonical valuation for the referential quantifier language* L' *iff for all sentences* A, B *and variables* x, y *of* L',

(a) $v(A) \in \{T, F\}$;

(b) if $v(x = y) = T$ and A is atomic, then $v(A) = v(y/x)A)$;

(c) $v(x = x) = T$;

(d) $v(A \,\&\, B) = T$ iff $v(A) = v(B) = T$;

(e) $v(\neg A) = T$ iff $v(A) = F$;

(f) $v((x)A) = T$ iff $v((y/x)A) = T$ for all variables y.

Proof: Let v be a canonical valuation for L'; then the only condition not obviously satisfied is the "if" part of (vi). But suppose that $v((x)A) = F$, and v induced by M and d. Then for some $d' =_x d$, $\sim M \vDash A[d']$. Since d is canonical, there is a variable y such that $d(y) = d'(x)$. By our theorem on unary substitution, $M \vDash (y/x)A[d]$ iff $M \vDash A[d']$; therefore, $\sim M \vDash (y/x)A[d]$. Hence $v((y/x)A) = F$.

On the other hand, let v satisfy conditions (i) through (vi) and let, for each variable x, $ev(x)$ be alphabetically the first variable y such that $v(y = x) = T$. Define $M = \langle f, D \rangle$ such that

$$D = \{ev(x) : x \text{ a variable of } L'\}$$

and f the function mapping all n-ary predicates of L' into D^n such that

$$f(P^n) = \{\langle x_1, \ldots, x_n \rangle : x_1, \ldots, x_n \in D \quad \text{and} \quad v(P^n x_1 \cdots x_n) = T\}$$

for each n. Finally, define the assignment

$$d : d(x) = ev(x).$$

Then d is a canonical assignment, and we maintain that v is the valuation induced by M and d. We have already shown that the canonical valuation v' induced by M and d satisfies conditions (a)–(f); to show that $v' = v$, it only remains to show that if A is atomic, then $v'(A) = v(A)$. But $v'(x = y) = T$ iff $d(x) = d(y)$, iff $ev(x) = ev(y)$, iff $v(x = y) = T$. And $v'(P^n x_1 \cdots x_n) = T$ iff $\langle d(x_1), \ldots, d(x_n) \rangle \in f(P^n)$ iff $\langle ev(x_1), \ldots ev(x_n) \rangle \in f(P^n)$ iff $v(P^n ev(x_1) \cdots ev(x_n)) = T$ iff $v(P^n x_1 \cdots x_n) = T$. So indeed $v' = v$.

This shows that the class of admissible valuations of a substitutional quantifier language can be defined entirely without recourse to models. So our reliance on the standard interpretation in our definition was not necessary after all. It is clear that quantificational logic is sound under the substitution interpretation; our definition makes this result immediate. But that this logic cannot have strong completeness here follows also from its soundness under the referential interpretation; for

$$\{(y_1/x)A, (y_2/x)A, \ldots\} \Vdash (x)A$$

(where $y_1, y_2, \ldots$ are all the variables) holds in a substitutional, but not in a referential, quantifier language.

It follows then that the syntactic description of the relation of semantic entailment cannot proceed in the present case by such elementary means as we have employed so far. We generalize the notion of a nonterminating branch of a tableau sequence in the following manner.[17]

DEFINITION. A set of sentences X of a QCS is a *model set* iff it satisfies

(a) X does not contain both A and $\neg A$ for any sentence A nor $x \neq x$ for any variable x;

(b) if $\neg \neg A \in X$, so is A;

(c) if $\neg (A \,\&\, B) \in X$, so is $\neg A$ or $\neg B$;

(d) if $(A \,\&\, B) \in X$, so are A and B;

(e) if $\neg (x)A \in X$, so is $\neg (y/x)A$ for at least one variable y;

(f) if $(x)A \in X$, so is $(y/x)A$ for each variable y;

(g) if $x = y$ and A are in X, so is $(y/x)A$.

We wish now to show that in a substitutional language L, $X \Vdash A$ iff $X \cup \{\neg A\}$ is not satisfiable, iff $X \cup \{\neg A\}$ is not contained in any model set. The first equivalence is obvious; the second is established by the following theorem.

Theorem. *If L is a substitutional quantifier language and X a set of sentences of L, then X is satisfiable if and only if X is contained in a model set.*

Proof: First, if v is a canonical valuation, then

$$\{A : v(A) = \mathrm{T}\}$$

is a model set; this is obvious. This shows that any satisfiable set is contained in a model set.

Second, let Y be a model set of L, and define the model $M = \langle f, D \rangle$ for the corresponding language L' by:

(a) if x is a variable free in Y, then ev(x) is alphabetically the first variable y such that $(y = x) \in Y$; or ev(x) is x;
(b) $D = \{y : y = \mathrm{ev}(x)$ for some variable $x\}$;
(c) $f(P^n) = \{\langle x_1, \ldots, x_n \rangle : x_1, \ldots, x_n \in D$ and $P^n x_1 \cdots x_n \in Y\}$ for each n-ary predicate P^n and each degree n.

Define the assignment d by $d(x) = \mathrm{ev}(x)$ when ev(x) is defined and $d(x)$ is alphabetically the first variable in D otherwise. Then d is canonical, and the canonical valuation v induced by M and d satisfies Y (by an argument parallel to that in the weak completeness proof for the standard interpretation).

Thus the set $\{\neg(x)A, (y_1/x)A, (y_2/x)A, \ldots\}$, where $y_1, y_2, \ldots$ are all the variables of L (of the corresponding referential quantifier language L'), is not satisfiable in L, because it is not included in a model set, but it is satisfiable in L'.

We end by presenting the most important relation between the referential and the substitution interpretation: their coincidence in the case of statements.[18]

Theorem. *If X is a set of statements and A a statement of a referential quantifier language L, then $X \Vdash A$ in L iff all canonical valuations that satisfy X also satisfy A.*

Proof: The "only if" part is obvious. On the other hand, suppose that $X \Vdash A$ does not hold. Then $X \cup \{\neg A\}$ is satisfiable; by the Löwenheim–Skolem theorem, there is an at-most-denumerable model M and assignment d in M such that $M \vDash B[d]$ for all B in $X \cup \{\neg A\}$. But all members B of this set are statements, so $M \vDash B$ for all B in $X \cup \{\neg A\}$. Now since M is denumerable, there exists a canonical assignment d' for M, and clearly the valuation induced by M and d' is a canonical valuation that satisfies X but not A.

This theorem should not be regarded as establishing an absolute asymmetry between statements and nonstatements. For we could also have implemented the substitution interpretation by singling out a subset V' of the variables as *names*, with the truth definition: $(x)A$ is true iff $(y/x)A$ is true for every member y of V'. If V' is infinite, we again would not have had compactness, and the asymmetry established in the above theorem would have been between sentences in which names occur free and sentences in which no names occur free. If we had added a special set of symbols $a_1, a_2, \ldots$ as names, rather than using variables for that purpose, this point would be clearer yet (for then the occurrences of "free" could be deleted from the preceding assertion).

The preceding theorem and the soundness and completeness theorems of Section 4 together establish that for any statement A, $\Vdash A$ in a substitutional quantifier language iff $\vdash A$ in quantificational logic. The following theorem extends this result to all sentences A, thus proving the soundness and weak completeness of quantificational logic under the substitution interpretation.

Theorem. *If A is any sentence of a substitutional quantifier language L, and $x_1, \ldots, x_n$ the variables free in A, then $\Vdash A$ in L iff $\Vdash (x_1) \cdots (x_n)A$ in L.*

Proof: The "if" part is obvious, for $(x_1) \cdots (x_n)A \Vdash A$. But if not $\Vdash (x_1) \cdots (x_n)A$ there is a canonical valuation v_d such that $v_d((x_1) \cdots$

$(x_n)A) =$ F. So there is an assignment d' that is like d except perhaps at $x_1, \ldots, x_n$ such that $v_{d'}(A) =$ F. This mapping d' is an assignment for the same model M with an at most denumerable domain D. Let $d''(x_i) = d'(x_i)$ for $i = 1, \ldots, n$ and let d'' map the other variables onto D. Then d'' and d' agree on all variables free in A, so $v_{d''}(A) =$ F also. In addition, $v_{d''}$ is canonical, so $\Vdash A$ does not hold in L.

We have now also established, in effect, that quantificational logic is adequate under the substitution interpretation for all arguments with finite sets of premises, and for all arguments whose premises and conclusion are statements.

10. Extensions of Quantificational Logic

The semantics of the referential interpretation may be extended by allowing a model to have an empty domain.[19] In that case there are, of course, no assignment functions for the model, so satisfaction of sentences that are not statements has no obvious sense. But truth of statements may be defined by: $(x)A$ is true; $\neg A$ is true iff A is not true; $(A \,\&\, B)$ is true iff A and B are true. There are, of course, various ways of extending this truth definition to sentences in general. The logic must be changed somewhat even for statements; for example, $(x) \neg (y)P'y \Vdash \neg(y)P'y$ does not hold anymore, nor does $\Vdash(Ex)(x = x)$.

We may further extend the logic by adding names (individual constants) to the syntax. If these are all regarded as having a denotation in the domain of discourse, it is necessary to add as axiom scheme

$$(x)A \supset (b/x)A,$$

where b is a name and $(b/x)A$ is the result of replacing all free occurrences of x in A by occurrences of b. If names are allowed not to have a denotation, the axiom scheme to be added is rather

$$(x)A \,\&\, (Ey)(y = b) \cdot \supset (b/x)A.$$

If, in addition, the variables are allowed not to have a denotation, the axiom scheme $(x)A \supset (y/x)A$ must be dropped in favor of

$$(x)A \ \& \ (Ez)(z = y) \cdot \supset (y/x)A,$$

where z is a variable distinct from y. Such extensions and modifications of quantificational logic are known as *free logics*.[20]

We can extend the syntax still further by adding function letters or a description operator; the latter makes the former superfluous. The description operator $\imath$ forms nouns from sentences; $(\imath x)A$ purports to denote the one and only individual b that satisfies A. [More precisely, the denotation of $(\imath x)A$ relative to assignment d for model M is b if and only if $M \vDash A[d']$ for any $d' =_x d$ just in case $d'(x) = b$.] Hence the following axiom scheme must be added:

$$\text{(FD)} \quad (y)(y = (\imath x)A \equiv \cdot (x)(A \supset x = y) \ \& \ (y/x)A),$$

with y a variable distinct from x. When $(\imath x)A$ does not have a denotation, one has various alternatives concerning its semantic treatment, and this has led to a variety of description theories.[21]

Finally, it is possible to add several styles of quantifiers, say one with a referential interpretation and one with a substitution interpretation, or several with referential interpretations in terms of different domains of discourse.[22]

NOTES

1. The semantics of quantificational logic is developed uniformly in terms of valuations in R. H. Thomason, *Symbolic Logic* (New York: Macmillan, 1970).
2. See D. Kalish and R. Montague, *Logic Techniques of Formal Reasoning* (New York: Harcourt, Brace & World, 1964), pp. 86–90, for the first usage; W. V. O. Quine, *Mathematical Logic*, rev. ed. (Cambridge, Mass.: Harvard University Press, 1958), p. 79, for the second usage.

3. When the language does not contain an identity predicate, "each" is too restrictive and is replaced by "some."

4. These terms are adopted from Kalish and Montague, *Logic Techniques*, p. 99.

5. Cf. H. Leblanc, *Techniques of Deductive Inference* (Englewood Cliffs, N.J.; Prentice-Hall, 1966), pp. 129–130.

6. See chap. III, note 4.

7. For perspicuity, consider the case of $F\overset{1}{x}$ and $\neg F\overset{1}{y}$. If x and y alone belong to the same elimination string, then suppose that x is eliminated in favor of y at stage r. Then $F\overset{1}{y}$ is a conjunct in every member of $\mathcal{B}$ beyond stage r; and $\neg F\overset{1}{y}$ must be a conjunct in every member of $\mathcal{B}$ beyond a certain stage r'. Hence the branch would terminate before stage $r + r'$.

8. Cf. E. W. Beth, *The Foundations of Mathematics* (Amsterdam: North-Holland, 1965), pp. 264–265.

9. The theorem can be generalized to read the cardinality of the variables where we have "denumerable" if that cardinality is not so restricted.

10. The theorem can be generalized to the cardinality of the set of sentences of the language; see the statement of the theorem in A. Mostowski, *Thirty Years of Foundational Studies* (New York: Barnes & Noble, 1966), p. 121.

11. Cf. J. Myhill, Contribution to a symposium "On the Ontological Significance of the Löwenheim–Skolem Theorem," *American Philosophical Association* (*Eastern Division*) *Proceedings*, 2 (1953), pp. 57–70, and M. D. Resnik, "On Skolem's Paradox," *Journal of Philosophy*, *63* (1966), pp. 425–437.

12. A. Tarski and R. L. Vaught, "Arithmetical Extensions of Relational Systems," *Compositio Mathematica*, *13* (1957), pp. 81–102.

13. *Ibid.*, Theorem 1.10; A. Robinson, *Introduction to Model Theory, and to the Metamathematics of Algebra* (Amsterdam: North-Holland, 1965), sec. 3.2.1., pp. 55–56.

14. Cf., e.g., Robinson, *Model Theory*, sec. 4.1.2, pp. 89–90.

15. See J. M. Dunn and N. D. Belnap, Jr., "The Substitution Interpretation of the Quantifiers," *Nous*, *2* (1968), pp. 177–185, and references therein; see also H. Leblanc, "A Simplified Account of Validity and Implication for Quantificational Logic," *Journal of Symbolic Logic*, *33* (1968), pp. 231–235.

16. In philosophical discussions especially it should not be overlooked that this assumption is not a necessary one; see Dunn and Belnap, *Nous*, *2* (1968), p. 183, and L. Henkin, "Some Notes on Nominalism," *Journal of Symbolic Logic*, *18* (1953).

17. The term "model set" was introduced by J. Hintikka.

18. Cf. Beth, *Foundations*, pp. 263–266.

19. See T. Hailperin, "Quantification Theory and Empty Individual Domains," *Journal of Symbolic Logic*, *18* (1953), pp. 197–200; W. V. O. Quine, "Quantification and the Empty Domain," *Journal of Symbolic Logic*, *19* (1954), pp. 177–179; A. Mostowski, "On the Rules of Proof in the Pure Functional Calculus of the First Order," *Journal of Symbolic Logic*, *16* (1956), pp. 129–136.

20. See K. Lambert, "Existential Import Revisited," *Notre Dame Journal of Formal Logic*, *4* (1963), pp. 288–292; B. van Fraassen, "The Completeness of Free Logic," *Zeitschrift für mathematische Logik und Grundlagen der Mathematik*, *14* (1966), pp. 219–234, and "A Topological Proof of the Löwenheim–Skolem Compactness and Strong Completeness Theorems for Free Logic," *Zeitschrift für Mathematische Logik und Grundlagen der Mathematik*, *14* (1968), pp. 245–254; H. Leblanc and R. H. Thomason, "Completeness Theorems for Some Presupposition-free Logics," *Fundamenta Mathematicae*, *62* (1968), pp. 125–164, and references therein.

21. See B. van Fraassen and K. Lambert, "On Free Description Theory," *Zeitschrift für mathematische Logik und Grundlagen der Mathematik*, *13* (1967), pp. 225–240.

22. See, e.g., N. Rescher, "On the Logic of Existence and Denotation," *Philosophical Review*, *68* (1959), pp. 157–180, and the references therein (especially in notes 30 and 31 on p. 175); B. van Fraassen, "Meaning Relations Among Predicates," *Nous*, *1* (1967), pp. 161–179; K. Lambert and B. van Fraassen, "Meaning Relations, Possible Objects, and Possible Worlds," in K. Lambert, ed., *Philosophical Problems in Logic* (Dordrecht, Holland: Reidel, 1970), pp. 1–20.

CHAPTER V

NONCLASSICAL LOGICS

There are many interesting logical systems other than classical logic (the classical propositional calculus or quantificational logic); some are extensions of classical logic, some are fragments, and some are neither extensions nor fragments. Some of the less radical departures from classical logic we have already discussed: logic valid for the empty domain, free logic, description theory. Other nonclassical logics are systems of many-valued logic and systems of modal logic; these are the best known. In these cases, one has nonclassical *connectors* in the language, or at least connectors with a nonclassical interpretation. We may also refer to the logic of presuppositions and the logic of tautological entailment as nonclassical logics.[1] In these cases, one studies nonclassical semantic *relations* among (sets of) sentences. In this chapter we shall study examples of both kinds of nonclassical logics. Finally, we shall discuss the concept of truth in the light of its role in the interpretation of nonclassical logics and formalize some aspects of a theory of truth applicable to arbitrary languages.

1. Many-Valued Logics

The terms "matrix," "*M*-assignment," "adequate matrix," "*M*-valuation," "*M*-propositional language" are defined in Chapter III, Section 5; we shall need these definitions, but not the results of that section. When the set of elements of a matrix is finite, we call the matrix *finite*.

a. Substitution and Lindenbaum Algebras

In the case of the familiar truth table, there is an easy algorithm for calculating the value (under a given assignment) of a complex formula, given the values of its components. We simply follow the rules:

1. Replace the components by the names of their values.
2. Replace (T & T) by T.
3. Replace (X & Y) by F.
4. Replace $\neg$T by F.
5. Replace $\neg$F by T.

where X, Y are ambiguous between T and F. (Note that 3 cannot be applied until 2 is no longer applicable.) We generalize this algorithm as follows:

Lemma 1. *If A is the expression $e_1 e_2 \cdots e_n$, and d is an M-assignment (on the PCS to which A belongs), then $d(A)$ is identical with the element $td(A) = td(e_1) \cdots td(e_n)$, where*
   $td(B) = d(B)$ *for any atomic sentence B,*
   $td(\&) = \cdot$,
   $td(\neg) = -$,
   $td(e_i) = e_i$ *if e_i is a parenthesis.*

The proof is by strong induction on the hypothesis that $d(C) = td(C)$ for any sentence C of length less than A:

1. A is atomic.   Then $td(A) = d(A)$.
2. A is (B & C).   Then $td(A) = (td(B) \cdot td(C))$.
   By hypothesis $td(B) = d(B)$, $td(C) = d(C)$.
   So $td(A) = d(B) \cdot d(C) = d(A)$.
3. A is $\neg C$.   Then $td(A) = -td(C)$. By hypothesis that is $-d(C) = d(A)$.

This leads at once to some helpful results about substitution in M-propositional languages. It is to be recalled that we recognize unary substitution, simultaneous substitution, and infinitary substitution. Each is a special case of the next, so "substitution" used without qualification is to be understood as "infinitary substitution."

Theorem. *In an M-propositional language, validity and unsatisfiability of sentence is preserved under substitution.*

It is sufficient to show that if $S^s(A)$ is sometimes undesignated (respectively, sometimes designated), then so is A, for any sentence A. This follows immediately from Lemma 1 and the following lemma (left as exercise).

Lemma 2. *If d and d' are M-assignments such that $d(p) = d'(s(p))$ for all atomic sentences p, then $d(A) = d'(S^s(A))$ for all sentences A.*

Theorem. *If A is a sentence for an M-propositional language such that for all admissible valuations v and all substitutions S^s, $v(A) = T$ iff $v(S^s(A)) = T$, then A is either valid or not satisfiable.*

Proof: If A is neither valid nor not satisfiable, then there are admissible valuations v and v' such that $v(A) = T$, $v'(A) \neq T$. This means that there are M-assignments d and d' such that $d(A)$ is designated and $d'(A)$ is not designated.

Let A have exactly $p_1, \ldots, p_n$ as its atomic constituents. We define a new M-assignment:

$d''(q_i) = d'(p_i)$ for $i = 1, \ldots, n$, where $q_1, \ldots, q_n$ are distinct atomic sentences other than $p_1, \ldots, p_n$,

$d''(q) = d(q)$ when q is an atomic sentence other than $q_1, \ldots, q_n$.

It follows at once that $d''(A) = d(A)$; $d''(S^s(A)) = d'(A)$ for $s(p_i) = q_i$; $s(q) = q$ for an atomic sentence q other than $p_1, \ldots, p_n$. The M-valuation v'' induced by d'' is such that $v''(A) = T$, $v''(S^s(A)) = T$. So if A is neither valid nor not satisfiable, then there is a valuation that assigns T to A but not to $S^s(A)$.

Carnap called a sentence *L-determinate* if it was either valid or not satisfiable. The two preceding theorems establish therefore an important connection between *L*-determinacy and invariance under substitution transformations.[2] This suggests that substitution has a deep semantic significance and that conclusion will be further strengthened by our next theorem. (We may note, as an aside, that satisfiability is not preserved under substitution in general, but is preserved under infinitary atomic substitution by one-to-one mappings.)

Theorem.   *If $LS = \langle Syn, T, \vdash \rangle$ is a logical system and Syn is a PCS, then there is an adequate matrix for LS iff T is closed under unary substitution.*

Proof: If M is an adequate matrix for LS, then T is exactly the set of valid statements of the M-propositional language with Syn as syntax. As we have seen, that set is closed under infinitary substitution. So if LS has an adequate matrix, T is closed under unary substitution.

On the other hand, suppose that T is closed under unary substitution; we now mean to construct a matrix that is adequate for LS. First we define an equivalence (that is, reflexive, symmetric, and transitive) relation R on the sentence of Syn: $R(A, B)$ iff for any sentence C and atomic sentence

$$p, S_p^A(C) \in T \quad \text{iff } S_p^B(C) \in T.$$

We define the equivalence class $E(A)$ of A as

$$E(A) = \{B: R(A, B)\}.$$

These equivalence classes will be the elements of the matrix $\langle E, D, \cdot, - \rangle = M(LS)$:

$$E = \{E(A): A \text{ is a sentence of Syn}\},$$
$$D = \{E(A): A \text{ is a theorem of } LS\},$$
$$E(A) \cdot E(B) = E(A \ \& \ B),$$
$$\overline{E(A)} = E(\neg A).$$

That all valid sentences are theorems is seen by considering the function $d: d(A) = E(A)$. That d is an $M(LS)$-assignment is clear:

$$d(B \ \& \ C) = E(B \ \& \ C) = E(B) \cdot E(C) = d(B) \cdot d(C),$$
$$d(\neg B) = E(\neg B) = \overline{E(B)} = \overline{d(B)}.$$

If A is valid, $d(A)$ is designated; that is, $E(A)$ belongs to D. But then A is a theorem, by the definition of D.

On the other hand, suppose A to be a theorem of LS, and let d' be an $M(LS)$-assignment. Recall that $d'(A) = td'(A)$, and let $d'(p_i) = E(B_i)$ for the atomic components $p_1, \ldots, p_n$ of A. Then $td'(A) = td(S^s(A))$, where d is the assignment defined above, and $s(p_i) = B_i$ for $i = 1, \ldots, n$. So $d'(A) = E(S^s(A))$.

The result of an infinitary substitution on a single sentence is just the result of some simultaneous substitutions. In the particular case,

$$S^s(A) = S_{p_1 \cdots p_n}^{B_1 \cdots B_n}(A),$$

which can be defined in terms of unary substitution. Since A is a theorem, and T is closed under unary substitution, it follows therefore that $S^s(A)$ is a theorem.

Hence $d'(A) = E(S^s(A)) \in D$. This argument being general in d', A is valid. This ends the proof.

The above theorem is essentially due to Lindenbaum and the matrix $M(LS)$ is therefore called the *Lindenbaum algebra* of LS.[3] The elements of the Lindenbaum algebra are often defined as the classes

$\{B : A \equiv B$ is a theorem of the system$\}$ (with $\equiv$ defined as usual),

which coincides with our definition just when the following principle holds:

$A \equiv B$ is a theorem if and only if for any sentence C, $S_p^A(C)$ is a theorem iff $S_p^B(C)$ is a theorem.

This is an important metatheorem for the classical propositional calculus and many other familiar systems.

b. Compactness and Finite Matrices

We recall from Chapter II, Section 10, that if a language is the union of a chain of its finitary fragments, then that language is compact and has finitary entailment. This provides us with the method of proof for the following theorem.

Theorem.   *If L is an M-propositional language for some finite matrix M, then L is compact and has finitary semantic entailment.*

Proof: We proceed by showing that L is the union of a chain of its finitary fragments (see Chapter II, Section 10). Let the atomic sentences of L, in alphabetic order, be $p_1, p_2, \ldots$, and let L_i be the M-propositional language with only $p_1, \ldots, p_i$ as atomic sentences, for $i = 1, 2, \ldots$. Then L_i is a finitary fragment of L, because there are only finitely many ways to map $\{p_1, \ldots, p_i\}$ into the (finite) set of elements of M, and hence only finitely many M-assignments (and M-valuations) for L_i.

Let $d_1 \subseteq d_2 \subseteq d_3 \subseteq \cdots$ be M-assignments   for $L_1, L_2, L_3, \ldots$, respectively, and let d be the union of this chain. Then $d(A) \in E$ for any sentence A of L, and if A belongs to L_i and B to L_j, with $i \leq j$, then

$$d(\neg A) = d_i(\neg A) = \overline{d_i(A)} = \overline{d(A)},$$
$$d(A \ \& \ B) = d_j(A \ \& \ B) = d_j(A) \cdot d_j(B) = d(A) \cdot d(B),$$

so d is an M-assignment for L.

Now if $v_1 \subseteq v_2 \subseteq v_3 \subseteq \cdots$ are admissible valuations for $L_1, L_2, L_3, \ldots$, respectively, then for each v_i there is a class D_i of M-assignments for L_i such that

$$v_i(A) = \text{T} \quad \text{iff } d(A) \in D \text{ for any } d \in D_i.$$

Moreover, if $d \subseteq D_{i+1}$, then there is a d' in D_i such that $d' \subseteq d$, and each D_i is finite. We have, therefore, a finitely branching tree, and no D_i is empty, so it has infinitely many nodes. (As in the proof in Chapter II, Section 10, let Λ be the origin, and let $\text{R}dd'$ for d in D_{i+1} iff $d' \in D_i$ and $d' \subseteq d$.) By Koenig's lemma this tree has infinite branch

$$d_1 \subseteq d_2 \subseteq d_3 \cdots$$

where $d_i \in D_i$ for $i = 1, 2, 3, \ldots$. We established above that the union d of this branch is an M-assignment; moreover, the union v of v_1, v_2,

$v_3, \ldots$ is a valuation on the syntax of L such that, for A a sentence of L_i,

$$v(A) = \text{T} \quad \text{iff } v_i(A) = \text{T}$$
$$\text{iff } d_i(A) \in D$$
$$\text{iff } d(A) \in D,$$

so v is the valuation induced by M and d and hence an admissible valuation for L. This is a simplified proof of a result due independently to P. Woodruff and B. Myers.

It must be pointed out that the restriction to finite matrices is essential. For example, let E be the set of natural numbers, and $D = \{1\}$, and let $\cdot$ be defined by

$$(x \cdot y) = \begin{cases} 1 & \text{iff } x < y, \\ 2 & \text{otherwise} \end{cases}$$

where $<$ is the *less-than* relation among natural numbers. Then the following set is not satisfiable, although each of its finite subsets is:

$$\{p_2 \cdot p_1, p_2 \cdot p_3, p_3 \cdot p_1, p_3 \cdot p_4, p_4 \cdot p_1, \ldots\}.$$

We can satisfy the first k members of this set by the assignment

$$d(p_1) = k + 1; \quad d(p_2) = 1; \quad d(p_3) = 2; \quad \ldots; \quad d(p_{k+1}) = k,$$

but the whole set cannot be satisfied except by giving natural numbers of strictly increasing size to $p_2, p_3, p_4, \ldots$, and a still greater number to p_1, which is impossible. (The above example is due to R. Meyer.) Significant compactness results for infinite matrices can be proved, but only with special conditions on the operations (see Appendix II).

2. Modal Logics

The construction of a semantics for modal logic by McKinsey, Tarski, Kanger, Hintikka, and Kripke is one of the most important developments in logic since the 1930s. Kripke gave this semantics what is essentially its current form, and provided weak completeness proofs for most of the known systems of modal logic.[4] Since completeness proofs in this area are readily available in a number of forms, we shall not take them up here. We shall concentrate instead on soundness, compactness, and cardinality questions.

a. Normal Propositional Modal Logics

The systems of propositional modal logic to which our discussion will be relevant are M (due to von Wright), B (what Becker called the "Brouwersche system"), and Lewis's S_4 and S_5. Their rules and axioms are as follows:

R0. If A is a theorem of the classical propositional calculus, $\vdash A$.
R1. If $\vdash A$ and $\vdash A \supset B$, then $\vdash B$.
R2. If $\vdash A$, then $\vdash \Box A$.
A1. $\vdash \Box A \supset A$.
A2. $\vdash \Box (A \supset B) \supset \cdot \Box A \supset \Box B$.
A3. $\vdash A \supset \Box \Diamond A$.
A4. $\vdash \Box A \supset \Box \Box A$.

Here each system has R0, R1, R2, A1, A2; B has in addition A3; S_4 has in addition A4, but not A3; S_5 has in addition both A3 and A4. To extend the system to the justification of arguments we add, as usual,

$$(ARG) \quad A_1, \ldots, A_n \vdash B \text{ if } \vdash \neg(A_1 \& \cdots \& A_n \& \neg B)$$

In addition, "$\Diamond$" is short for "$\neg \Box \neg$" and "$A \supset B$" short for "$\neg(A \& \neg B)$," where $\neg$ and $\&$ are the signs for negation and conjunction, respectively. We shall finally use τ as an index, ranging over $\{m, b, 4, 5\}$, and use "system τ" to refer to system M if $\tau = m$, B if $\tau = b$, S_4 if $\tau = 4$, and S_5 if $\tau = 5$.

The syntax for each system is the same.

DEFINITION. The syntactic system Synt is the triple $\langle \mathscr{A}, \mathscr{S}, W \rangle$ where $\mathscr{A}$ is a denumerable set—the *atomic sentences*; $\mathscr{S}$ is the set

{&, ¬, □,), (}—the *logical signs*; and W is the least set containing $\mathscr{A}$ and such that if A, B are in W, so are $(A \ \& \ B)$, $\neg(A)$, $\Box(A)$—the set of *sentences*.

The languages that we discuss here shall be called (with obvious reference to the systems M, B, S_4, S_5) L_m, L_b, L_4, L_5. We need several preliminary definitions. The intuitive idea behind the interpretation of $\Box$ is that $\Box A$ is true iff A is true in all possible worlds. Since truth is itself relative to a possible world, it is more accurate to say that $\Box A$ is true in a given possible world α iff A is true in each world that is *possible relative* to α. The set of possible worlds with the possible-relative-to relation on it will be called a *model structure*. The languages are distinguished by the properties of this possible-relative-to relation.

DEFINITION.   A τ-*model structure* (τ-ms) is a couple $M = \langle K, R \rangle$, where K is a nonempty set (the "possible worlds") and R a dyadic reflexive relation on K, and such that R is symmetric if $\tau = b$, transitive if $\tau = 4$, and both transitive and symmetric if $\tau = 5$.

We read "$\alpha R \beta$" as "β is possible relative to α," or better, as "There is access from α to β."

DEFINITION.   A *valuation over* a τ-ms $M = \langle K, R \rangle$ is a mapping v of $K \times W$ into {T, F} subject to the conditions that for all α in K and A, B in W:

$v_\alpha(\neg A) = \mathrm{T}$ iff $v_\alpha(A) = \mathrm{F}$,

$v_\alpha(A \ \& \ B) = \mathrm{T}$ iff $v_\alpha(A) = v_\alpha(B) = \mathrm{T}$,

$v_\alpha(\Box A) = \mathrm{T}$ iff $v_\beta(A) = \mathrm{T}$ for all β in K such that $\alpha R \beta$, where we designate v relativized to α in K as v_α and omit parentheses where convenient.

If there is a τ-ms $M = \langle K, R \rangle$ and member α of K such that $v' = v_\alpha$, we call v' a τ-*valuation*.

The language L_τ is the couple $\langle \mathrm{Synt}, V_\tau \rangle$, where V_τ is the set of all τ-valuations. We call W the set of sentences of L_τ and V_τ the set of admissible valuations of L_τ, and denote the valuation space of L_τ as H_τ.

Theorem. *For each index τ, system τ is argument sound for L_τ.*

Proof: That the classical propositional calculus is sound for L_τ is clear (R0 and R1).

Suppose that $\Vdash A$ in L_τ, and let $v' = v_\alpha$ be a τ-valuation over a τ-ms $M = \langle K, R \rangle$. Then for all β such that $\alpha R\beta$, $v_\beta(A) = T$, just because all τ-valuations assign T to A. Therefore, $v'(\Box A) = v_\alpha(\Box A) = T$. This shows the soundness of R2.

Because R is reflexive, if $v_\beta(A) = T$ for all β such that $\alpha R\beta$, then $v_\alpha(A) = T$. Therefore, if $v_\alpha(\Box A) = T$, then $v_\alpha(A) = T$. This shows the soundness of A1, and the case of A2 may be proved similarly.

Suppose now that $\tau = b$, so that R is symmetric, and let $v_\alpha(A) = T$. Now if $\alpha R\beta$, then $\beta R\alpha$, so there is a possible world relative to β in which A is true (namely, α). Therefore, $v_\beta(\Diamond A) = T$. This proof is general in β, so we have the result that for all β such that $\alpha R\beta$, $v_\beta(\Diamond A) = T$. So $v_\alpha(\Box \Diamond A) = T$.

Finally, suppose that $\tau = 4$, so that R is transitive, and that $v_\alpha(\Box A) = T$. Then for all β possible relative to α, $v_\beta(A) = T$. Suppose that β is possible relative to α, and that γ is possible relative to β. Then $\alpha R\gamma$ also; therefore, $v_\gamma(A) = T$. This proof is general in γ, so if β is possible relative to α, then $v_\beta(\Box A) = T$. And similarly it follows then that $v_\alpha(\Box\Box A) = T$.

The result for S_5 and L_5 follows from the preceding considerations.

Theorem. *Every ultrafilter on H_τ converges.*

Proof: Let $\mathscr{F}(\tau)$ be the family of all ultrafilters on H_τ. We define the relation $R(\tau)$ on $\mathscr{F}(\tau)$ as follows:

if $\mathscr{F}, \mathscr{F}' \in \mathscr{F}(\tau)$, then $\mathscr{F}R(\tau)\mathscr{F}'$ iff for all $A \in W$ such that $H_\tau(\Box A) \in \mathscr{F}$, $H_\tau(A) \in \mathscr{F}'$.

Lemma 1. $M(\tau) = \langle \mathscr{F}(\tau), R(\tau) \rangle$ *is a τ-ms.*

Lemma 2. *The mapping v of $\mathscr{F}(\tau) \times W$ into $\{T, F\}$ such that $v_\mathscr{F}(A) = T$ iff $H_\tau(A) \in \mathscr{F}$, for all $A \in W$, for all $\mathscr{F}$ in $\mathscr{F}(\tau)$, is a valuation over $M(\tau)$.*

It is clear that each ultrafilter $\mathscr{F}$ on H_τ converges to the τ-valuation $v_{\mathscr{F}}$. Hence it remains only to prove the lemmas.

Proof of Lemma 1: In L_τ, $\Box A \Vdash A$; hence $H_\tau(\Box A) \subseteq H_\tau(A)$; hence $R(\tau)$ is reflexive. In L_b, $A \Vdash \Box \Diamond A$; let $\mathscr{F}R(b)\mathscr{F}'$ and $H_b(\Box B) \in \mathscr{F}'$. If $H_b(B) \notin \mathscr{F}$, then $H_b(\neg B) \in \mathscr{F}$ [because an ultrafilter on H_b contains either $H_b(B)$ or $H_b - H_b(B)$], so then $\mathscr{F}'$ would contain $H_b(\Diamond \neg B) = H_b(\neg \Box B)$. But $H_b(\Box B) \cap H_b(\neg \Box B) = \Lambda$, so this is impossible. Hence $R(b)$ is also symmetric.

In L_4, $\Box A \Vdash \Box \Box A$; hence $H_4(\Box A) \subseteq H_4(\Box \Box A)$. Therefore, if $\mathscr{F}R(4)\mathscr{F}'$, and $H_4(\Box A) \in \mathscr{F}$, then $H_4(\Box A) \in \mathscr{F}'$. Hence $R(4)$ is also transitive. In L_5 we prove similarly that $R(5)$ is both symmetric and transitive.

Proof of Lemma 2: Because an ultrafilter $\mathscr{F}$ must contain either $H_\tau(B)$ or $H_\tau - H_\tau(B)$ for any sentence B, $v_{\mathscr{F}}(\neg B) = \text{T}$ iff $v_{\mathscr{F}}(B) \neq \text{T}$. Because an ultrafilter contains $H_\tau(B \mathbin{\&} C) = H_\tau(B) \cap H_\tau(C)$ iff it contains both $H_\tau(B)$ and $H_\tau(C)$, $v_{\mathscr{F}}(B \mathbin{\&} C) = \text{T}$ iff $v_{\mathscr{F}}(B) = v_{\mathscr{F}}(C) = \text{T}$.

That $v_{\mathscr{F}}(\Box B) = \text{T}$ iff $v_{\mathscr{F}'}(B) = \text{T}$ for all $\mathscr{F}'$ such that $\mathscr{F}R(\tau)\mathscr{F}'$, we prove in two steps.

    (a) If $H_\tau(\Box A) \in \mathscr{F}$, then $H_\tau(A) \in \mathscr{F}'$ for all $\mathscr{F}'$ such that $\mathscr{F}R(\tau)\mathscr{F}'$; this follows by the definition of $R(\tau)$.

    (b) If $H_\tau(\Box A) \notin \mathscr{F}$, then $\mathscr{F}^* = \{H_\tau(\neg A)\} \cup \{H_\tau(B) : H_\tau(\Box B) \in \mathscr{F}\}$ is a family of sets such that each of its finite subfamilies has a nonempty intersection. For it if were not so, then there would be sentences $B_1, \ldots, B_n$ such that $B_1, \ldots, B_n \Vdash A$ holds in L_τ and $H_\tau(\Box B_1), \ldots, H_\tau(\Box B_n) \in \mathscr{F}$. But then $\Box B_1, \ldots, \Box B_n \Vdash \Box A$ would hold in L_τ [let $v_\alpha(\Box A) = \text{F}$ and $v_\alpha(\Box B_i) = \text{T}$ for $i = 1, i, \ldots, n$; then there is a β such that $\alpha R \beta$ in the relevant model structure and $v_\beta(B_i) = \text{T}$ for $i = 1, \ldots, n$, but $v_\beta(A) = \text{F}$]; so then $H_\tau(\Box A)$ would be in $\mathscr{F}$. We conclude that $\mathscr{F}^*$ is a filter base on H_τ, included in an ultrafilter $\mathscr{F}'$. Clearly, $\mathscr{F}R(\tau)\mathscr{F}'$ and $H_\tau(A) \notin \mathscr{F}'$.

Corollary. *For each index τ, L_τ is compact and has finitary semantic entailment.*

Proof by the preceding theorem and the theorems in Chapter II.

This compactness proof can be extended to quantificational modal logic in the manner of Chapter IV, Section 5, and then yields also a Löwenheim–Skolem theorem.[5]

Since each model structure contains a number of worlds, the question of cardinality may also be raised for model structures. We can certainly find sets of sentences which cannot be satisfied in finite model structures; for example, the set with the members

$$\diamondsuit p_1,$$
$$\diamondsuit(p_1 \And p_2), \diamondsuit(p_1 \And \neg p_2),$$
$$\diamondsuit(p_1 \And p_2 \And p_3), \diamondsuit(p_1 \And p_2 \And \neg p_3), \diamondsuit(p_1 \And \neg p_2 \And p_3),$$
$$\diamondsuit(p_1 \And \neg p_2 \And \neg p_3),$$

and so on. But the construction given in the preceding theorem used a nondenumerable model structure. We may reasonably expect a Skolem-like result for modal logic: that each satisfiable set is satisfied in some at-most-denumerable model structure. And this we shall prove now.

A set X is satisfiable iff $\{H(A): A \in X\}$ is a filter base; let us call X a *maximal satisfiable set* if

$$X = \{A: H(A) \in \mathscr{F}\}$$

for some ultrafilter $\mathscr{F}$ on the valuation space. Every satisfiable set can therefore be extended into a maximal satisfiable set; let us use the axiom of choice to introduce a function that assigns each satisfiable set such an extension:

The function $\delta\tau$ is defined for each satisfiable set of sentences of L_τ and if X is such a set, then $\delta\tau(X)$ is a maximal satisfiable set of sentences of L_τ that contains X.

Now, if X is a satisfiable set of sentences, we choose for each of its members of form $\diamondsuit A$ a world in which A is true; since X is denumerable we need only choose denumerably many worlds to accomplish this.

These worlds will themselves have sentences of form $\Diamond B$ true in them, so the process must be repeated ad infinitum. But $\aleph_0$ times $\aleph_0$ still equals $\aleph_0$, so this does not rule out that the total number of worlds chosen can be denumerable. This is the basis of the proof below.

Theorem. *Every satisfiable set of sentences of L_τ is satisfied by a valuation over a denumerable τ-ms.*

Proof: Let X be a satisfiable set of sentences of L. Define the following sequence of sets

$$\Gamma_i = \{\delta\tau(X)\},$$
$$\Gamma_{2i} = \{\{A\} \cup \{B \colon \Box B \in Y\} \colon \Diamond A \in Y, \; Y \in \Gamma_{2i-1}\},$$
$$\Gamma_{2i+1} = \{\delta\tau(Y) \colon Y \in \Gamma_{2i}\}$$

for $i = 1, 2, 3, \ldots$. Now we define a large family

$$\Gamma = \bigcup_{i=0}^{\infty} \Gamma_{2i+1}$$

the union of all the odd-numbered sets constructed above. Γ_1 has only one member and Γ_2 is at most denumerable. In going from Γ_{2i} to Γ_{2i+1} we replace each member by another set using the function $\delta\tau$, so the cardinality of Γ_{2i+1} equals that of Γ_{2i}. The only place a problem might be expected is in going from Γ_{2i-1} to Γ_{2i}. There we choose for each set Y in Γ_{2i-1} a denumerable family of new sets to put in Γ_{2i}. If Γ_{2i-1} is itself denumerable, the cardinality of Γ_{2i} is therefore ($\aleph_0$ times $\aleph_0$) = $\aleph_0$. So each Γ_j is denumerable, and Γ is again of cardinality $\aleph_0$ times $\aleph_0 = \aleph_0$.

If we now define YRZ iff $\{B \colon \Box B \in Y\} \subseteq Z$ for all Y and Z in Γ, then $M = \langle \Gamma, R \rangle$ is a denumerable τ-ms. The proof of this is as for Lemma 1. Second, the mapping v of $\Gamma \times W$ into $\{T, F\}$ such that $v_Y(A) = T$ iff $A \in Y$ for all $Y \in \Gamma$, $A \in W$, is a valuation over M. This is proved as for Lemma 2. And so X is satisfied by the τ-valuation v_Y such that $Y = \delta\tau(X)$, which is a valuation over the denumerable τ-ms M.

The similarity of this proof to that of the preceding theorem suggests certain modifications in the latter proof. That is, using the operation

$\delta\tau$, or an analogous operation on filter bases, we could have shown that every ultrafilter converges to a valuation over a denumerable model structure, and the present theorem would also have been a corollary. But clarity suggested otherwise.

b. Transformation Semantics for Modal Logics

Which sentences (in a given language) we consider true is to some extent, perhaps even mainly, determined by linguistic commitments that we might consider changing. For example, as Poincaré argued, whether or not space is Euclidean depends on what conventions we adopt concerning spatial congruence. And we may distinguish such conventions from some much better entrenched linguistic commitments (say concerning the meaning of "congruence") so that we can freely admit arbitrary choices in regions of our conceptual scheme without lapsing immediately into trivial linguistic conventionalism. But without entering into difficult philosophical questions here, we may note that "necessary" may be taken to mean "true and such that its truth value is invariant under all admissible changes in (transformations of) point of view, frame of reference, linguistic conventions, ..." This interpretation of necessity is the one that leads to the semantics for modal logic developed in this section.[6]

We shall say that $L = \langle \text{Synt}, \text{Val}, T, V \rangle$ is a *transformational modal language* iff Val is a set of bivalent valuations of Synt, T a set of transformations on Val, and V (the set of admissible valuations) is a subset of Val defined by

A member v of Val is in V if and only if, for all $A, B \in W$,
(a) $v(\neg A) = \text{T}$ iff $v(A) = \text{F}$;
(b) $v(A \mathbin{\&} B) = \text{T}$ iff $v(A) = v(B) = \text{T}$;
(c) $v(\Box A) = \text{T}$ iff $t(v)(A) = \text{T}$ for all $t \in T$.

We shall henceforth write tv for $t(v)$. It is to be noted that the regular capital letter T is still being used to stand for "True," while the italic capital letter T is used to denote a set of transformations. We use the lowercase Greek letter τ again as an index, ranging over $\{m, b, 4, 5\}$, and define the following classes of transformational languages:

$L = \langle \text{Synt, Val}, T, V \rangle$ belongs to $C(\tau)$ iff the set τ of conditions is fulfilled:

m. (i) For all t in T and v in Val, if $v \in V$, then $tv \in V$.

(ii) For each v in V, T contains an element t such that $tv = v$.

b. (i), (ii), and

(iii) For each v in V, each t in T, T contains an element t^* such that $t^*(tv) = v$.

4. (i), (ii), and

(iv) For each v in V, and each t, t' in T, T contains an element t'' such that $t(t'v) = t''v$.

5. (i), (ii), (iii), and (iv).

We note that (ii) is satisfied if T has an identity element (element i such that $iv = v$ for all $v \in$ Val), that (iii) is satisfied if T has for every member t an inverse (element t^* such that $t^*t = i$), and the (iv) is satisfied if T is closed under composition (tt' is a member of T if t and t' are). The question whether these stronger conditions would alter the set of valid arguments we leave as exercise.

Now it is easily proved that system τ is sound for any language in $C(\tau)$. In addition, we argue that if $X \vdash A$ does not hold in system τ, then there is some language L in $C(\tau)$ such that $X \Vdash A$ does not hold in L. This we prove with reference to the preceding subsection, by showing that if v is a τ-valuation, then it is also an admissible valuation for some language L in $C(\tau)$.

Let $M = \langle K, R \rangle$ be a τ-ms and v a valuation over M. We define

$$\text{Val} = \{v_\alpha : \alpha \in K\},$$

and for each α in K we define a transformation t_α on Val:

$$t_\alpha v_\beta = \begin{cases} v_\alpha & \text{if } \beta R\alpha, \\ v_\beta & \text{otherwise,} \end{cases}$$

and $T = \{t_\alpha : \alpha \in K\}$.

We claim now that $L = \langle \text{Synt, Val}, T, V \rangle$ as defined is a member of $C(\tau)$ and that $V = \text{Val}$, so that every τ-valuation v_α over M is an admissible valuation for L. We establish this claim in four steps.

(1) $V = $ Val. To show this, note that every member of Val satisfies the conditions (a)–(c) on V. Concerning (c) we have to note specifically that $\{v_\beta : \alpha R\beta\} = \{t_\beta v_\alpha : \beta \in K\}$, because $\alpha R\beta$ iff $t_\beta v_\alpha = v_\beta$; in all other cases $t_\beta v_\alpha = v_\alpha$, and $\alpha R\alpha$.

(2) Because $V = $ Val, condition (i) on T is fulfilled; to show that condition (ii) is fulfilled, note that $t_\beta v_\beta = v_\beta$ for all $\beta \in K$.

(3) If R is symmetric, then if $\alpha R\beta$, $t_\alpha t_\beta v_\alpha = t_\alpha v_\beta = v_\alpha$; if not $\alpha R\beta$, then $t_\beta t_\beta v_\alpha = t_\beta v_\alpha = v_\alpha$—therefore condition (iii) is met.

(4) If R is transitive, then condition (iv) is met. For if $\alpha R\beta$ and $\beta R\gamma$, then $t_\gamma t_\beta v_\alpha = v_\gamma$, but then $\alpha R\gamma$, so $t_\gamma v_\alpha = v_\gamma$; and this is the only case for which the condition could fail.

As an example we shall discuss briefly the case of $\tau = b$.

Suppose $M = \langle K, R \rangle$ is a b-ms and α a member of K; let $\{\beta : \alpha R\beta\}$ have the structure

$$V = \text{Val} = \,\{v_\alpha, v_\beta, v_\gamma\}$$
$$T = \{t_\alpha, t_\beta \; t_\gamma\}$$

Then $t_\alpha v_\gamma = v_\alpha$ but $t_\gamma v_\alpha = v_\gamma$, so that $t_\gamma t_\alpha v_\gamma = v_\gamma$; thus the effect of t_α on v_γ can be reversed, and similarly for the effect of other transformations on other valuations. But condition (iv) is not met, for $t_\beta t_\alpha v_\gamma = t_\beta v_\alpha = v_\beta$, but there is no t in T such that $t v_\gamma = v_\beta$ (for $t_\alpha v_\gamma = v_\alpha$; $t_\beta v_\gamma = v_\gamma$; $t_\gamma v_\gamma = v_\gamma$).

We have now shown that the set of arguments validated by system τ is exactly the set of arguments valid in all languages in the class $C(\tau)$, for each index τ.

3. Logic of Presuppositions

The term "presupposition" is sometimes used in the sense of "assumption," sometimes in the sense of "consequence." But there is also a more significant sense, aptly characterized by P. F. Strawson, a sense corresponding to a notion of presupposition that has played an important role in many philosophical discussions. Strawson wrote:

> "Does he care about it?" "He neither cares nor doesn't care; he's dead." The answer shows that the question is inappropriate to the circumstances. . . It does not show that the statement that he cared and the statement that he did not care would both be false; it shows rather that the question of which is true does not arise, because the conditions of its arising are not fulfilled.[7]

Strawson then arrived at the following precise formulation:

> It is self-contradictory to conjoin S with the denial of S' if S' is a necessary condition of the truth, simply, of S. It is a different kind of logical absurdity to conjoin S with the denial of S' if S' is a necessary condition of the *truth or falsity* of S. The relation between S and S' in the first case is that S entails S'. We need a different name for the second case; let us say, as above, that S presupposes S'.

There has been much discussion of the relation of presupposition introduced by Strawson, and much confusion in this discussion. The two major causes of the confusion appear to have been the underdeveloped state of the study of nonbivalent languages, and the fact that natural language provides for more than one kind of negation, at the least exclusion negation and also what we shall call "choice negation" below. (The reader may note that in the second sentence in quotation marks in our first quotation from Strawson, the negations expressed by "neither . . . nor" and "doesn't" cannot both be exclusion negation, if that sentence is to be satisfiable.) We shall now study formal languages that admit of signficant cases of Strawsonian presuppositions.[9]

a. Presupposition and Semantic Entailment

The semantic relation of presupposition may be defined in our terms by

> DEFINITION.   If A and B are sentences of L, then A *presupposes B* in L iff, for every admissible valuation v of L, if $v(A) = T$, then $v(B) = T$ and if $v(A) = F$, then $v(B) = T$.

This may be generalized to sets of sentences, of course, in several ways. The relation of presupposition is most easily studied if L has *choice negation*, that is, if L has for every sentence A some sentence $\sim A$ such that $v(A) = $ T (respectively, F) iff $v(\sim A) = $ F (respectively, T), for every admissible valuation v of L. In that case, A presupposes B iff $A \Vdash B$ and $\sim A \Vdash B$. Hence, in that case, the study of presupposition forms a proper part of the study of the relation of semantic entailment.

It is clear from the above definition that presupposition is a trivial relation if the language is bivalent; for then A presupposes B if and only if B is valid. To make the same point in a different way: If A has a presupposition that fails to be true, then A is neither true nor false. So to have a nontrivial presupposition relation, a language must not be bivalent. But Strawson argued furthermore that, at the same time, natural language has nontrivial presuppositions *and* that arguments in natural language may be appraised by classical logic. So we shall here study how logic is affected when presuppositions are admitted, and accept as a criterion that presuppositions are to be introduced in such a way that any logic that was sound before their introduction remains sound afterward. We shall call the admissible valuations of the old language the *classical valuations*. Then we add a new relation N of sets of sentences to sentences; we call this *nonclassical necessitation*. And then we define the admissible valuations of the new language in such a way that valid arguments in the old language are valid in the new, and if XNA, then the argument from X to A is also valid in the new language.

The definition of presuppositional language that we shall give will be rather broad, in that we shall omit the requirement of choice negation, which would not play any role in our theorems. We need some preliminary definitions. First, let Syn be a syntactic system, V a set of valuations of Syn, N a relation of sets of sentences of Syn to sentences of Syn. Then X is a $(V, $ N$)$-*saturated set of sentences* of Syn iff X is a set of sentences of Syn; some member of V satisfies X; if all members of V that satisfy X also satisfy A, then $A \in X$; and if YNA for some subset Y of X, then $A \in X$.

In the last section of Chapter III we introduced the notion of a supervaluation and showed how to construct from a given language L a new language L^* with the same semantic entailment relation. We shall now generalize this construction to suit our present purposes.

Let us start out with a language $L = \langle \text{Syn}, V \rangle$ and a relation N as above. If X is any set of sentences of Syn, a *V-supervaluation* of Syn *induced by* X is a valuation s of Syn such that:

(a) $s(A) = \text{T}$ iff $v(A) = \text{T}$ for all $v \in V$ that satisfy X;
(b) $s(A) = \text{F}$ iff $v(A) = \text{F}$ for all $v \in V$ that satisfy X;
(c) $s(A)$ is undefined otherwise.

Now we will use the notions of (V, N)-saturation and V-supervaluation to define a new language $L^* = \langle \text{Syn}, V, \text{N}, \text{C}, V^* \rangle$ which is the result of admitting as valid arguments all members of N into the old language L.

> DEFINITION. A presuppositional language L is a quintuple $\langle \text{Syn}, V, \text{N}, \text{C}, V^* \rangle$ such that
> (a) Syn is a syntactic system (the *syntax* of L);
> (b) V is a set of valuations on Syn (the *classical valuations* of L);
> (c) N is a relation of sets of sentences of Syn to sentences of Syn (*nonclassical necessitation*);
> (d) C is the relation of sets of sentences of Syn to sentences of Syn such that $X\text{C}A$ iff all members of V that satisfy X also satisfy A (*classical necessitation*);
> (e) V^* is a set of V-supervaluations of Syn induced by (V, N)-saturated sets of sentences of Syn (the *admissible valuations* of L).

From now on we shall simply say "supervaluation" and "saturated" when the context specifies Syn, V, and N. We also say "$X\text{N}A$ in L" and "$X\text{C}A$ in L" when L is a presuppositional language $\langle \text{Syn}, V, \text{N}, \text{C}, V^* \rangle$.

Theorem. *If L is a presuppositional language, and X classically or nonclassically necessitates A in L, then $X \Vdash A$ in L.*

Proof obvious. We cannot immediately inquire into the converse, because the set V^* is not *defined*, but only restricted, in terms of V and N.

b. Policies on Presupposition

There are, of course, many possible ways to complete the definition of the set of admissible valuations for a presuppositional language. Each such completion—or policy—defines a species of presuppositional languages. We shall here address ourselves to two extreme policies, the radical and the conservative. The former admits as many super-valuations as our restrictions will allow, and the latter very few. More specifically, the radical policy is to allow that a sentence may be neither true nor false for reasons not reflected in V or N, while the conservative policy is to insist that all reasons for truth-value gaps be reflected in V or N.

To be precise, a presuppositional language $L = \langle \text{Syn}, V, \text{N}, \text{C}, V^* \rangle$ is *radical* iff V^* is the set of all V-supervaluations induced by (V, N)-saturated sets of sentences of Syn.

> DEFINITION. If L is a presuppositional language and X a set of sentences of L, then $\text{CNL}(X)$ is the smallest set of sentences Y such that Y contains X, and is closed under C and N (that is, if a subset of Y classically or nonclassically necessitates A, then $A \in Y$).

Theorem. *If L is a radical presuppositional language, then $X \Vdash A$ in L iff $A \in \text{CNL}(X)$.*

Proof: The "if" part follows from the preceding theorem. Second, note that either $\text{CNL}(X)$ is a saturated set, or $\text{CNL}(X)$ is not satisfiable by a classical valuation. In the first case, $\text{CNL}(X)$ induces a supervaluation s such that if $A \notin \text{CNL}(X)$, then s satisfies X but not A; hence $X \Vdash A$ does not hold in this case unless $A \in \text{CNL}(X)$. In the second case, $X \text{C} A$ for every sentence A in L; hence $X \Vdash A$ *and* $A \in \text{CNL}(X)$ for every sentence A in L.

Turning now to the conservative policy, we must first provide it with a precise definition. The policy has at least the assumptions that all presuppositions of a given sentence are reflected in N, and if all these presuppositions are satisfied, the sentence is either true or false. It would seem reasonable therefore to stipulate that a saturated set X induces an admissible supervaluation only if it satisfies the condition if all the presuppositions of A in L belong to X, so does either A or $\sim A$.

This supposes that the language L contains choice negation. That supposition concerns specifically the syntax and classical valuations of L, and we prefer here to be neutral on those features as far as possible.

There is, however, a more serious objection to the course of taking the above condition as defining the conservative policy. When we first introduced this policy, we said that it assumed also that *the reasons for which a sentence can lack a truth value are all reflected in* N *and* V. That the proposed explication does not fulfill this assumption is seen when we ask the question: If a set satisfies the above conditions, how could it fail to be maximal among the saturated sets satisfied by a given valuation v?

Suppose that X satisfies the condition but is not maximal in this sense; that is, suppose that v satisfies a saturated set X' of which X is a proper subset. Let A_1 belong to X' but not to X. Then neither A_1 nor $\sim A_1$ belongs to X. So A_1 must have a presupposition A_2 that does not belong to X. It belongs to X', however, because A_1 does. Now A_2 belongs to X' but not to X; hence A_2 has a presupposition A_3 that does not belong to X. But A_3 belongs to X', because A_2 does . . . ; and so on, and so forth. Thus we obtain an infinite chain $A_1, A_2, \ldots, A_k, \ldots$ such that for each i, A_i is neither true nor false, because it presupposes A_{i+1}, and A_{i+1} is neither true nor false. Could this be because the whole set $(A_1, \ldots, A_k, \ldots)$ has an untrue presupposition B? Certainly not, for then B belongs to X', hence its negation does not belong to X (and so on). The fact that a truth-value gap occurs is never explained in terms of N, but always in terms of N and an additional truth-value gap. If we deny this possibility, we arrive at the conclusion that X must be maximal after all. This gives us the correct definition of the conservative policy.

DEFINITION. A presuppositional language $L = \langle \text{Syn}, V, \text{N}, \text{C}, V^* \rangle$ is *conservative* iff: $s \in V^*$ iff s is a V-supervaluation induced by some (V, N)-saturated set that is maximal among the (V, N)-saturated sets satisfied by a certain $v \in V$.

When we are concerned with maximal elements, the obvious tool to use is Zorn's lemma. But it is hard to see how this could be used unless C and N are *finitary relations*, that is, unless

XCA iff YCA for some finite subset Y of X,

XNA iff YNA for some finite subset Y of X.

Theorem. *If $L = \langle Syn, V, N, C, V^* \rangle$ is a conservative presuppositional language, and C and N are finitary, then $X \Vdash A$ in L iff $A \in CNL(X)$.*

Proof: Again the "if" part follows from a preceding theorem. To prove the "only if" part is somewhat more complicated.

Let us suppose that A does not belong to $CNL(X)$. Since $CNL(X)$ is closed under C, it follows that A is not a classical consequence of $CNL(X)$. Hence there must be a classical valuation v that assigns T to every member of $CNL(X)$, but not to A. We must now show that from this it follows that there is an admissible supervaluation that satisfies $CNL(X)$ but not A.

Well, $CNL(X)$ is a saturated set satisfied by v. Let $\mathscr{F}$ be the family of all saturated sets that contain $CNL(X)$ and are satisfied by v. This family is partially ordered by set inclusion. Consider the chain

$$\cdots \subseteq C_i \subseteq C_{i+1} \subseteq \cdots$$

of elements of $\mathscr{F}$. The union of all the sets C_i is again satisfied by v. This union is closed under C and N because each of the sets C_i is and these are finitary relations. So this union also belongs to the family $\mathscr{F}$: It is an upper bound of that chain in $\mathscr{F}$. The argument being general, we conclude that each chain in $\mathscr{F}$ has an upper bound in $\mathscr{F}$. Therefore, by Zorn's lemma, $\mathscr{F}$ has a maximal element M. This set M must also be maximal among the saturated sets satisfied by v, for any larger such set would contain M, and hence $CNL(X)$, and hence belong again to $\mathscr{F}$. So M induces an admissible supervaluation. This supervaluation satisfies M, and hence $CNL(X)$, but cannot assign T to A: for v does not assign T to A, so A cannot belong to M. Hence if $A \notin CNL(X)$, then $X \Vdash A$ does not hold in L.

c. Epitheoretic Arguments*

As we noted in the first section of Chapter III, Gentzen introduced rules of the form

$$\frac{X_1 \vdash A_1, \ X_2 \vdash A_2, \ \ldots}{X \vdash A}$$

to help catalogue the deductive consequences in a logical system. While the usual rules of deduction, that is, rules of form "X, hence A," remain sound even after we begin to countenance presuppositions, Gentzen rules may not. For example, the Gentzen or natural deduction rule

$$\text{(N)} \quad \frac{A \vdash B \qquad \neg A \vdash B}{\vdash B}$$

is sound in propositional logic. But if we extend this logic by adding

$$A \vdash B$$
$$\neg A \vdash B$$

for those cases in which A presupposes B, rule (N) would allow us to deduce $\vdash B$: All presuppositions would have to be valid. Similarly the rule

$$\text{(I)} \quad \frac{A \vdash B}{\vdash A \supset B}$$

would yield that if A presupposes B, $A \supset B$ and $\neg A \supset B$ are valid. But together with the classically valid statement $(A \supset B) \ \& \ (\neg A \supset B) \cdot \supset B$ and modus ponens, this would mean again that B is valid. So some of the Gentzen rules for classical propositional logic cease to apply when nontrivial presuppositions exist.

Because ordinary arguments remain sound here, and the arguments justified by Gentzen rules do not, Gentzen rules are essentially stronger than ordinary rules. A Gentzen formulation of logic is essentially

* Some of the following originally appeared in my article in K. Lambert (ed.), *The Logical Way of Doing Things* (New Haven: Yale University Press, 1969).

richer than an axiomatic formulation.[10] And this is not at all surprising, since Gentzen rules license arguments *about* ordinary arguments.[11]

It is an interesting question just to what extent the valid arguments about arguments in a language may be destroyed by the countenancing of presuppositions. To answer this question we must first make it precise.

Adapting some terminology introduced by Curry, we call

$$X \Vdash A$$

an *epistatement* with antecedent X and consequent A. This epistatement is *true in L* if and only if the argument from X to A is valid in L. We use E, with or without subscripts, to range over epistatements.

An *epitheoretic argument* is an argument whose premises and conclusion are epistatements. A minimal sense of *validity* for such an argument in a language L would be: Either not all its premises are true in L or its conclusion is true in L, However, the notion of validity is not interesting when we are considering only one interpretation of the premises and conclusion, validity is an interesting notion only in the presence of a certain degree of abstraction. In the present context, it is more relevant to abstract from the content of N. If L and L' are both radical or both conservative languages, we shall call L' a *necessitation extension* of L if and only if L' and L have the same syntax and class of classical valuations, but the relation N′ of nonclassical necessitation of L' contains the corresponding relation N of L.

DEFINITION. The epitheoretic argument

$$\frac{E_1; \ldots; E_k; \ldots}{E}$$

is *valid in* a radical or conservative presuppositional language L if and only if for every necessitation extension L' of L either E is true in L' or not all of $E_1; \ldots; E_k; \ldots$ are true in L'.

We wish now to characterize the set of epistatements $X \Vdash A$ which can be deduced from a set K of epistatements by means of the transitivity of $\Vdash$. It is necessary to take into account the infinitary case; $A \Vdash (x)Fx$ should be considered a consequence of

$$A \Vdash Fx_1; \ldots; A \Vdash Fx_k; \ldots$$

(where $x_1, \ldots, x_k, \ldots$ are all the substituents for x) under the substitution interpretation of the quantifier. (We do limit ourselves to at most countable sets of epistatements, although this makes little difference to our argument.) Hence we define:

> Definition. $\mathrm{CONL}(X, K)$ is the smallest set Y satisfying
> (a) X is contained in Y;
> (b) if for every member A of X_i, $Y \Vdash A$ is true in L and $X_i \Vdash B$ is either true in L or a member of K, then B is in Y.

Note that Y is closed under $\Vdash$, and hence under C and N.

Theorem. *If L is a radical or conservative presuppositional language, and A belongs to $\mathrm{CONL}(X, K)$, then the epitheoretic argument from K to $X \Vdash A$ is valid in L.*

It is clear that if every member of K is true in L', then any admissible valuation for L' that satisfies X will satisfy every member of $\mathrm{CONL}(X)$—for if $Y \Vdash A$ in L, then $Y \Vdash A$ in L'—for every necessitation extension L' of L. This proves the theorem.

Theorem. *If L is a radical presuppositional language, and A does not belong to $\mathrm{CONL}(X, K)$, then the epitheoretic argument from K to $X \Vdash A$ is not valid in L.*

Proof: To show that "K, hence $X \Vdash A$" is not valid in L we must find a necessitation extension L' of L in which every member of K, but not $X \Vdash A$, is true. We construct L' by setting $Y N'B$ if YNB, and also if $Y \Vdash B$ is a member of K. Note that $\mathrm{CONL}'(X, K) = \mathrm{CONL}(X, K)$; the extension of N to N' is chosen so as not to increase the set of sentences semantically entailed by $\mathrm{CONL}(X, K)$. So $\mathrm{CONL}'(X, K)$ is a saturated set of L' not containing A. Thus $X \Vdash A$ is not true in L'; but, clearly, each member of K is true in L'.

Theorem. *If L is a conservative presuppositional language with* C *and* N *finitary, and A does not belong to* CONL(X, K), *then the epitheoretic argument from K to X $\Vdash$ A is not valid in L.*

Proof: In this case we must take care, in our construction of L', to keep N' finitary. We begin with the stipulation that $YN'B$ if YNB, and also if Y is finite and $Y \Vdash B$ belongs to K. If $Y \Vdash B$ belongs to K and Y is not finite, there are two cases to be considered. If Y is included in CONL(X, K) we choose alphabetically the first sentence in Y, say D, and set $\{D\}N'B$ (if Y is empty let D be alphabetically the first valid sentence of L). If Y is not included in CONL(X, K) we choose alphabetically the first sentence of Y that does not belong to CONL(X, K), say D, and set $\{D\}N'B$. Now each member of K is true in L'; yet CONL$'(X, K)$ = CONL(X, K). So now CONL(X, K) is a saturated set of L' not containing A. As in the preceding subsection, it can be extended into a maximal saturated set not containing A. Thus $X \Vdash A$ is not true in L'.

4. Concept of Truth

The notion of truth has been discussed by philosophers throughout the Western tradition; indeed, Aristotle's discussion of the subject is still one of the most important.[12] In the present century, the most widely discussed theory of truth is certainly Tarski's, a theory that led to important results concerning limitations upon expressibility in language.[13] But much of the discussion of truth in this century, including Tarski's, has implicitly or explicitly restricted itself to bivalent languages, and this makes the discussion rather limited in some respects.[14] The purpose of this section is to discuss the notion of truth in any language, bivalent or nonbivalent.

a. Truth and Bivalence

Through the writings of Tarski, and others, the following principle has widely been accepted as correct:

1. [A] is true if and only if A,

where A is any sentence and $[A]$ a name of that sentence. This principle has such seemingly innocuous instances as

1'. "Snow is white" is true if and only if snow is white,

and it has widely been accepted that any adequate theory of truth must have all these instances [the range of A restricted to the object language(s) that the theory concerns] as consequences. This has furthermore in philosophical circles led to the "redundancy theory of truth" according to which "$[A]$ is true" is but a redundant way of rendering the informative content of A.

Now this leads to certain difficulties when we consider nonbivalent languages. Let us symbolize "$[A]$ is true" as $T(A)$. Then the problem is this: Clearly $T(A)$ is true if and only if A is true. But what is the truth value of $T(A)$ if A is not true? If one answers "false," then $T(A)$ is no longer semantically on a par with A in all cases, since A may now be neither true nor false, while $T(A)$ is false. If one answers "the same truth value as A," then $T(A)$ and A remain semantically on a par, but then one's metalanguage is not bivalent either. And we are so used to discussing the structure of languages ourselves in the usual language of ordinary (that is, classical) logic that this may appear as a drawback. That is, if the metalanguage is not bivalent, then it does not seem to be a correct model of the part of natural language that we actually *use* to discuss the object language.

Here it may be countered that it may just not be possible to remain in the secure enclave of the language of ordinary logic. The semantic paradoxes (such as Epimenides's liar paradox) tend to show this. But even if that is correct, we can maintain that we can use that simple language to discuss simple subjects, such as the nonbivalent languages studied in this book, and wish to take advantage of this possibility.[15] A second point is that even if we find it necessary to go to a non-bivalent metalanguage, we can at least try to preserve the soundness of ordinary logic, so that our uncritical reasoning will be valid insofar as that is possible.

The whole discussion so far has been rather abstract, so let us see specifically what happens when principle 1 is applied in a nonclassical context. In Chapter 9 of *De Interpretatione* Aristotle apparently found it necessary to give up bivalence; but he wished to retain *excluded middle*, that is, the principle that any sentence of form (*A or not A*) is valid.[16] The Kneales have questioned his consistency at this point[17] by roughly the following argument:

2. (a) P or (not P)   premise
   (b) P if and only if T(P)   from 1
   (c) T(P) or (not P)   (a), (b) sub. equiv.
   (d) (not P) if and only if T(not P)   from 1
   (e) T(P) or T(not P)   (c), (d) sub. equiv.
   (f) False (P) iff T(not P)   definition
   (g) T(P) or False(P)   (e), (f) sub. equiv.

By "sub. equiv." we mean the operation of substitution of equivalent sentences for equivalent sentences. In the last step this is justified by the equivalence of "It is false that P " as "It is true that (not P)." While this equivalence might or might not always be acceptable, we shall not quibble with it here; certainly Aristotle seemed to accept it in this context.

What conclusion can we draw from this? It is not possible to agree that Aristotle is inconsistent here, since we have studied languages in which excluded middle holds although bivalence fails. So we must conclude that either 1 must be given up, or the meaning of "if and only if" in 1 is not such as to license the substitution of the left-hand side for the right-hand side everywhere. Either way the redundancy theory of truth seems to be in trouble: If T(A) and A are redundantly equivalent, it is hard to see how either 1 or the substitution of T(A) for A could possibly be wrong.

Of course, the rule of sub. equiv. is a rather powerful one, usually proved as a metatheorem rather than assumed. (And it is known that it fails, in its most familiar form, in modal contexts.) But the argument is easily pared down to a much more manageable form:

3. (a) If P , then T(P)   from 1
   (b) If not T(P), then not P (a), contrapos.
   (c) If not P , then T(not P)   from 1
   (d) If not T(P), then T(not P)   (b), (c) transit.

The conclusion (d) seems to amount to bivalence, because a sentence P such that neither $T(P)$ nor $T(\text{not } P)$ is true would seem to be a counter-example to this implication. The choice seems now to be between giving up 1, or saying that the meaning of "if" in 1 is such that even the most familiar reasoning involving implications is not sound.

We propose that the trouble lies in the move from (a) to (b) in 3. For suppose the antecedent is true: P is not true. Then P is either false or neither true nor false. But only if P is false will the consequent (not P), be true. But in that case 3(a) cannot be true unless it does not express or entail the material conditional that it seems to express or entail.

This analysis supposes that we have accepted the definitional equivalence of

$$[P] \text{ is false}$$

and

$$[\text{not } P] \text{ is true,}$$

which seems innocuous enough. But, of course, other approaches are possible.

What can we save from the long-cherished principle 1? Near the beginning of this discussion we said that the important question determining our alternatives was: What truth value will $T(A)$ have if A is not true? We can leave this question *entirely open*, and still accept that the following holds in any adequate theory of truth:

4. $A \Vdash T(A)$ and $T(A) \Vdash A$

[for any sentence A, in a language in which A as well as $T(A)$ appears]. For 4 says only that $T(A)$ is true if and only if A is true. This principle must form the core of a theory of truth with application to non-classical as well as classical logics.

b. Designation of True Sentences

With only principle 4 of the preceding section as an absolute require-ment, there are of course many different ways of constructing languages in which truth may be asserted. In this section we shall consider one kind of construction, which begins with a referential quantifier language,[18] and in the next section we shall consider another kind of construction, which begins with an arbitrary language. In both cases the construction is such that classical logic is sound in the new language; this is achieved through the use of supervaluations.

Let L be a language that has a QCS as syntax. We adopt the following terminology.

DEFINITION. In L, monadic predicate P (*semantically*) *represents truth with respect to* the mapping g of sentences into variables *for valuation v* iff for any sentence A, $v(A) = T$ iff $v(Pg(A)) = T$, and *strongly represents truth with respect to g* iff it represents truth with respect to g for all admissible valuations of L.

Now, when $g(\neg Px) = x$, then we cannot have P representing truth with respect to g and any bivalent valuation v. The simple restriction that $g(A)$ should not occur in A does not remove the difficulty entirely, since we might still have $v(x = y) = T$ and $g(\neg Px) = y$. However, we might then hope that, identities aside, we could satisfy whatever set of sentences we wished to satisfy. [That is, we would then hope to prove, for example, that if L is a referential quantifier language, and X a satisfiable set of sentences in which P does not occur, nor any identity statements in which variables $g(A)$ occur, then X is satisfiable by a valuation for which P represents truth with respect to g.] But this is not very general, nor very interesting.

We shall here consider the problem of constructing a language in which truth is strongly represented in the above sense, and in which the satisfiability of sets of sentences in which the predicate P and the variables in the range of g do not occur is not affected. Because of the paradoxical cases discussed above, such a language cannot be bivalent.

Let L_0 be a referential quantifier language, P a monadic predicate of L_0, and g a mapping of the sentences of L_0 into the variables of L_0. We shall henceforth write $Pg(A)$ as $T(A)$. Let N_0 be the smallest relation such that

$$\{A\}N_0 T(A)$$
$$\{T(A)\}N_0 A$$

(this will be the relation of nonclassical necessitation; see the section on the logic of presuppositions above). We define the language L to be the presuppositional language

$$L = \langle \text{Syn}, V, N_0, C, V^* \rangle$$

where Syn is the syntax of L_0, V the set of admissible valuations of L_0, C the relation of semantic entailment of L_0, and V^* the set of all V-supervaluations of Syn induced by (V, N_0)-saturated sets of sentences of Syn (the radical policy; it is easy to see that the conservative policy would lead to the same results here, since N_0 is finitary).

From our results in Section 3 we know that semantic entailment in L can be characterized exactly in terms of C and N_0. In addition, it is immediate that P strongly represents truth with respect to g in L. Because of the paradoxical cases that may occur due to the nature of g, however, one might still doubt the usefulness of L for any purpose but that for which we explicitly designed it. It is hoped that the adequacy proof in Appendix III will lay these doubts to rest.

c. Truth Assertions in General

When discussing the structure of a given language L we normally do not assume that L is bivalent, nor that L has the familiar structure that L_0 was assumed to have in the preceding section. We do tend to assume, on the other hand, that our own assertions of truth in L are bivalent, and combined into complex assertions in the familiar way studied in classical logic. We shall now construct a language L^* that plays a role vis-à-vis L that satisfies these assumptions.[19] The atomic sentences of L^* will be exactly the sentences of L. We introduce the unary connectors T and $\sim$, and the binary connector & (not expressions of L): $T(A)$ is to mean that A is true, $\sim A$ that A is false, $A \,\&\, B$ that A is true and B is true. There is no doubt again more than one way to implement these stipulations, but the way we choose has some interesting connections with modal logic.

The syntax of L^* is the triple $\langle \mathscr{A}, S, W \rangle$, where $\mathscr{A}$ is the set of sentences of L, S the set $\{T, \neg, \&\}$, and W the least set containing $\mathscr{A}$

such that if A and B are in W, so are $T(A)$, $\sim(A)$, $(A \,\&\, B)$. A *model* for L^* is any admissible valuation for L. An *assignment* d over a model M is a bivalent valuation of $\mathscr{A}$ such that

$$d(A) = \text{T} \quad \text{if } M(A) = \text{T},$$
$$d(A) = \text{F} \quad \text{if } M(A) = \text{F}, \qquad \text{for all } A \in \mathscr{A}.$$

We define the truth value of a sentence A in a model M relative to an assignment d over M, $|A[d]|^M$, as follows (suppressing the superscript M when only one model is referred to in the context):

(a) $|A[d]| \in \{\text{T, F}\}$ for all A in W.
(b) $|A[d]| = d(A)$ if $d(A)$ is defined.
(c) $|\sim A[d]| = \text{T}$ iff $|A[d]| = \text{F}$.
(d) $|(A \,\&\, B)[d]| = \text{T}$ iff $|A[d]| = |B[d]| = \text{T}$.
(e) $|\text{T}(A)[d]|^M = \text{T}$ iff $|A[d']|^M = \text{T}$ for every assignment d' over M.

The value of a sentence A in M, $|A|^M$ is defined to be T(F) if $|A[d]|^M = \text{T(F)}$ for all assignments d over M, and is undefined otherwise. An admissible valuation for L^* is any function v defined only on sentences of L^* for which there is a model M for L^* such that

$$v(A) = |A|^M \qquad \text{for all } A \text{ in } W$$

(where we momentarily regard $t = t'$ as true when neither exists). We note that $|T(A)|^M = \text{T}$ iff $|A|^M = \text{T}$ for any sentence A. Therefore, if we define

$$\text{T}(X) = \{\text{T}(A) : A \in X\},$$

we deduce immediately that $T(X)$ is satisfiable iff X is satisfiable, and $X \Vdash A$ iff $T(X) \Vdash T(A)$, in L^*. Also, any sentence $T(A)$ has a truth value—T or F—in every model for L^*. It is now easy to show that the following logical system LT pertaining to the syntax of L^* is sound for L^*.

$LT: X \vdash A$ in LT iff $T(X) \vdash T(A)$ in S_5 with T as necessity symbol (we mean simply that in S_5 in the usual formulation the necessity sign is the box $\square$, and we wish to consider it formulated with T instead of $\square$ as necessity sign).

What is LT like? Well, in S_5 we have $\vdash\square(\square A \supset A)$, so in LT we have

1. $\vdash T(A) \supset A$.

However, $\square(A \supset \square A)$ is not a theorem of S_5, so that $A \supset T(A)$ is not a theorem of LT. However, $\square A \vdash \square\square A$ in S_5, so we have in LT

2. $A \vdash T(A)$

and, of course,

3. $\vdash T(A) \supset TT(A)$.

Also, $\vdash\square(\sim\square A \supset \square(\sim\square A))$ in S_5, so in LT

4. $\vdash \sim T(A) \supset T(\sim T(A))$.

Finally, we have

5. $\vdash T(A \supset B) \supset \cdot T(A) \supset T(B)$,

6. If $\vdash A$, then $\vdash T(A)$,

as well as ordinary propositional logic and modus ponens. We do not have that if $A \vdash B$, then $\vdash A \supset B$, but only if $A \vdash B$, then $\vdash T(A) \supset T(B)$, and if $T(A) \vdash T(B)$, then $\vdash T(A) \supset T(B)$.

We now want to prove a kind of completeness theorem: We want to show that if A cannot be deduced from X in LT, then there is a language L (whose sentences form the set $\mathscr{A}$) such that $X \Vdash A$ does not hold in L^*. First a definition and a lemma.

DEFINITION. $X \vdash^1 A$ iff $X \vdash A$ in S_5 with T as necessity sign.

Lemma 1. *If $X \vdash^1 A$, then $X \vdash A$ in LT.*
This has as corollary that $\vdash^1 A$ iff $\vdash A$ in LT, but this will already have been clear from 1 and 6 above. We shan't prove the lemma, which is quite straightforward.

Keeping in mind that we wish to show completeness for the case of L arbitrary, we shall call M a *general model* of L^* if M is any mapping of a subset of $\mathscr{A}$ into $\{T, F\}$. We shall call a set X consistent iff not $X \vdash A$ for some sentence A (for example, $B \,\&\, \sim B$), and say that X is *1-consistent* iff not $X \vdash^1 A$ for some sentence A. Now we have $X \Vdash A$ in L^* iff $X \cup \{\sim T(A)\}$ is not satisfiable in L^*, so the following theorem suffices to show soundness and strong completeness.

Theorem. *A set of sentences X is satisfiable by a general model of L^* iff X is consistent in LT.*

Proof: We have already commented on the soundness ("only if" part) of this theorem. Now suppose that X is consistent in LT. Then by the definition of $\vdash$ in LT, $T(X)$ is 1-consistent. So $T(X)$ can be extended into a maximal 1-consistent set Y, by Zorn's lemma and the fact that deducibility is a finitary relation in S_5. But then Y is satisfiable by a valuation v over a general model M of L^* (Lemma 2). So M satisfies the sentences in Y that have the form $T(A)$; and this includes $T(X)$. But then M satisfies X.

Lemma 2. *If Y is a maximal 1-consistent set of sentences of L^*, then Y is satisfied by a valuation v over a general model M of L^*.*

Proof: Define M to be the mapping $M(A) = T$(respectively, F) iff $A \in \mathscr{A}$ and $T(A) \in Y$(respectively, $T(\sim A) \in Y$). Define a relation **R** among the maximal 1-consistent sets Z of sentences of L^* by

$$Z \mathbf{R} Z' \quad \text{iff} \{B : T(B) \in Z\} \subseteq Z'$$

and define v_Z to be the bivalent valuation on W mapping exactly the members of Z into T. Then it is easily proved (by strong induction; see similar proofs in Section 2a) that v is a valuation over M iff $v = v_Z$ for some Z such that $Y \mathbf{R} Z$. Thus v_Y is the valuation over M that we were looking for.

   In conclusion I wish to point out that we can define connectives in L^* that correspond to familiar matrix operations. This is due to the bivalence of truth assertions in L^*. Thus if we write $-A$ for $\sim T(A)$, we find that we have exclusion negation: $-A$ is false when A is true, and true otherwise. Similarly, if "$(A \cdot B)$" is short for $(T(A) \& T(B))$, then $A \cdot B$ is true exactly when A and B are both true, and false otherwise. These connectives correspond to the operations of the matrix M_3^{**} studied in Section 5 of Chapter III. The operations of the matrix M_3 studied there may be similarly represented.

NOTES

1. For the logic of tautological entailment, see A. R. Anderson and N. D. Belnap, Jr., "Tautological Entailments," *Philosophical Studies*, *13* (1962), pp. 9–24, and B. C. van Fraassen, "Facts and Tautological Entailments," *Journal of Philosophy*, *66* (1969), pp. 477–487.

2. There have been few attempts to apply invariance theory in logic or formal semantics; see R. Carnap, *Logical Foundations of Probability* (Chicago: University of Chicago Press, 1950), p. 109.

3. Cf. E. W. Beth, *The Foundations of Mathematics* (Amsterdam, North-Holland, 1965), sec. 85, pp. 250–251.

4. S. Kripke, "Semantical Analyses of Modal Logic I: Normal Propositional Calculi," *Zeitschrift für mathematische Logik und Grundlagen der Mathematik*, *9* (1963), pp. 67–96; and R. H. Thomason, "Some Completeness Results for Modal Predicate Calculi" (in press). See also G. E. Hughes and M. J. Cresswell, *An Introduction to Modal Logic* (London: Methuen, 1968).

5. See B. van Fraassen, "Compactness and Löwenheim–Skolem Proofs in Modal Logic," *Logique et Analyse*, *12* (1969), pp. 167–178.

6. See B. van Fraassen, "Meaning Relations and Modalities," *Nous*, *3* (1969), pp. 155–167, and K. Lambert and B. van Fraassen, "Meaning Relations, Possible Objects, and Possible Worlds" in K. Lambert, ed., *Philosophical Problems in Logic* (Dordrecht, Holland: Reidel, 1970), pp. 1–20.

7. P. F. Strawson, *Introduction to Logical Theory* (London: Methuen, 1952), p. 18.

8. *Ibid.*, p. 175.

9. This subject was developed in B. van Fraassen, "Presupposition, Implication, and Self-reference," *Journal of Philosophy*, *65* (1968), pp.

136–152, and "Presuppositions, Supervaluations, and Free Logic" in K. Lambert, ed., *The Logical Way of Doing Things* (New Haven: Yale University Press, 1969), pp. 67–91.

10. For an exposition of the development of logical systems (logic of pure implication, absolute logic, minimal logic, logic of strict negation, intuitionistic logic, and classical logic) by means of Gentzen rules, see J. Dopp, *Logiques construites par une méthode de déduction naturelle* (Louvain: Editions Nauwelaerts, 1962), and H. Curry, *Foundations of Mathematical Logic* (New York: McGraw-Hill, 1963).

11. *A note on natural deduction.* Many logic texts use neither the axiomatic nor the Gentzen method, but the method of *subproofs* (often called "natural deduction," although that term is sometimes used to include Gentzen methods). Examples are I. Copi, *Symbolic Logic* (New York: Macmillan, 1954); F. Fitch, *Symbolic Logic—An Introduction* (New York: Ronald Press, 1952); and D. Kalish and R. Montague, *Logic— Techniques of Formal Reasoning* (New York: Harcourt, Brace & World, 1964). The method is described systematically in F. Fitch and R. Orgass, *Minimal Logic and Computers—I. The Method of Subordinate Proofs* (IBM Research Report RC 2503, 1969). First some rules are given which can be stated in the form "From $A_1, \ldots, A_n$, infer B." A first-order proof from premises X is a sequence of sentences each of which either belongs to X or follows from preceding members of the sequence by the given rules. Subject to certain restrictions, which constitute further rules, a sequence of sentences and first-order proofs is a second-order proof, a sequence of sentences and first- or second-order proofs is a third-order proof, and so on. It is clear that in the higher-order proofs one is utilizing arguments about arguments, just as in the Gentzen method. Thus the rules describing higher-order proofs are vulnerable when presuppositions are introduced in just the same sense as the Gentzen rules. For informative discussions concerning the relations among the various methods, see H. Curry, *Foundations of Mathematical Logic*, chap. 5, secs. B and E8; chap. 6, sec. C 1–3.

12. Aristotle, *Metaphysics*, Book IV: chap. 7 (1011b, 25–30), and Book IX: chap. 10 (1051b, 5–1952a, 4).

13. A. Tarski, "The Concept of Truth in Formalized Languages," in his *Logic, Semantics, Metamathematics*, J. H. Woodger, trans. (Oxford: Clarendon, 1956), pp. 152–278.

14. For a good selection of papers, see C. Pitcher, *Truth* (Englewood Cliffs, N.J.: Prentice-Hall, 1964).

15. If 1 (or its instances) can be expressed in the language, the nonbivalent sentences *A* must occur in the language. But the part of the language in which the shortest sentences all begin with T could be kept ordinary; this part of the metalanguage is what we are discussing here.

16. Aristotle, *On Interpretation*, chap. 9 (18a, 30–19b, 4).

17. W. and M. Kneale, *The Development of Logic* (Oxford: Oxford University Press, 1962), pp. 46–48.

18. Cf. B. van Fraassen, "Truth and Paradoxical Consequences" in R. Martin, ed., *The Liar* (New Haven: Yale University Press, in press).

19. This construction was first described in B. van Fraassen, "A propos Kaplan's *R*," mimeographed, Indiana University, 1968. The constructed system bears some relation to those of B. Skyrms, "Return of the Liar: Three-Valued Logic and the Concept of Truth," mimeographed, University of Illinois at Chicago Circle, 1968; and S. McCall, "Notes Toward a Non-classical Theory of Truth," mimeographed, University of Pittsburgh, 1968. The first mentioned paper was a reaction to mimeographed notes of D. Kaplan (University of California at Los Angeles, 1968).

APPENDIX I

COMPLETENESS OF THE CALCULUS OF SYSTEMS

In Section 6 of Chapter II we gave a set of principles (a)–(g) that may be taken as a set of axioms for a general calculus of systems. We noted there that these were essentially the axioms of the theory of lattices. We shall here use some results from that theory to show that no further principle expressible in those terms (such as distributivity or modularity) holds in general for systems in languages of arbitrary structure.

If L is a language, let us denote by $\underline{\text{SYST}}(L)$ the set of systems in L. Then the study of the relations among systems of L, using the notions we have so far introduced, is the study of the mathematical structure $\langle \underline{\text{SYST}}(L), \cap, \dot\cup, \subseteq \rangle$, which we shall call the *calculus of systems in L*-CS(L). To see what kind of structure this is we formally introduce the notion of a *lattice*.

DEFINITION. A *lattice* is a quadruple $\langle X, \wedge, \vee, \leq \rangle$ such that X is a nonempty set, $\wedge$ and $\vee$ binary operations on X, and $\leq$ a partial ordering of X, such that

(a) $a \wedge b \leq a; a \wedge b \leq b$;
(b) $a \leq a \vee b; b \leq a \vee b$;
(c) if $c \leq a$ and $c \leq b$, then $c \leq a \wedge b$;
(d) if $a \leq c$ and $b \leq c$, then $a \vee b \leq c$

for all elements a, b, c of X.

175

We call $a \wedge b$ the *greatest lower bound* (glb) or *meet* of a and b, $a \vee b$ their *lowest upper bound* (lub) or *join*. It is easy to check that $\mathrm{CS}(L)$ is a lattice, with $\cap$ as meet, $\dot{\cup}$ as join, and $\subseteq$ as partial ordering.

There are interesting kinds of lattices, the most familiar being the distributive lattices (for example, classical propositional logic, Boolean algebra, the lattice of subsets of a given set). A calculus of systems is a distributive lattice iff the following laws hold (for all systems X, Y, Z, in the language in question):

(e) $X \cap (Y \dot{\cup} Z) \subseteq (X \cap Y) \dot{\cup} (X \cap Z)$

(f) $(X \dot{\cup} Y) \cap (X \dot{\cup} Z) \subseteq X \dot{\cup} (Y \cap Z)$

But this is not always the case. For example, let L have only the sentences $p, q, p \to q$; and let its admissible valuations be the bivalent valuations v on these sentences such that if $v(p) = v(p \to q) = \mathrm{T}$, then $v(q) = \mathrm{T}$. We clearly have

$$\{p\}, \{q\}, \quad \text{and} \quad \{p \to q\} \text{ are systems,}$$

$$\{q\} \cap (\{p\} \dot{\cup} \{p \to q\}) = \{q\} \cap \{p, p \to q, q\}$$

$$= \{q\},$$

$$(\{q\} \cap \{p\}) \dot{\cup} (\{q\} \cap \{p \to q\}) = \Lambda \dot{\cup} \Lambda = \Lambda.$$

Since $\{q\} \neq \Lambda$, law (e) does not hold for the systems $X = \{q\}$, $Y = \{p\}$, and $Z = \{p \to q\}$. However, we must point out that if we take $p, q, p \to q$ to belong to a bivalent propositional language L', with $p \to q$ defined as $\neg(p \,\&\, \neg q)$, then the law does not fail in this way. For then we must set

$$X = \{A : q \Vdash A\} \neq \{q\},$$

$$Y = \{A : p \Vdash A\} \neq \{p\},$$

$$Z = \{A : p \to q \Vdash A\} \neq \{p \to q\}$$

and, furthermore,

$$p \vee q \in X \cap Y,$$

$$(p \to q) \vee q \in X \cap Z,$$

so

$$p \vee q, (p \to q) \vee q \in (X \cap Y) \dot{\cup} (X \cap Z),$$

but then $q \in (X \cap Y) \mathbin{\dot{\cup}} (X \cap Z)$. There is, in fact, a proof that $CS(L)$ is a distributive lattice when L is a bivalent propositional language.[1] But we are here concerned with the general case.

We shall now prove that the laws that hold in any calculus of systems are exactly those that make it a lattice, and no others. First we must make this precise. We shall use the notation $\varphi(X_1, \ldots, X_n)$ to refer to a sentence made up of variables $X_1, \ldots, X_n$ and the symbols, $\wedge, \vee, \leq$. We say that $\varphi(X_1, \ldots, X_n)$ *holds in* a lattice iff it is true for all values of the variables $X_1, \ldots, X_n$ in that lattice, where $\wedge, \vee, \leq$ are interpreted as standing for the meet, join, and partial ordering of that lattice. We shall also need a lemma from lattice theory that we shall not prove.[2]

Lemma. *There exists a denumerable* free *lattice, that is, a denumerable lattice* **A** *such that any sentence* $\varphi(X_1, X_2, \ldots)$ *holds in* **A** *if and only if it holds in all lattices.*

Theorem. *A sentence* $\varphi(X_1, \ldots, X_n)$ *holds in every calculus of systems if and only if it holds in all lattices.*

Proof: Let $\mathbf{A} = \langle W, \wedge, \vee, \leq \rangle$ be a denumerable free lattice, and L the language whose sentences are the elements of W, and whose admissible valuations are the mappings of W into $\{T, F\}$ such that

1. if $v(b) = T$ and $a \leq b$, then $v(a) = T$;
2. if $v(a) = v(b) = T$, then $v(a \vee b) = T$

for all elements a, b of W.

We shall concentrate on those systems in L that are axiomatizable by means of a single sentence. For brevity, we define

$$[a] = \{b : a \Vdash b \text{ in } L\},$$
$$[W] = \{[a] : a \in W\}.$$

The structure $\mathbf{A}^* = \langle [W], \cap, \mathbin{\dot{\cup}}, \subseteq \rangle$ is a lattice of systems in L, and we assert that $\mathbf{A}^*$ is isomorphic to $\mathbf{A}$, by the mapping f of W into $[W]$ such that $f(a) = [a]$.

To prove this, we note first that $[a] = \{b:b \leq a\}$. By 1, if $b \leq a$, then $b \in [a]$. Second, the valuation $v:v(b) = \text{T}$ iff $b \leq a$, $v(b) = \text{F}$ otherwise, is an admissible valuation (if $c \leq b$, $b \leq a$, then $c \leq a$, so 1 holds; if $c \leq a$, $b \leq a$, then $c \vee b \leq a$, so 2 holds). We may also note about any system that it contains the join of any two of its elements, because of 2. We can now prove the isomorphism in four steps.

(a) If $[a] = [b]$, then $a = b$, because if $a \leq b$ and $b \leq a$, then $a = b$.

(b) $a \leq b$ iff $[a] \leq [b]$, by our first observation above.

(c) $[a \wedge b] = \{x:x \leq a \wedge b\} = \{x:x \leq a \text{ and } x \leq b\} = \{x:x \leq a\} \cap \{x:x \leq b\} = [a] \cap [b]$.

(d) $[a \vee b] = [a] \,\dot\cup\, [b]$. By definition, $[a] \,\dot\cup\, [b]$ is the smallest system including both $[a]$ and $[b]$. If a system contains both a and b, it contains $a \vee b$, and hence includes $[a \vee b]$. On the other hand, $a \leq a \vee b$ and $b \leq a \vee b$, hence $[a \vee b]$ contains both a and b, and so includes both $[a]$ and $[b]$.

Because of this isomorphism, a lattice theoretic sentence $\varphi(X_1, \ldots, X_n)$ will hold in $\mathbf{A}^*$ iff it holds in $\mathbf{A}$. But $\mathbf{A}$ is free, so this is equivalent to $\varphi(X_1, \ldots, X_n)$ holding in all lattices. On the other hand, $\mathbf{A}^*$ is part of $\text{CS}(L)$, so if $\varphi(X_1, \ldots, X_n)$ does not hold in $\mathbf{A}^*$, then it does not hold in $\text{CS}(L)$. We conclude that if φ does not hold in all lattices, then it does not hold in $\text{CS}(L)$, and so the general calculus of systems is complete.

NOTES

1. E. W. Beth, *The Foundations of Mathematics* (Amsterdam: North-Holland, 1965), p. 548.
2. See C. Birkhoff, *Lattice Theory*, rev. ed. (New York: American Mathematical Society, 1948), pp. viii, 29.

APPENDIX II

TOPOLOGICAL MATRICES

When the elements of a matrix are taken to be the points in a topological space, we call the matrix a topological matrix. This extension of the theory of matrices will enable us to prove a general compactness result of which the compactness theorem of Section 1b of Chapter V is a corollary.[1] It will be necessary to introduce some notions and results from point-set topology.[2]

DEFINITION. A *topological space* is a couple $\langle E, \mathcal{O} \rangle$, where E is a nonempty set (the *points* or *elements*) and $\mathcal{O}$ a family of subsets of E (the *open sets*) such that

(a) $\Lambda \in \mathcal{O}$, $E \in \mathcal{O}$;

(b) if $O_1, O_2 \in \mathcal{O}$, then $O_1 \cap O_2 \in \mathcal{O}$;

(c) If $\mathcal{O}' \subseteq \mathcal{O}$, then $\bigcup \mathcal{O}' \in \mathcal{O}$.

When $\langle E, \mathcal{O} \rangle$ is a topological space, we also say that $\mathcal{O}$ is a *topology on E*. The relative complement in E of a member of $\mathcal{O}$ is called a *closed* set in this space.

The notion of compactness for a topological space, when defined in terms of open sets, resembles that of U-compactness for a valuation space.

DEFINITION. A topological space $\langle E, \mathcal{O} \rangle$ is *compact* iff every family $\mathcal{O}' \subseteq \mathcal{O}$ such that $\bigcup \mathcal{O}' = E$ (an *open cover*) has a finite subfamily $\mathcal{O}''$ such that $\bigcup \mathcal{O}'' = E$ (a finite *subcover*).

Two new topics must be covered before we can turn to topological matrices proper: Cartesian products of spaces, and continuous functions.

We begin by generalizing products of sets as follows: Where I is the set of the first n natural numbers, or the set of all natural numbers, $\prod(\{Y_i\}, i \in I)$ is the set of sequences whose ith member is an element of Y_i, $i \in I$. For example, $\prod(\{X_i\}, i \in \{1, 2\})$ is the Cartesian product of X_1 with X_2, and hence X^2 when $X_1 = X_2 = X$. When all the X_i are the same, and I is the set of *all* natural numbers, we designate $\prod(\{X_i\}, i \in I)$ as X^ω (X to the power omega). More generally we shall write X^I for $\prod(\{X_i\}, i \in I)$ when $X = X_i$ for each i in I.

We shall now use topologies on given sets to produce a topology on their products.

> DEFINITION. When the families $\{\mathcal{O}_i\}$, $i \in I$ are topologies on the sets $\{E_i\}$, $i \in I$, then the corresponding *product* topology on $\prod(\{E_i\}, i \in I)$ is the family of products $\prod^*(\{O_i\}, i \in I) = \{\prod(\{Q_i\}, i \in I): Q_i \in \mathcal{O}_i$ for each $i \in I$, and $Q_i = E_i$ for all but finitely many indices $i\}$.

That $\prod^*(\{\mathcal{O}_i\}, i \in I)$ is indeed a topology on $\prod(\{E_i\}, i \in I)$ may readily be checked.[3] When all the sets E_i equal E, and all the sets $\mathcal{O}_i$ equal $\mathcal{O}$, then the resulting topological space is designated as $\langle E, \mathcal{O} \rangle^I = \langle E^I, \mathcal{O}_I \rangle$, where $\mathcal{O}_I$ is the product topology in question.

The following theorem is a special case of a famous result known as Tychonoff's theorem, its proof may be found in any text.

Theorem. *If a topological space is compact, then all its Cartesian powers are compact.*

We turn now to continuous functions.

When f maps E into E', we shall also say that it maps any space $\langle E, \mathcal{O} \rangle$ into any space $\langle E', \mathcal{O}' \rangle$. And then we call f *continuous* if, whenever $O \subseteq E'$ is an open set, its *inverse image* $f^{-1}(O) = \{x \in E: f(x) \in O\}$ is again an open set. We call f an *n-ary operation* on E if it maps E^n into E, and a continuous *n-ary operation on* $\langle E, \mathcal{O} \rangle$ if it maps $\langle E, \mathcal{O} \rangle^I$ continuously into $\langle E, \mathcal{O} \rangle$, where $I = \{i, \ldots, n\}$. It can readily be checked that for a continuous mapping, the inverse images of closed sets are again closed.

The theory of continuous mappings is an interesting subject, from which we shall need several lemmas.

Lemma 1. *If f is a continuous n-ary operation on $\langle E, \mathcal{O} \rangle$ then $f^*: f^*(d) = f(\langle d(1), \ldots, d(n) \rangle)$ defined for all d in E^I, where $\{1, \ldots, n\} \subseteq I \subseteq \omega$, is a continuous mapping from $\langle E, \mathcal{O} \rangle^I$ into $\langle E, \mathcal{O} \rangle$.*

Proof: Suppose that O is an open set on E. Then if f is continuous, $f^{-1}(O)$ is an open set on E^n, hence is a product $\prod (\{O_i\}, i \in 1, 2, \ldots, n\})$ of open sets on E. But the inverse image of O under f^* is just $f^{-1}(O) \times E \times E \times \cdots$, and so an open set on E^I.

Lemma 2. *If g is a continuous mapping of $\langle E_1, \mathcal{O}_1 \rangle$ into $\langle E_2, \mathcal{O}_2 \rangle$, and f a continuous mapping of $\langle E_2, \mathcal{O}_2 \rangle$ into $\langle E_3, \mathcal{O}_3 \rangle$, then the composite function fg is a continuous mapping of $\langle E_1, \mathcal{O}_3 \rangle$ into $\langle E_3, \mathcal{O}_3 \rangle$.*

Proof: The function fg is defined by $fg(x) = f(g(x))$, so that function is the set of couples

$$\{\langle x, y \rangle : x \in E_1, Y \in E_3, \text{ and there is a } z \in E_2 \text{ such that } g(x) = z,$$
$$f(z) = y\}.$$

It can then readily be seen that $fg^{-1}(O) = g^{-1}(f^{-1}(O))$. So if O is open, then $f^{-1}(O)$ is open and then $g^{-1}(f^{-1}(O))$ is open, provided f and g are continuous.

Lemma 3. *If g_1 and g_2 are continuous mappings of spaces S_1 and S_2 into S, and f is a continuous mapping of S^2 into S, then the composite function $h(x, y) = f(\langle g_1(x), g_2(y) \rangle)$ is a continuous mapping of the product of S_1 and S_2 into S.*

Proof: This can be reduced to the previous lemma if we can prove it for the case

$$h'(x, y) = \langle g_1(x), g_2(y) \rangle$$

because then $h(x, y) = fh'(x, y)$. To prove the case for h' is straightforward: If O is open in S, then its inverse image under h' is just the product of $g_1^{-1}(O)$ with $g_2^{-1}(O)$. If the functions g_1 and g_2 are continuous, the components of that product are open, and hence so is the product itself.

Now, at long last, we can return to topological matrices. Again we consider matrices with only two operations.

DEFINITION. A *topological matrix* is a quintuple $M = \langle E, \mathcal{O}, D, \cdot, - \rangle$, where $\langle E, D, \cdot, - \rangle$ is a matrix and $\mathcal{O}$ a topology on E.

We shall now study the class of topological matrices $\langle E, \mathcal{O}, D, \cdot, - \rangle$ with continuous operations $\cdot$ and $-$. We shall use the terms "M-assignment," "M-propositional language," and so on, as before. If L is an M-propositional language, where $M = \langle E, \mathcal{O}, D, \cdot, - \rangle$, and $\mathscr{A}$ its set of atomic sentences, there is a one-to-one correspondence between E^ω and the set of M-assignments—the natural correspondence of the restriction of each M-assignment to atomic sentences (for what the M-assignment assigns to the atomic sentences determines it uniquely).

In addition, because of Lemmas 2 and 3, there will be for each sentence A a continuous n-ary operation a on E, where A contains alphabetically the nth but no later atomic sentences, such that

$$d(A) = a(d(p_1), \ldots, d(p_n)).$$

By Lemma 1, a can be extended into a continuous operation a^* on E, so that

$$d(A) = a^*(d),$$

where M-assignments are now identified with elements of E^ω in the natural manner described above.

Henceforth we shall call $\mathrm{T}(A) = \{d \in E^\omega : d(A) \in D\}$ the *truth sets* for the M-propositional language.

Lemma 4. *If L is an M-propositional language with set of atomic sentences $\mathscr{A}$ and $M = \langle E, \mathcal{O}, D, \cdot, - \rangle$ such that $\cdot$ and $-$ are continuous operations on $\langle E, \mathcal{O} \rangle$, then*
(a) if D is open in $\langle E, \mathcal{O} \rangle$, the truth sets are open in $\langle E, \mathcal{O} \rangle^\omega$;
(b) if D is closed in $\langle E, \mathcal{O} \rangle$, the truth sets are closed in $\langle E, \mathcal{O} \rangle^\omega$.

Proof: *The truth sets*

$$T(A) = \{d \in E^\omega : d(A) \in D\}$$
$$= \{d \in E^\omega : a^*(d) \in D\}$$

are the inverse images of D under the continuous functions a^*. Hence if D is open, the truth sets are open, and if D is closed, the truth sets are closed.

Theorem. *If L is an M-propositional language, where $M = \langle E, \mathcal{O}, D, \cdot, - \rangle$ such that*
(a) $\langle E, \mathcal{O} \rangle$ is compact,
(b) $\cdot, -$ are continuous operations on $E, \mathcal{O}$,
then L is U-compact if D is open, I-compact if D is closed, and has finitary entailment if D is both open and closed.

Proof: Let $\mathscr{A}$ be the set of atomic sentences and assume the conditions of the theorem. By Tychonoff's theorem $\langle E, \mathcal{O} \rangle^\omega$ is compact.

(a) Let D be open. Then, by Lemma 4, the truth sets are open in $\langle E, \mathcal{O} \rangle^\omega$. If X is a set of sentences such that each admissible valuation satisfies a member of X, then

$$\bigcup_{A \in X} T(A) = E^\omega.$$

By the compactness of $\langle E, \mathcal{O} \rangle^\omega$, this cover contains a finite subcover; hence X has a finite unassailable subset.

(b) Suppose D is closed. Then the truth sets are closed. It follows that any finite intersection of truth sets is closed. Suppose that for each finite subset Y of X, $T(Y) = \bigcap_{A \in Y} T(A)$ is nonempty. Then the sets $E^\omega - T(Y)$ are open sets not equal to E, and correspond to the finite unions of complements of truth sets of members of X. By compactness we conclude that the union $\bigcup \{E^{\omega} - T(A) : A \in X\}$ does not cover E; hence the intersection $T(X)$ is not empty.

(c) Suppose D is both open and closed. Then, by Lemma 4, the truth sets are both open and closed. Then if $X \Vdash A$,

$$\bigcap \{T(B) : B \in X\} \subseteq T(A);$$
$$\bigcap \{T(B) : B \in X\} \cap (E^{\omega} - T(A)) = \Lambda.$$

But $T(A)$ is open, so $(E^{\omega} - T(A))$ is closed, and we have here an infinite intersection of closed sets that is empty. By compactness and (b) above, this has a finite subintersection that is empty, so X has a finite subset Y such that

$$\bigcap \{T(B) : B \in Y\} \cap (E^{\omega} - T(A)) = \Lambda;$$

that is, $Y \Vdash A$.

The compactness result of Section 1b of Chapter V is a corollary to this. For a topology on a finite set of elements must itself be finite, so that compactness holds automatically. Second, we can choose this topology on the set of elements to be simply the family of all its subsets, so that each subset is both open and closed.

NOTES

1. Cf. C. C. Chang and H. J. Keisler, *Continuous Model Theory* (Princeton, N.J.: Princeton University Press, 1966) for a more general development of this subject.
2. See, e.g., S. A. Gaal, *Point Set Topology* (New York: Academic Press, 1964).
3. Cf. Gaal, *Point Set Topology*, p. 59, lemma 2.

APPENDIX III

SATISFIABILITY AND SEMANTIC PARADOXES

In Section 4b of Chapter V we constructed a language L from a language L_0 in which for every sentence A there is a name $g(A)$ and predicate P such that A and $Pg(A)$ semantically entail each other in L. The mapping g of sentences into names has no restrictions placed on it, so paradoxical cases may result. We shall now prove that these paradoxes do not infect the rest of the language; that is, if a set of sentences does not involve the predicate P or the names $g(A)$, and it is ordinarily satisfiable, then it is satisfiable in L.

To prove this result, we shall need a famous theorem concerning quantificational logic which we have not proved.[1]

Craig's Lemma. *Let $\vdash A \supset B$ in quantificational logic. Then if some predicates occur in both A and B, there is a sentence C such that $\vdash A \supset C$ and $\vdash C \supset B$, and any predicate or free variable in C is a predicate or free variable both in A and in B. If no predicates occur in both A and B, then either $\vdash \neg A$ or $\vdash B$.*

Corollary. *If X is a set of sentences and A a sentence of L_0, and X is satisfiable in L_0, then $X \Vdash A$ in L_0 if and only if there is a sentence B of L_0 such that all the predicates and free variables in B are predicates and free variables in X and in A and $X \Vdash B$, $B \Vdash A$ in L_0; or $\Vdash A$ in L_0.*

This corollary follows immediately from Craig's lemma by the compactness, soundness, and completeness theorems for quantificational logic.

Let SY be the set of sentences of L in which the predicate P and the variables $g(A)$, A a sentence, do not appear, and let L, L_0 be as in Section 4b of Chapter V.

Theorem. *If X is a subset of SY and satisfiable in L_0, then X is satisfiable in L.*

Proof: We perform the following construction:

$$X_1 = X,$$
$$X_{2i} = \{A : X_{2i-1} \Vdash A \text{ in } L_0\}, \qquad X^1 = \bigcup_{j=1}^{\infty} X_j$$
$$X_{2i+1} = X_{2i} \cup \{T(A) : A \in X_{2i}\}.$$

We assert that X^1 is satisfiable in L. To prove this, note that $\Vdash$ in L_0 is finitary, and so is N_0. Therefore X^1 is closed under both classical and nonclassical necessitation for L. It remains to prove that X^1 is satisfied by some admissible valuation of L_0: Then X^1 will be N_0-saturated, and induce an admissible (super)valuation that satisfies it and hence X.

We claim first that if $B \in X_{2i}$, then there are sentences $A_1, \ldots, A_m \in X$ and $T(A_{m+1}), \ldots, T(A_n) \in X_{2i-1}$ such that $A_1, \ldots, A_m, T(A_{m+1}), \ldots, T(A_n) \Vdash B$ in L_0. This is obvious for cases $i = 1$, $i = 2$; mathematical induction quickly shows the rest.

Now if X^1 is not satisfiable in L_0, it contains a contradiction ($p \mathbin{\&} \neg p$); this contradiction will be found in X_{2i} for some i. But then we have $A_1, \ldots, A_m \in X$, $Px_{m+1}, \ldots, Px_n \in X_{2i-1}$ such that $A_1, \ldots, A_m, Px_{m+1}, \ldots, Px_n \Vdash (p \mathbin{\&} \neg p)$ in L_0. This means that $A_1 \mathbin{\&} \cdots \mathbin{\&} A_m \Vdash \neg(Px_{m+1} \mathbin{\&} \cdots \mathbin{\&} Px_n)$ in L_0. Now the $A_i \in X \subseteq SY$, so the antecedent and consequent have no predicates in common. By Craig's lemma, either the antecedent is a contradiction or the consequent is a tautology. The former cannot be because X is satisfiable in L_0. The latter cannot be because a conjunction of atomic sentences is never contradictory. Therefore, X^1 must be satisfiable in L_0, as we meant to prove.[2]

NOTES

1. See, e.g., A. Robinson, *Introduction to Model Theory and to the Meta-mathematics of Algebra* (Amsterdam: North-Holland, 1965), p. 116. A simplified proof is given by B. Dreben and H. Putnam, "The Craig Interpolation Lemma," *Notre Dame Journal of Formal Logic, 8* (1967), pp. 229–233, and a more semantic proof by J. R. Schoenfield, *Mathematical Logic* (Reading, Mass.: Addison-Wesley, 1967), pp. 79–81.

2. Cf. B. van Fraassen, "Truth and Paradoxical Consequences" in R. Martin, ed., *The Liar* (New Haven: Yale University Press, in press).

PROBLEMS

Chapter I

Section 1

1.1 Prove, using the principles of abstraction and extensionality, and the definitions of the set-theoretic symbols:

(a) $\Lambda \subseteq X$.

(b) If $X \subseteq Y$ and $Y \subseteq Z$, then $X \subseteq Z$.

(c) If $X \subseteq Y$ and $X \subseteq Z$, then $X \subseteq Y \cap Z$.

(d) $X - (X - Y) \subseteq Y$.

(e) If $X \subseteq \bar{Z}$ for every member Z of a family F, then $X \subseteq \bigcap_{Z \in F} \bar{Z}$.

X, Y, and Z stand for sets.

Section 2

2.1 If there is a one-to-one mapping from X into Y and also a one-to-one mapping from Y into Z, then there is a one-to-one mapping from X into Z.

2.2 Every one-to-one mapping has an *inverse*; that is, if f is a one-to-one mapping from X onto Y, then there is a mapping f' from Y onto X such that $f(x) = y$ if and only if $f'(y) = x$, for any members x of X and y of Y.

2.3 If a mapping has a unique inverse (see 2.2), then it is one-to-one.

2.4 The intersection of a family of functions is a function.

2.5 Show that having the same cardinality ($\equiv$) is an *equivalence relation* among sets, that is, that it is *reflexive* ($X \equiv X$), *symmetric* (if $X \equiv Y$, then $Y \equiv X$), and *transitive* (if $X \equiv Y$ and $Y \equiv Z$, then $X \equiv Z$).

2.6 (Cantor) $|\{Y : Y \subseteq X\}| > |X|$.

2.7 (a) Where N is the set of natural numbers, $|N^2| = |N|$.

(b) The union of denumerably many countable sets is countable.

(c) The Cartesian product of two countable sets is countable.

(d) The set of all finite sequences of members of a given countable set is again countable.

(e) The set of all countable sequences of members of a given countable set is not countable.

Section 3

3.1 Use Zorn's lemma to prove that a nonempty family D of lines in a plane must have a maximal subset D' such that if 1 and $1'$ belong to D', they do not intersect.

3.2 "Everything is conditioned to exist by something. Hence, there exists something (an 'absolute') which is not conditioned to exist by anything other than itself." Make explicit any further assumptions needed for this to follow by Zorn's lemma. Will it also follow that this "absolute" conditions all else to exist?

3.3 Can a tree with the finite branching property have nondenumerably many branches?

Section 4

4.1 The *sum* $\sum_{i=1}^{n} a_i$ of the first n members of the sequence $\langle a_1, a_2, \ldots, a_i, \ldots \rangle$ is defined recursively by

(a) $\displaystyle\sum_{i=1}^{1} a_i = a_1.$

(b) $\displaystyle\sum_{i=1}^{k+1} a_i = \left(\sum_{i=1}^{k} a_i \right) + a_{k+1}.$

Define similarly the *product* $\prod_{i=1}^{n} a_i$ of the first n members of this sequence.

4.2 With reference to the definition in Exercise 4.1, prove the following by natural induction:

(a) $\displaystyle\sum_{i=1}^{n} ra_i = r \sum_{i=1}^{n} a_i.$

(b) $\displaystyle\sum_{i=1}^{n} (a_i + b_i) = \sum_{i=1}^{n} a_i + \sum_{i=1}^{n} b_i.$

(c) $\displaystyle\sum_{i=1}^{n} i = \frac{n(n+1)}{2}.$

4.3 Prove by strong induction and some simple premises about the human race that each human is a descendant of Adam or Eve. (These premises might include, for example, that all but Adam and Eve have parents, and that each person is a descendant both of himself and of whomever his parents are descendants. *Hint:* Assign each person a rank.)

Section 5

5.1 Assuming that a given machine (or person) can multiply numbers less than 10 and can add any two numbers, construct an algorithm by which it (he) can multiply any two numbers less than 100. Carry it out for 24×23.

5.2 Construct an algorithm for transforming an expression into its reverse, and carry it out for *abc*. [*Hint*: Mark the first letter, move marked letters to the right; a marked letter should stop moving to the right when either (a) there is nothing to its right or (b) a marked letter is on its right. Finally, erase the marks.]

Chapter II

Section 2

2.1 Show that two PCS have the same sentences if they have the same atomic sentences and the same logical signs.

2.2 Prove that if P does not occur in B, then $S_p^A(B) = B$.

2.3 Prove that $S_{p_1 \cdots p_n}^{B_1 \cdots B_n}(A) = S^s(A)$ for a mapping s such that $s(p_i) = B_i$ for $i = 1, \ldots, n$, and if q occurs in A but is not one of the p_i, then $s(q) = q$. (The case $n = 1$ is a theorem proved in this section.)

Section 3

3.1 Show that infinitary substitution preserves validity in a bivalent propositional language. What does this show about unary and simultaneous substitution?

3.2 From the definition of bivalent propositional language, show that $\{A, B, \neg(A \ \& \ B)\}$ is not a satisfiable set, and that X is not a satisfiable set iff $X - \{A\} \Vdash \neg A$ holds, in such a language, if $A \in X$.

3.3 Prove clauses (b)–(d) of the theorem on the properties of the semantic entailment relation.

Section 4

4.1 Let H be the valuation space of a bivalent propositional language. Show informally that

   (a) the intersection of a finite family of elementary classes is an elementary class,

   (b) the intersection of an infinite family of elementary classes may not be an elementary class.

4.2 If H is the valuation space of a bivalent language L with exclusion negation, and v, v' are distinct points in H, then there are elementary classes $H(A)$, $H(B)$ such that $v \in H(A)$, $v' \in H(B)$, and $H(A) \cap H(B) = \Lambda$.

4.3 $\Vdash A \supset B$ iff $H(A) \subseteq H(B)$ for all sentences A, B in a bivalent propositional language L with valuation space H. [Use the identities $H(A \ \& \ B) = H(A) \cap H(B)$, $H(\neg A) = H - H(A)$.]

4.4 Using Exercise 4.3, show the validity of the following sentences in a bivalent propositional language:

   (a) $(A \supset B \cdot \supset A) \supset A$.

   (b) $A \supset B \cdot \supset \cdot (A \ \& \ C) \supset B$.

   (c) $\neg(\neg A \ \& \ (\neg A \supset A))$.

   (d) $A \supset (\neg A \supset B)$.

4.5 Show that if L has a sentence f such that $H(f) = \Lambda$ and L has finitary semantic entailment, then L is I-compact.

Section 5

5.1 If for all sentences A of L, $X \Vdash A$ iff $Y \Vdash A$ in L, then X and Y are semantically equivalent in L.

5.2 Define $\mathbf{C}(X) = \{A : X \Vdash A \text{ in } L\}$, that is $\mathbf{C}(X)$ is the least system in L that contains X. Prove that

   (a) $X \subseteq \mathbf{C}(X)$.

   (b) $\mathbf{C}(\mathbf{C}(X)) \subseteq \mathbf{C}(X)$.

   (c) if $X \subseteq Y$, then $\mathbf{C}(X) \subseteq \mathbf{C}(Y)$.

   (d) $\mathbf{C}(X \cup Y) = \mathbf{C}(\mathbf{C}(X) \cup \mathbf{C}(Y))$.

   [*Note*: By definition, $\mathbf{C}$ is a *closure operation* (on the sets of sentences of L) iff conditions (a)–(c) hold.]

5.3 Let Nx mean that x is a natural number, and consider the set of true sentences formed by the use of quantification, the identity predicate $=$, conjunction, negation, and predicate N. Is this set finitely axiomatizable?

Section 6

6.1 With reference to Exercise 5.2, note that $X \mathbin{\dot\cup} Y = \mathbf{C}(X \cup Y)$. Use Exercise 5.2 to show that if X, Y, Z are systems and $X \subseteq Z$, $Y \subseteq Z$, then $X \mathbin{\dot\cup} Y \subseteq Z$.

6.2 Find a counterexample to the assertion that the general calculus of systems is distributive, that is, to $X \cap (Y \mathbin{\dot\cup} Z) \subseteq (X \cap Y) \mathbin{\dot\cup} (X \cap Z)$.

Section 7

7.1 Find a language in whose calculus of systems $\overline{X \mathbin{\dot\cap} Y} = \dot X \mathbin{\dot\cup} \dot Y$ does not hold.

7.2 Show that $\overline{X \mathbin{\dot\cap} Y} = \dot X \cup \dot Y$ holds for finitely axiomatizable systems X, Y in a bivalent propositional language.

Section 8

8.1 Suppose that $\mathscr{B}$ is a nonempty family of subsets of X such that any *two* members of $\mathscr{B}$ have a nonempty intersection. Does it follow that $\mathscr{B}$ is a filter base?

8.2 In the example of a bivalent propositional language, with exactly *two* atomic sentences, each subset of H is an elementary class. Why is this so?

8.3 Show that if $\mathscr{F}$ is a filter on X and contains the union of Y and Z iff it contains Y or Z, for all subsets Y and Z of X, then $\mathscr{F}$ contains either Y or $X - Y$ (for all subsets Y of X).

8.4 Show that if H is I (U)-compact, then every ultrafilter on H is I(U)-convergent.

8.5 Show that if $\mathscr{F}$ is an ultrafilter on Z, then if $X \subseteq Z$ and $X \cap Y \neq \Lambda$ for all Y in $\mathscr{F}$, then X is in $\mathscr{F}$.

8.6 Show that I-compactness does not entail U-compactness.

8.7 If A is a sentence of language L, define $L(A)$ to be the language with the same syntax as L and whose admissible valuations are exactly those admissible valuations of L that do not satisfy A. Show that L has finitary semantic entailment iff for every sentence A of L, $L(A)$ is I-compact.

Section 9

9.1 Let L be a language with the following syntax and semantics:
   (a) L has denumerably many atomic sentences, and if A, B are sentences, so is $(A|B)$.
   (b) A valuation v is admissible for L iff v maps all sentences into $\{T, F\}$, and is such that $v(A|B) = F$ iff $v(A) = v(B) = T$.
   Show that the valuation space H of L admits all ultraproducts.[1]

Section 10

10.1 Show that if a language L is the union of a chain of its finitary fragments, then L is U-compact.

10.2 Let L be the language defined in Exercise 9.1; show that L is the union of a chain of its finitary fragments.

Chapter III

Section 1

1.1 Show that (c) if $X \subseteq Y$ and $X \Vdash A$, then $Y \Vdash A$ follows from (a) $X \Vdash A$ if $A \in X$, and (b) if $X \Vdash A$ for all A in Y and $Y \Vdash B$, then $X \Vdash B$.

1.2 Show that if $LS = \langle \text{Syn}, \text{Th}, \vdash \rangle$ is a normal logical system, then $\text{Th} = \text{Cn}(\text{Th}) = \text{Cn}(\Lambda)$, and also that Th is the intersection of all sets $\text{Cn}(X)$, X a set of sentences of Syn.

1.3 Show from the definition that if Cn is a closure operator, then $\text{Cn}(X \cup Y) \subseteq \text{Cn}(\text{Cn}(X) \cup \text{Cn}(Y))$.

1.4 Let Cn be a closure operator on the sets of sentences of syntax Syn, and define the relation $\vdash$ by $X \vdash A$ iff $A \in \text{Cn}(X)$. Prove that
   (a) $X \vdash A$ if $A \in X$.
   (b) If $X \vdash A$ for all $A \in Y$ and $Y \vdash B$, then $X \vdash B$.

1.5 With references to Exercise 1.4, prove that if Cn is a closure operator on the sets of sentences of syntax Syn, then $\text{Cn}(\text{Cn}(X) \cup$

Cn(Y) $\subseteq$ Cn($X \cup Y$). (*Note:* Compare Exercises 1.3 and 1.5 with Exercise 5.2 of Chapter II.)

1.6 If L has an absurd sentence f ($H(f) = \Lambda$), and there is a logical system LS sound and strongly complete for L with $\vdash$ in LS a finitary relation, then L is I-compact. (*Note:* This is the usual form of compactness proofs in standard texts.)

1.7 Let Syn be a PCS, and the relation $\vdash$ be given by

(a) any sentence of form $\neg(A \mathbin{\&} \neg A)$ belongs to Th $= \{A : \Lambda \vdash A\}$.

(b) if $\vdash A$ and $\vdash B$, then $\vdash A \mathbin{\&} B$.

(c) $\{A\} \vdash \neg\neg A$.

Show that the system $LS = \langle \text{Syn}, \text{Th}, \vdash \rangle$ is sound, but neither statement nor argument complete, for a bivalent propositional language with syntax Syn.

Section 2

2.1 Prove that $\vdash A \supset A$ in Sobocinski's system.

2.2 Prove Sobocinski's axioms by the Beth algorithm.

2.3 Prove that if $\vdash$ is the deducibility relation in propositional logic, and Cn(X) $= \{A : X \vdash A\}$ for all sets of sentences X of a given PCS, Cn is a closure operator.

Section 3

3.1 Prove that $v(A_1 \vee \cdots \vee A_n) = F$ iff $v(A_1) = \cdots = v(A_n) = F$.

3.2 Prove that if the tableau sequences of A and $A \supset B$ terminate, so does the tableau sequence of B.

Section 5

5.1 Let $M = \langle E, \{0\}, \cdot, - \rangle$ be a matrix with E the set of integers and $\cdot, -$ the operations of multiplication and subtraction from zero. Which of the following mappings are homomorphisms of M into M?

$$f : f(x) = -x,$$
$$g : g(x) = |x|,$$
$$h : h(x) = 1 + x,$$
$$j : j(x) = x^2.$$

5.2 For a matrix $M = \langle E, D, \cdot, - \rangle$ let M^2 be the matrix $\langle E^2, (E \times D) \cup (D \times E), \wedge, \sim \rangle$ with the operations defined by

$$\langle x_1, y_1 \rangle \wedge \langle x_2, y_2 \rangle = \langle x_1 \cdot x_2, y_1 \cdot y_2 \rangle,$$
$$\sim \langle x, y \rangle = \langle -x, -y \rangle.$$

Construct the matrix B_2^2, and compare it with the matrix B_4 defined in this section.[2]

5.3 With M^2 defined as in Exercise 5.2, show there are homomorphisms from M into M^2 and from M^2 into M which take undesignated elements into undesignated elements.[3] What does this show about matrix interpretations of propositional logic?

5.4 Investigate the statement and argument soundness and completeness of classical propositional logic with respect to $M_3^* = \langle \{1, b, 0\}, \{1\}, \cdot, - \rangle$, with the operator diagrams

$\cdot$	1	b	0		$-$	
1	1	1	0		1	0
b	1	1	0		b	1
0	0	0	0		0	1

5.5 Show that for any n-valued matrix there is an $(n + 1)$-valued matrix with the same valid sentences.[4]

Section 6

6.1 Let L be a bivalent propositional language with exactly two atomic sentences, and L^* the language with the same syntax as L but with the supervaluations for L being the admissible valuations for L^*. Show that L^* is a matrix-propositional language for a four-element matrix M_4. Can you generalize this result?

Chapter IV

Section 1

1.1 What sentences are $(x/y)((x)(Fxy \vee (y)(Ex)(y \neq x)))$, and $f((x)(Fxy \vee (y)(Ex)(y \neq x)))$, where $f(y) = x, f(x) = z, f(z) = y$? How are these sentences related?

1.2 Prove the theorems in this section whose proofs were said to be immediate.

Section 2

2.1 Show that the tableau sequences of the axioms terminate.

2.2 In what sense is rule **Ur** justified by the axiom system?

Section 3

3.1 Show that the rule of *generalization* preserves validity under the standard interpretation.

3.2 Show that $M \vDash (Ey)(Fy \supset (x)Fx)$ for any model M, where F is a unary predicate.

3.3 Show by explicit counterexample (that is, by a model M and assignment function d for M) that $\{Fy : y$ a variable$\} \vDash (x)Fx$ does not hold in a referential quantifier language.

Section 5.

5.1 Prove Lemma 2.

5.2 Show that regular valuations could be defined without recourse to models, that is, in terms of the values assigned to component sentences, as in the case of bivalent propositional languages.

Section 6

6.1 Let L be a referential quantifier language with only one predicate, P, of degree 2; and $M = \langle D, R \rangle$ a model for L with $D = \{1, 2, 3\}$, $R = \{\langle 1, 2 \rangle, \langle 2, 3 \rangle\}$. For the following models, consider whether they are submodels of, elementary submodels of, or elementarily equivalent to M.

$$M_1 = \langle \{1, 2\}, \{\langle 1, 2 \rangle\} \rangle,$$
$$M_2 = \langle \{1, 2\}, \Lambda \rangle,$$
$$M_3 = \langle \{0, 1, 2\}, \{\langle 0, 2 \rangle, \langle 2, 1 \rangle\} \rangle.$$

6.2 If M' is an extension of M, and M'' is an elementary extension of both M and M', then M' is an elementary extension of M.

6.3 If A does not contain any quantifiers and $B = (y_1)(y_2) \ldots (y_n)A$ holds in M, then B holds in all submodels of M.

Section 8

8.1 We consider a language with one (binary) predicate P. Let N be the set of nonnegative integers, $\leq$ the usual less-than-or-equal-to relation on N, and consider the models $M = \langle N, \leq \rangle$, $M' = \langle \{2i : i \in N\}, \{\langle 2i, 2j \rangle : i \leq j\} \rangle$. Show that M' is elementarily equivalent to M, but that M' is not an elementary submodel of M.

Section 9

9.1 Define $X \to A$ to hold in substitutional quantifier language L iff $f(X) \Vdash f(A)$ in L for all one-to-one substitution functions f. Show that $X \to A$ in L iff $X \Vdash A$ in the corresponding referential quantifier language L^*.

9.2 Calling substitutional quantifier language L' an extension of similar language L if all expressions of L are expressions of L' and all predicates of L' are predicates of L, define $X \to A$ to hold in L iff $X \Vdash A$ holds in all extensions of L. Show that $X \to A$ in L iff $X \Vdash A$ in the corresponding referential quantifier language L^*.

Section 10

10.1 Show that if the Beth algorithm is applied to a syntactic system formed by adding names to a QCS, the tableau sequence of $(x)Fx \ \& \ (Ey)(y = b) \cdot \supset Fb$ terminates, provided rule I is extended to apply to names.

10.2 Show that $\vdash F(\imath x)Fx$ and $\vdash (Ey)Fy \supset F(\imath y)Fy$ cannot be added as axiom schemes to free description theory without disastrous results.

10.3 Show that the addition of either of the following axiom schemes to free description theory would lead to equivalent theories:
   (a) $\vdash \neg(Ey)(y = t) \ \& \ \neg(Ey)(y = t') \cdot \supset t = t'$.
   (b) (1) $\vdash (x)(Fx \equiv Gx) \supset (\imath x)Fx = (\imath x)Gx$.
       (2) $\vdash t = (\imath x)(x = t)$.

Chapter V

Section 1

1.1 Prove Lemma 2.

1.2 Show that one-to-one substitution of atomic sentences for atomic sentences preserves satisfiability in a matrix-propositional language.

1.3 If $M \equiv \langle E, D, \cdot, - \rangle$ and $M' = \langle E', D', \wedge, \sim \rangle$ define $M \; \boxed{x} \; M'$ to be $\langle E \times E', \; D \times D', \; \cap, \; \div \rangle$, where $\langle u, u' \rangle \cap \langle v, v' \rangle = \langle u \cdot v, u' \wedge v' \rangle$ and $\div \langle u, u' \rangle = \langle -u, \sim u' \rangle$. Show that the sentences valid in $M \; \boxed{x} \; M'$ are exactly those valid in both M and M'. (*Hint:* Define products of matrix assignments.)[5]

1.4 With M and M' as in Exercise 1.3, let $M \; \textcircled{x} \; M'$ be like $M \; \boxed{x} \; M'$ except that the set of designated elements is $(E \times D') \cup (D \times E')$. Show that the sentences valid in $M \; \textcircled{x} \; M'$ are exactly those valid in either M or M'. (For a hint, see Exercise 1.3.)[6]

Section 2a

2a.1 Show that sentence $\tau(\tau = m, b, 4, 5)$ below is valid in language L_τ, without appeal to the relevant logical systems. (p is an atomic sentence and $\Diamond A$ is defined as $\neg \Box \neg A$.)

m. $p \supset \Diamond p$

b. $\Diamond \Box p \supset p$

4. $\Diamond \Diamond p \supset \Diamond p$

5. $\Diamond p \supset \Box \Diamond p$

2a.2 Show that the sentence b of 2a.1 is not valid in L_m, that 4 is not valid in L_b, and that 5 is not valid in L_4.

2a.3 In Section 2a an infinite set of sentences was indicated which is not satisfiable in any finite model structure. Show that this is so, and also show that the set is, nevertheless, satisfiable.

Section 2b

2b.1 Prove that system τ is sound for every language in $C(\tau)$, $\tau = m, b, 4, 5$.

2b.2 Certain stronger conditions entailing (b), (c), and (d) are suggested; show that the set of sentences valid in all members of $C(\tau)$ remains the same ($\tau = m, b, 4, 5$) when (b), (c), and (d) are replaced by these stronger conditions.[7]

Section 3a

3a.1 Let $L = \langle \text{Syn}, V \rangle$ be a referential quantifier language, and let the relation N be the least relation such that $\langle\{A\}, (Ex)(x \neq y)\rangle \in N$ for every sentence A with y free in A and x a variable distinct from y. Characterize the set of valid sentences of the presuppositional language $L^* = \langle Syn, V, N, C, V^*\rangle$ with C as usual and V^* the set of all V-supervaluations of Syn induced by (V, N)-saturated sets.

Section 3b

3b.1 Let $L = \langle Syn, V\rangle$ be a bivalent propositional language with atomic sentences $p_1, p_2, p_3, \ldots$, and let N be the least relation such that $\{p_i\}Np_{2i}$ and $\{\neg p_i\}Np_{2i}$, for each index i. Show that there is a member v of V such that some set maximal among the (V, N)-saturated sets satisfied by v contains either p_i or $\neg p_i$ if and only if $i = 2^n \cdot 3$, for some nonnegative integer n.

Section 3c

3c.1 The following are Gentzen rules for classical logic. Check each to see whether it would remain valid no matter what presuppositions are introduced (assume the radical policy).

(a) $\dfrac{A \vdash B}{A \,\&\, C \vdash B}$.

(b) $\dfrac{A \vdash B \quad A \vdash C}{A \vdash B \,\&\, C}$.

(c) $\dfrac{A \vdash B \quad C \vdash B}{A \lor C \vdash B}$.

(d) $\dfrac{A \vdash B}{A \vdash B \lor C}$.

(e) $\dfrac{A \vdash B}{A, \neg B \vdash C}$.

(f) $\dfrac{A, B \vdash C \quad A, B \vdash \neg C}{A \vdash \neg B}$.

(g) $\dfrac{A \vdash B}{(x)A \vdash B}$.

(h) $\dfrac{A \vdash B}{A \vdash (x)B}$, provided x is not free in A.

Section 4b

4b.1 Characterize the set of valid sentences of the presuppositional language L constructed in this section (using the radical policy on presuppositions), considering specifically its classical satisfiability.

Section 4c

4c.1 Show directly that the following hold in L^*.
- (a) $\Vdash T(A) \supset A$.
- (b) $\Vdash T(A \supset B) \supset \cdot T(A) \supset T(B)$.
- (c) $\Vdash A \supset T \sim T \sim A$.
- (d) $\Vdash T(A) \supset TT(A)$.
- (e) $A \Vdash T(A)$.

4c.2 Prove Lemma 1: If $X \vdash^1 A$, then $X \vdash A$ in LT.

4c.3 Prove the remark that precedes the theorem: $X \Vdash A$ in L^* iff $X \cup \{ \sim T(A) \}$ is not satisfiable in L^*.

4c.4 With $-$ and $\cdot$ as defined in this section, consider the fragment L_2^* of L^* whose sentences are those made up of atomic sentences of L^* by the connectives $-$ and $\cdot$, and whose models are the general models of L^*. Show that classical logic is sound and strongly complete for L_2^*.

NOTES

1. The vertical stroke denotes a single truth function in terms of which all other truth functions in a bivalent language may be defined; cf., e.g., W. V. O. Quine, *Mathematical Logic*, rev. ed. (Cambridge, Mass.: Harvard University Press, 1958), pp. 48–49.
2. Cf. N. Rescher, *Many-Valued Logic* (New York: McGraw-Hill, 1969), chap. 2, sec. 16.
3. *Ibid.*
4. *Ibid.*, chap. 2, sec. 15.
5. *Ibid.*, chap. 2, sec. 16.
6. *Ibid.*
7. See K. Lambert and B. van Fraassen, "Meaning Relations, Possible Objects, and Possible Worlds" in K. Lambert, ed., *Philosophical Problems in Logic* (Dordrecht, Holland: Reidel, 1970), pp. 1–20, Appendix, for a completeness proof using these stronger conditions and covering quantification.

SOLUTIONS
TO
SELECTED
PROBLEMS

Chapter I

2.3 Assume that function f has a unique inverse $f^*:f(x) = y$ if and only if $f^*(y) = x$ for all x in the domain of f and all y in the domain of f^*, and no function other than f^* satisfies this condition. Assume *per absurdum* that f is not one-to-one, so that there are elements v, w such that $f(v) = f(w)$ and $v \neq w$. Let f' be like f^* except at $f(v)$, and yet $f'(f(v))$ is either v or w. Then f' is also an inverse of f.

2.6 Suppose there is a one-to-one mapping f of the members of X onto the subsets of X. That means that if $x \in X$, then $f(x) \subseteq X$. Let $Y = \{x \in X : x \notin f(x)\}$. Since $Y \subseteq X$ there must be an element y of X such that $Y = f(y)$. We now ask whether y is in Y; if $y \in Y$, then $y \in f(y)$ so $y \notin Y$ by the definition of Y, but if $y \in Y$, then $y \notin f(y)$, so $y \notin Y$ by the definition of Y. This reduces our supposition to absurdity.

2.7 (a) One strategy is to divide N^2 into denumerably many finite sets first; say $N^2 = R_1 \cup R_2 \cup \cdots$ with $|R_i| = n_i \in N$. Then R_1 can be mapped one-to-one onto $\{1, \ldots, n_1\}$, R_2 onto $\{n_1 + 1, \ldots, n_1 + n_2\}$, and so on, thus yielding a one-to-one mapping of N^2 onto N. To divide N^2 into denumerably many finite sets, we assign each couple $\langle x, y \rangle$ the index $x + y$. This index is a natural number, so there are at most denumerably many such indices. In addition, each natural number from $2 = 1 + 1$ on is such an index. So we set $R_i = \{\langle x, y \rangle : x + y = i + 1\}$. But R_i must be finite, because there are only finitely many couples $\langle x, y \rangle$ such that x, y are each smaller than $(i + 1)$, so there are less than $(i + 1) \cdot (i + 1)$ such couples.

(b) Let the sets be $X_1, X_2, \ldots$ and let each be denumerated in some way: $X_i = \{x_1^i, x_2^i, \ldots\}$. Then the mapping

$$f(x_j^i) = \langle i, j \rangle$$

is a one-to-one mapping of their union onto N^2 [see (a)].

(c) Let $X = \{x_1, x_2, \ldots\}$ and $Y = \{y_1, y_2, \ldots\}$. Then the mapping

$$f(\langle x_i, y_j \rangle) = \langle i, j \rangle$$

is again one-to-one onto N^2.

(d) Let X be countable, and note the obvious one-to-one correspondence between X^{n+1} and the Cartesian product of X^n with X. By natural induction and (c) above we therefore find that X^n is countable for all natural numbers n. By (b), result (d) follows.

(e) Suppose we denote the ith element of such a sequence d of members of countable set X as d_i, and suppose that f maps a set of such sequences one-to-one onto N. If we now construct a new sequence d' such that $d_i' \neq d_i$ when $f(d_i) = i$, then clearly f is not defined for d'. Hence any such denumeration fails to be exhaustive.

3.1 Let $\mathscr{F} = \{E \subseteq D$: no two members of E intersect$\}$. The family $\mathscr{F}$ is partially ordered by set inclusion, and if $\mathscr{C}$ is a chain in $\mathscr{F}$, then $\bigcup \mathscr{C}$ is an upper bound of $\mathscr{C}$. But $\bigcup \mathscr{C}$ belongs to $\mathscr{F}$, for any two members of $\bigcup \mathscr{C}$ are members of some member of $\mathscr{C}$ and hence do not intersect. By Zorn's lemma, $\mathscr{F}$ has a maximal element.

3.3 Let T be the *full binary tree*: Each node has exactly two nodes directly below it, a *left* node and a *right* node. Now let X be a denumerable set $\{x_1, x_2, \ldots\}$. We begin by associating with each node of T a subset of X: With the origin we associate $\wedge$, with each left node of rank n we associate the set associated with its direct ancestor, with each right node of rank n we associate the set associated with its direct ancestor plus $x_{n-1}(n = 2, 3, \ldots)$. Now with each branch of T we associate the union of the sets associated with the nodes on that branch. This establishes a one-to-one correspondence between the branches of T and the subsets of X. By Exercise 2.6, our result follows.

4.2 (c) $\displaystyle\sum_{i=1}^{1} i = 1 = \frac{1(1+1)}{2}$.

Assume that $\displaystyle\sum_{i=1}^{k} i = \frac{k(k+1)}{2}$.

$$\sum_{i=1}^{k+1} i = \sum_{i=1}^{k} i + (k+1)$$

$$= \frac{k(k+1)}{2} + (k+1)$$

$$= \frac{k(k+1) + 2(k+1)}{2} = \frac{k^2 + 2k + 2}{2}$$

$$= \frac{(k+1)(k+2)}{2}$$

5.1 Commands C_1. $(xy, a) \to (x0, a) + (y, a)$
C_2. $(x0, a) \to (x, a)0$
C_3. $(x, yz) \to ((x, y)0 + (x, z))$
C_4. $(x, y) \to b$, where b is the product of x and y.
C_5. $(a) \to a$
C_6. $a + b \to c$, where c is the sum of a and b.

Here x, y range over integers less than 10, and a, b over integers less than 100 (all nonnegative); termination consists in being blocked.

5.2 There are at least two answers. First reversing algorithm:
C_1. $\alpha\beta xy \to \alpha y\beta x$
C_2. $\beta xy \to y\beta x$
C_3. $\alpha x \to \alpha\beta x$
C_4. $\alpha\beta x \to x\alpha$
C_5. $\alpha \to \cdot$
C_6. $\to \alpha$

Second reversing algorithm:

C_1. $\alpha x y \rightarrow y \alpha x$

C_2. $\alpha x + \rightarrow \beta + x$, where $+$ is another auxiliary symbol.

C_3. $\alpha x \rightarrow \beta + x$

C_4. $x\beta \rightarrow \beta x$

C_5. $\beta x \rightarrow \alpha x$

C_6. $\beta + x \rightarrow x\beta$

C_7. $\beta \rightarrow \cdot$

C_8. $\rightarrow \alpha$

Chapter II

2.3 Recall that simultaneous substitution has been defined in terms of unary substitution. In addition, each unary substitution S_p^B is equivalent to an infinitary substitution $s : s(p) = B, s(q) = q$ when $q = p$. It is therefore sufficient to prove that the result of performing a series of infinitary substitution is again an infinitary substitution (which is obvious), and that the precautions taken in the definition of simultaneous substitution in terms of unary substitution are not nullified in the process.

3.1 By our previous results that unary and simultaneous substitution are definable in terms of infinitary substitutions, it follows that these will also preserve validity. To prove the first part, suppose that v is an admissible valuation such that $v(S^s(A)) = F$. Define $v^*(B) = v(S^s(B))$ for all sentences B; then $v^*(A) = F$, so it will suffice to show that the mapping v^* is again an admissible valuation. This is straightforward; for example, $v^*(B \& C) = v(S^s(B \& C)) = v(S^s(B) \& S^s(C)) = T$ iff $v(S^s(B)) = v(S^s(C)) = T$ iff $v^*(B) = v^*(C) = T$.

4.2 If $v \neq v'$, then $v(A) = T \neq v'(A)$, for some sentence A; so $v'(A) = F$. But $H(A) \cap H(\neg A) = \wedge$.

4.3 $\Vdash A \supset B$ iff $H(A \supset B) = H$ iff $H(\neg(A \& \neg B)) = H$ iff $H(A \& \neg B) = \wedge$ iff $H(A) \cap H(\neg B) = \wedge$ iff $H(A) \subseteq H - H(\neg B)$ iff $H(A) \subseteq H(B)$.

5.2 (d) For any set X of sentences of L, $\mathbf{C}(X)$ is semantically equivalent to X. Hence we have $X \cup Y$ semantically equivalent to $\mathbf{C}(X \cup Y)$, and also $\mathbf{C}(X) \cup \mathbf{C}(Y)$ semantically equivalent to $\mathbf{C}(\mathbf{C}(X) \cup \mathbf{C}(Y))$. It remains to show that $X \cup Y$ is thus equivalent to $\mathbf{C}(X) \cup \mathbf{C}(Y)$. But v satisfies $X \cup Y$ iff it satisfies both X and Y iff it satisfies both $\mathbf{C}(X)$ and $\mathbf{C}(Y)$ iff it satisfies $\mathbf{C}(X) \cup \mathbf{C}(Y)$.

5.3 This set contains sentences which formulate that there are at least two natural numbers, at least three natural numbers, at least four natural numbers, and so on $((Ex)(Ey)(Nx \ \& \ Ny \ \& \ x \neq y)$, $(Ex)(Ey)(Ez)(Nx \ \& \ Ny \ \& \ Nz \ \& \ x \neq y \ \& \ y \neq z \ \& \ x \neq z), \ldots)$. These form a chain of increasing strength; hence the set cannot be finitely axiomatized.

6.1 Because X, Y, Z, $X \cup Y$ are systems, we have, for example, $Z = \mathbf{C}(Z)$, $X \cup Y = \mathbf{C}(X \cup Y) = \mathbf{C}(\mathbf{C}(X) \cup \mathbf{C}(Y))$. Now if $X \subseteq Z$ and $Y \subseteq Z$ then $\mathbf{C}(X) \subseteq \mathbf{C}(Z)$ and $\mathbf{C}(Y) \subseteq \mathbf{C}(Z)$, so $\mathbf{C}(X) \cup \mathbf{C}(Y) \subseteq \mathbf{C}(Z) = Z$; hence $X \cup Y = \mathbf{C}(\mathbf{C}(X) \cup \mathbf{C}(Y)) \subseteq \mathbf{C}(Z) = Z$.

6.2 Let L be a language with exactly three sentences (p, q, r) and as admissible valuations exactly those mappings v of $\{p, q, r\}$ into $\{T, F\}$ such that if v satisfies both p and q, then v satisfies r (think of q as saying that p implies r). Then $\{r\} \cap (\{p\} \cup \{q\}) = \{r\} \cap \{p, q, r\} = \{r\}$. But $(\{r\} \cap \{p\}) \cup (\{r\} \cap \{q\}) = \Lambda \cup \Lambda = \Lambda$.

7.1 Let L have exactly two sentences (p, q) and as admissible valuations all mappings of $\{p, q\}$ into $\{T, F\}$. Then $\{p\} \cap \{q\} = \Lambda$ and its system complement is $\{p, q\}$. But the system complements of $\{p\}$ and $\{q\}$ are both empty, so their system union is also empty.

7.2 In such a language, each finitely axiomatizable set is axiomatizable by a single sentence. In addition, if $X = \{A : B \Vdash A\}$ and $Y = \{A : C \Vdash A\}$, then $\dot{X} = \{A : \neg B \Vdash A\}$, $\dot{Y} = \{A : \neg C \Vdash A\}$, and $\dot{X} \cup \dot{Y} = \{A : \neg B \ \& \ \neg C \Vdash A\} = \{A : \neg (B \vee C) \Vdash A\}$, where disjunction is defined as usual. But also, $X \cap Y = \{A : B \vee C \Vdash A\}$.

8.3 Suppose that $\mathscr{F}$ is a filter on X and contains $Y \cup Z$ iff it contains Y or Z, for all $Y, Z \subseteq X$. Every filter on X contains X; $X = (X - Y) \cup Y$ when $Y \subseteq X$; hence by our assumption $\mathscr{F}$ contains $X - Y$ or Y.

8.4 (a) Let $\mathscr{F}$ be an ultrafilter on H which is not I-convergent. Then there is no point v contained by every elementary class $H(A)$ in $\mathscr{F}$. Hence the intersection of all elementary classes in $\mathscr{F}$ is empty; but $\mathscr{F}$ being a filter, the intersection of any finite collection of elementary classes in $\mathscr{F}$ is not empty. Therefore, the elementary classes in $\mathscr{F}$ provide a counterexample to the hypothesis that H is I-compact.

(b) Let $\mathscr{F}$ be an ultrafilter on H which is not U-convergent. Then for every point v in H there is an elementary class $H(A)$ containing v which does not belong to $\mathscr{F}$. These elementary classes cover H; the question is whether any finite union of them covers H. Suppose $H(A_1) \cup \cdots \cup H(A_n)$ is such a finite union. Then, being equal to H, it belongs to $\mathscr{F}$. $\mathscr{F}$ being an ultrafilter, it contains one of the components of that union. But this is contrary to assumption.

8.5 Suppose $\mathscr{F}$ is an ultrafilter on Z and $X \cap Y \neq \Lambda$ for all Y in $\mathscr{F}$, but $X \notin \mathscr{F}$. Then $Z - X \in \mathscr{F}$. So by assumption, $X \cap (Z - X) \neq \Lambda$, which is impossible.

9.1 Let $V = \{v_i\}$, $i \notin I$ be a subset of the valuation space H of L, $\mathscr{U}$ an ultrafilter on I, and v an ultraproduct of V generated by $\mathscr{U}$. Then we have, for any sentence A,

$$v(A) = \mathrm{T} \quad \text{iff } \{i : v_i(A) = \mathrm{T}\} \in \mathscr{U}.$$

Let us add

$$v(A) = \mathrm{F} \quad \text{iff } v(A) \neq \mathrm{T}, \qquad \text{for all sentences } A \text{ of } L.$$

It remains then to show that v, thus defined, is an admissible valuation of L.

(a) $v(A \mid B) = \mathrm{F}$ iff $\{i : v_i(A \mid B) = \mathrm{T}\} \notin \mathscr{U}$
   iff $I - \{i : v_i(A \mid B) = \mathrm{T}\} \in \mathscr{U}$
   iff $\{i : v_i(A \mid B) = \mathrm{F}\} \in \mathscr{U}$
   iff $\{i : v_i(A) = v_i(B) = \mathrm{T}\} \in \mathscr{U}$
   iff $\{i : v_i(A) = \mathrm{T}\} \cap \{i : v_i(B) = \mathrm{T}\} \in \mathscr{U}$
   iff $\{i : v_i(A) = \mathrm{T}\}, \{i : v_i(B) = \mathrm{T}\} \in \mathscr{U}$
   iff $v(A) = v(B) = \mathrm{T}$.

10.1 Let language L be the union of its finitary fragments $L_1, L_2, \ldots,$ with L_i a fragment of L_{i+1} ($i = 1, 2, \ldots$). Suppose that X is an infinite set of sentences of L such that each finite subset of X fails to be satisfied by some admissible valuation for L. Let X_i be the set of sentences of L_i belonging to X; for each index i we have a valuation v_i of L whose restriction to L_i does not satisfy X_i. Since L_i is finitary, X_i is equivalent to some finite set of sentences of L_i. We construct a tree as before, the nodes of rank i being the valuations of L_i not satisfying X_i; the union of an infinite branch of this tree (existing by Koenig's lemma) is an admissible valuation of L that does not satisfy X.

Chapter III

1.4 (b) Suppose that $X \vdash A$ for all A in Y and $Y \vdash B$. That means that $Y \subseteq \mathrm{Cn}(X)$ and so $\mathrm{Cn}(Y) \subseteq \mathrm{Cn}(\mathrm{Cn}(X)) = \mathrm{Cn}(X)$. But also $B \in \mathrm{Cn}(Y)$ so $B \in \mathrm{Cn}(X)$; that is, $X \vdash B$.

1.5 From Exercise 1.4 we infer that if $Y \subseteq \mathrm{Cn}(X)$, then $\mathrm{Cn}(Y) \subseteq \mathrm{Cn}(X)$. So we need only to show that $\mathrm{Cn}(X) \cup \mathrm{Cn}(Y) \subseteq \mathrm{Cn}(X \cup Y)$. But that follows because both $\mathrm{Cn}(X)$ and $\mathrm{Cn}(Y)$ are included in $\mathrm{Cn}(X \cup Y)$, owing to the fact that X and Y are included in $X \cup Y$.

1.7 The system is not complete because, for example, $\neg(\neg p \mathbin{\&} p)$ cannot be deduced; it is not an axiom, not a conjunction, and does not begin with a double negation.

3.1 By the soundness and completeness theorems, this reduces to showing that if A and $A \supset B$ are valid, so is B.

5.2 Setting $\langle 1, 1 \rangle = 1$, $\langle 0, 1 \rangle = a$, $\langle 1, 0 \rangle = b$, $\langle 0, 0 \rangle = 0$ we see that the only difference between B_2^2 and B_4 is that here one more element is designated. (See Exercise 1.4 of Chapter V for a more general treatment.)

5.3 Define $f(x) = \langle x, x \rangle$ and $g(\langle x, y \rangle) = x$; these are homomorphisms taking undesignated elements into undesignated elements. Hence M is an adequate matrix iff M^2 is an adequate matrix.

5.4 The function $f(1) = 1$, $f(0) = 0$ is a homomorphism of B_2 into M_3^* taking undesignated elements into undesignated elements. Hence the propositional calculus is statement complete for an M_3^*-propositional language (and argument complete for the same reason: a counterexample in B_2 is again a counterexample in M_3^*). Statement soundness must be proved directly, using the tableau method. To prove argument soundness it then suffices to show that $\Vdash\neg(A \& \neg B)$ iff $A \Vdash B$ in an M_3^*-propositional language— that is, that if $d(\neg(A \& \neg B)) = d(A) = 1$, then $d(B) = 1$ for any M_3^*-assignment d. But if $d(\neg(A \& \neg B)) = 1$, then $d(A \& \neg B)$ equals either 0 or b. But $d(A \& \neg B) = d(A) \cdot d(\neg B)$, so it cannot equal b. If $d(A) \cdot d(\neg B) = 0$ and $d(A) = 1$, then $d(\neg B) = 0$; hence $d(B) = 1$.

5.5 Let c be an element of M and add an element b which is like c in all respects to form M'. Then $f(x) = x$ is a homomorphism of M into M', and $g(b) = c, g(y) = y$ when $y \neq b$ is a homomorphism of M' into M.

6.1 We let M be the matrix $\langle E, D, \cdot, - \rangle$ such that

$$E = \{0, 1\}^4, \qquad D = \{\langle 1, 1, 1, 1\rangle\},$$

$$-\langle x, y, z, w\rangle = \langle -x, -y, -z, -w\rangle,$$

$$\langle x, y, z, w\rangle \cdot \langle x', y', z', w'\rangle = \langle x \cdot x', y \cdot y', z \cdot z', w \cdot w'\rangle$$

Then the supervaluations of L correspond exactly to M-assignments; for example, if s is the supervaluation corresponding to the set $\{v_1, v_2\}$ of valuations, then s corresponds to the M-assignment $d(A) = \langle v_1(A), v_2(A), v_2(A), v_2(A)\rangle$. We can generalize this in two ways: (a) for sentences with at most n atomic components the super-valuation approach is equivalent to the use of a finite matrix with 2^{2^n} elements; (b) we have here a construction of powers of matrices (M being the fourth power of B_2) which yield the same set of valid sentences as the original matrix (see Exercise 1.3 of Chapter V).

Chapter IV

3.1 The rule has two parts; we must show that if $\Vdash A$ then $\Vdash(x)A$, and that if y is not free in A, and $\Vdash(y/x)A$, then $\Vdash(x)A$. [Note that in the second case, $(y/x)A$ is exactly like an alphabetic variant of A except that it has free occurrences of y wherever A has free occurrences of x.] We prove the second case. Suppose $\sim M \Vdash (x)A[d]$. Then for some $d' =_x d$, $\sim M \Vdash A[d']$. Let $d'' =_y d'$, $d''(y) = d'(x)$, so that $d''(y) = d''(x)$. Then we can apply the unary substitution theorem to d'' by itself: $d'' =_x d''$ and $d''(x) = d''(y)$. Hence $M \Vdash A[d'']$ iff $M \vDash (y/x)A[d'']$. In addition, since y is not free in A, d'' agrees with d' on all variables free in A, so that $\sim M \vDash A[d'']$.

3.2 Suppose $\sim M \vDash (Ey)(Fy \supset (x)Fx)[d]$; that is, $M \vDash (y)(Fy \,\&\, \neg(x)Fx)[d]$. Then for any $d' =_y d$, $M \vDash Fy[d']$ and $\sim M \vDash (x)Fx[d']$. So there must be $d'' =_x d'$ such that $M \vDash \neg Fx[d'']$. Now let $d''' =_y d''$, $d'''(y) = d''(x)$. Since y does not occur in $\neg Fx$, $M \vDash \neg Fx[d''']$. But also, by the unary substitution theorem $M \vDash \neg Fx[d''']$ iff $M \vDash \neg Fy[d''']$, since $d''' =_x d'''$, $d'''(y) = d'''(x)$. On the other hand, d''' agrees with d on all variables free in $(y)(Fy \,\&\, \neg(x)Fx)$—none—so $M \vDash (y)(Fy \,\&\, \neg(x)Fx)[d''']$ and hence $M \vDash Fy[d''']$. But this is absurd.

5.1 We prove by strong induction on the length of A that $M \vDash A^*[d]$ iff $M \vDash A[d^*]$. The only part which is not obvious is that if $M \vDash A^*[d]$, then $M \vDash A[d^*]$ when A has the form $(x)B$. Suppose that $M \vDash A^*[d]$, that is, $M \vDash (x^*)B^*[d]$, so for each $d' =_{x^*} d$, $M \vDash B^*[d']$. By hypothesis, for each such d', $M \vDash B[d'^*]$. It will suffice to show now that if $d'' =_x d^*$, then $d'' = d'^*$ for some $d' =_{x^*} d$. This can be done by explicit constructions; given $d'' =_x d^*$, we define

$$d'(y^*) = d''(y) \qquad \text{for all variables } y,$$
$$d'(z) = d(z) \qquad \text{when } z \neq y^* \text{ for any } y.$$

We clearly have that $d'' = d'^*$, and need to show that $d' =_{x^*} d$. This amounts to: If $y \neq x$, then $d'(y^*) = d(y^*)$. But $d'(y^*) = d''(y) = d^*(y)$ when $y \neq x$, and $d^*(y) = d(y^*)$, so $d'(y^*) = d(y^*)$ when $y \neq x$.

6.2 Note that any sequence d in M is also a sequence in M'. For such a sequence d and any sentence A we have therefore $M \vDash A[d]$ iff $M'' \vDash A[d]$ iff $M' \vDash A[d]$.

6.3 Let M' be a submodel of M. Then, since A is quantifier free, $M' \vDash A[d]$ iff $M \vDash A[d]$ for any sequence d in M' (this can be proved by an easy induction). Now $M \vDash B$ iff $M \vDash A$. So if $M \vDash B$, then, $M \vDash A[d]$ for all sequences d in M, hence $M \vDash A[d']$ for all sequences d' in M'. But then $M' \vDash A[d']$ for all sequences d' in M'; hence $M' \vDash B$.

8.1 To show that M and M' are elementarily equivalent it suffices to show that they are isomorphic. Define f: $f(i) = 2i$. We clearly have that $\langle f(i), f(j)\rangle \in \{\langle 2i, 2j\rangle : i \leq j\}$ iff $\langle i, j\rangle \in \leq$; moreover f is one-to-one and onto, so f is an isomorphism. To show that M' is not an elementary submodel of M, let $d(x) = 0$, $d(y) = 2$. Then $M \vDash (Ez)(x \leq z \ \& \ z \leq y \ \& \ z \neq x \ \& \ z \neq y)[d]$, but this does not hold for M', although d is a sequence in M'.

9.1 If $X \Vdash A$ in L^*, then $f(X) \Vdash f(A)$ in L^*, for all one-to-one substitution functions f, hence $f(X) \Vdash f(A)$ in L for all such f, hence $X \to A$ in L. On the other hand, suppose that $X \Vdash A$ does not hold in L^*; then L^* has a denumerable model $M = \langle f, D\rangle$ with assignment d such that d satisfies $X \cup \{\neg A\} = X'$ in M. Let $f(x_i) = x_{2i}$; as in Section 5, we conclude that some d' for M satisfies $f(X')$. Let d'' agree with d' on all even variables, and map the odd variables onto D; then d'' satisfies $f(X')$ and is canonical. But then d'' satisfies $f(X)$ and not $f(A)$; hence $f(X) \Vdash f(A)$ does not hold in L.

10.2 Let Fx be $(Cx \ \& \ \neg Cx)$ in the first case, let it be $(Ez)(z = x)$ in the second, and apply principle FD.

Chapter V

1.1 Note that $td(p) = td'(s(p))$ for all atomic sentences p; by induction $td(A) = td'(S^s(A))$ for all sentences A. If d' exists, so does d.

1.2 Let M-assignment d satisfy set X and let s be a one-to-one substitution function. Define d': $d'(s(p)) = d(p)$, $d'(q) = d(q)$ when $q \neq s(p)$ for any atomic sentence p. Because s is one-to-one, d' exists when d exists. By Lemma 2, d' now satisfies $\{S^s(A) : A \in X\}$.

1.3 If d, d' are assignments for M, M', respectively, define $d \times d'$ to be the assignment $d \times d'(A) = \langle d(A), d'(A) \rangle$. It is easily shown that any $M \boxed{x} M'$ assignment is such a product of M and M' assignments, and conversely. Moreover, $d \times d'(A)$ is designated exactly if $d(A)$ and $d'(A)$ are both designated, so A is valid in $M \boxed{x} M'$ iff A is valid in both M and M'.

2a.3 Let Y be the least set containing p_1 and such that if A is a sentence with atomic components $p_1, \ldots, p_n$ which belongs to Y, then both $A \& p_{n+1}$ and $A \& \neg p_{n+1}$ belong to Y. Then the set in question may be defined as $X = \{\Diamond B : B \in Y\}$. The members of Y form a tree with p_1 as origin and *being part of* as ancestor relation. The members of a branch of this tree are jointly satisfiable, but the union of any two branches is not satisfiable; moreover, there are infinitely many branches. So X is not satisfiable in a finite model structure. But we can take the set $\mathscr{B}$ of branches of this tree as possible worlds; then $\langle \mathscr{B}, \mathscr{B}^2 \rangle$ is a 5-ms, and X is satisfied in each member α of $\mathscr{B}$ by the valuation $v_\alpha : v_\alpha(p_i) = T$ iff p_i occurs as a conjunct in some member of branch α. It is also possible to construct a denumerable m.s.; take a specific branch B, say the leftmost, and consider the set $\mathscr{C}$ of rightmost branches passing through members of B. $\mathscr{C}$ is countable because B is countable, and $\langle \mathscr{C}, \mathscr{C}^2 \rangle$ is again a suitable 5-ms.

2b.1 (**ad R_2**) If not $\Vdash \Box A$ in $L = \langle \text{Synt}, \text{Val}, T, V \rangle$ then there is a v in V such that for some t in T, $tv(A) \neq T$. But by (i), $tv \in V$, so not $\Vdash A$ in L.

(**ad A_2**) If $v(\Box(A \supset B)) = v(\Box A)$, then for all t in T, $tv(A \supset B) = tv(A) = T$, so $tv(B) = T$. But then $v(\Box B) = T$.

(**ad A_1**) If $v(\Box A) = T$, then $tv(A) = T$ for all $t \in T$; by (ii), $v(A) = T$.

(**ad A_3**) If $v(A) = T$ and $v' = tv$, then by (iii), $v = t^* v'$, so $v'(\Diamond A) = T$. Since this is so for all t in T, $v(\Box \Diamond A) = T$.

(**ad A_4**) If $v(\Box A) = T$, then for all t in T, $tv(A) = T$. By (iv), if $v' = t'(t(v))$, then $v' = t''v$ for some t'' in T; hence $v'(A) = T$. So for any t, $tv(\Box A) = T$; so $v(\Box \Box A) = T$.

2b.2 That the soundness results follow holds *a fortiori*; in addition, the completeness proof given in this section continues to go through, because the identity $\{v_\beta : \alpha R \beta\} = \{tv_\alpha : t \in T\}$ continues to hold.

3a.1 In L^*, A is valid iff $(Ex)(Ey)(x \neq y) \Vdash A$ in L. First, to show that $(Ex)(Ey)(x \neq y)$ is valid in L^*, we note that any (V, N)-saturated set will contain $y = y$, and hence $(Ex)(x \neq y)$, and hence $(Ey)(Ex)(x \neq y)$, for any pair of distinct variables x and y. Second, to show that only the sentences quantificationally deducible from $(Ex)(Ey)(x \neq y)$ are valid in L^*, let $X = \{(Ex)(Ey)(x \neq y)\}$ and $C(X) = \{A : XCA\}$. We maintain that $C(X)$ is (V, N)-saturated and provides therefore a counterexample to the validity of any sentence not deducible from $(Ex)(Ey)(x \neq y)$. It suffices here to show that $(Ex)(Ey)(x \neq y) \Vdash (Ez)(z \neq w)$ in L when z and w are distinct variables, which can be shown, for example, by semantic tableau.

3b.1 Let v be the admissible valuation for L such that $v(p_i) = T$ iff $i = 2^n \cdot 3$ for some nonnegative integer n. Then if X is a (V, N)-saturated set satisfied by v, and $j \neq 2^n \cdot 3$ for any such n, then neither p_j nor $\neg p_j$ can belong to X. For if either belonged, so would p_{2j}, so $v(p_{2j}) = T$, so $2j = 2^m \cdot 3$ for some m, so $j = 2^{m-1} \cdot 3$, counter to assumption. In addition, N is finitary, so any (V, N)-saturated set satisfied by v can be extended into a maximal such set. It will now suffice, therefore, to prove that $Y = \{p_j : j = 2^n \cdot 3$ for some nonnegative integer $n\}$ is included in some (V, N)-saturated set satisfied by v. But clearly $X = \{A : Y \Vdash A$ in $L\}$ is such a set, since Y is already closed under N and X does not contain any atomic sentences or negations of atomic sentences that do not belong to Y.

3c.1 (a), (b), (d), (e), (g) hold. This can be proved by considering the construction of CONL (X, K). Thus for (a) let $X = \{A \ \& \ C\}$, $k = \{A \Vdash B\}$; since $A \ \& \ C \Vdash A$ holds classically, $B \in \text{CONL}(X, K)$. For (b) we assume $A \Vdash B$ and $A \Vdash C$, so that both B and C belong to the consequences of $\{A\}$; by the classical $B, C \Vdash B \ \& \ C$, it follows that $B \ \& \ C$ also belongs to these consequences under our assumptions.

But the others need not hold, for example, if Fy presupposes Fx, we have $Fy \Vdash Fx$, but not (necessarily) $Fy \Vdash (x)Fx$.

4b.1 The only principle that would have to be added to quantificational logic is that if A is a theorem, so is $T(A)$. To prove this we note first that if A belongs to any saturated set, do does $T(A)$. Therefore, the rule is sound. [Indeed, the stronger principle $A \vdash T(A)$ is sound, but we are here only considering valid sentences.] The important question is completeness. Let Y be the least set of sentences closed under deduction in quantificational logic such that if A is in Y, so is $T(A)$. That Y is closed under N is clear; we need to prove that Y is satisfied by some valuation of L_0. We can do this by noting that Y is the union of the sets

$$X_1 = \text{set of valid sentences of } L_0,$$
$$X_{2i} = X_{2i-1} \cup \{T(A) : A \in X_{2i-1}\},$$
$$X_{2i+1} = \{A : X_{2i} \Vdash A \text{ in } L_0\}.$$

For convenience, let $Y_i = \{T(A) : A \in X_{2i-1} \text{ and } T(A) \notin X_{2i-1}\}$, so that $X_{2i} = X_{2i-1} \cup Y_i$. Indeed, all members of X are semantically entailed by the union Y of the sets Y_i. We define the model $\langle f, D \rangle$ as follows: D is the set of variables occurring in members of Y, $f(P) = \{x \in D : Px \in Y\}$, $f(P') = \Lambda$ for any other predicate P'. Now the assignment $d : d(x) = x$ if $x \in D$, $d(x)$ is alphabetically the first variable in D otherwise, satisfies the set Y in this model.

4c.2 We have $X \vdash A$ iff $T(X) \vdash_1 T(A)$, and $Y \vdash_1 B$ iff $Y \vdash B$ in S_5. So we must prove that if $X \vdash A$ in S_5, then $T(X) \vdash T(A)$ in S_5, with T as necessity sign. Given the soundness and completeness of S_5 for L_5 (see Section 2a) it suffices to show that if $X \Vdash A$ in L_5 and $T(X)$ is satisfied in a 5-ms, then so is $T(A)$, which is straightforward.

4c.3 If $\sim T(A)$ is satisfied in M, then there is a d over M that does not satisfy A. Hence if $X \cup \{\sim T(A)\}$ is satisfied in M, so is X but not A. Conversely, suppose that X but not A is satisfied in M. Then some d over M does not satisfy A; but then $\sim T(A)$ is satisfied in M.

4c.4 It suffices to show that L_2^* can be regarded as an M_3^{**}-propositional language. This means that to a model M of L^* there corresponds an M_3^{**}-assignment d such that $d(A) = 1$ iff $|A|^M =$

T, $d(A) = 0$ iff $|A|^M = $ F, and $d(A) = b$ otherwise, for all sentences A of L^*. Conversely, for every M_3^{**}-assignment d we have a general model M of L^* such that these conditions are satisfied. Both cases are easily proved.

INDEX

217

INDEX OF SYMBOLS